Women in Patriarchy

Cross-Cultural Readings

Edited by

Jasbir Jain

RAWAT PUBLICATIONS

Jaipur • New Delhi • Bangalore • Guwahati • Kolkata

ISBN 978-81-7033-906-9

Reprinted, 2017

Published by
Prem Rawat for **Rawat Publications**
Satyam Apts, Sector 3, Jawahar Nagar, Jaipur 302 004 (India)
Phone: 0141 265 1748 / 7006 Fax: 0141 265 1748
E-mail: info@rawatbooks.com
Website: www.rawatbooks.com

New Delhi Office
4858/24, Ansari Road, Daryaganj, New Delhi 110 002
Phone: 011 2326 3290

Also at *Bangalore, Guwahati* and *Kolkata*

Printed and bound in India

to the future and the hope for a better world

Contents

Preface

Women in Patriarchy is an anthology of cross-cultural readings, which tell their own story across the boundaries of nation, religion and time. The stories, essays and extracts included here trace the history of women's struggle for space in political and social structures, against hegemonic control and oppression, and their ongoing questioning of the role models thrust upon them.

This articulation of women's experience has shaken up the foundation of earlier epistemologies which have been based largely on male experience, specially in the fields of psychology and literary aesthetics. The assumptions of political ideologies, which base their approaches on the universal concept of 'man' rather than on the more inclusive 'human', has also been questioned. In fact, the last two centuries have been a journey where women have pushed against the boundaries of knowledge, have deconstructed the concept of personhood in order to reconstruct it as inclusive of woman, and have travelled through the different phases of protest, acceptance of challenges, assertion of individual positions and struggle for legal rights to reformulate the concept of the word 'human'.

The struggle is not yet over. It cannot be over. Gender is a cultural construct and has constantly to negotiate age-old practices and traditions as well as to work at the frameworks that have been internalised by women themselves from generation to generation.

Every society also has its own questionings and its own forms of resistance. This anthology of fiction and non-fiction from America, New Zealand, India, Canada, South Africa, England, Australia and France, includes voices from the socially marginalised categories like the blacks, the third world, the tribals, the dalits and the 'lower' castes. Education, marriage, political rights, religious positions, emotional expressions and the psychology of deprivation all find a place here. The reworking of myths also has a gender dimension. These readings unfold a narrative of their own and reflect the history of women across ages and across geographical spaces.

This anthology has been in the making for a long time as I have, at a personal level, moved through similar confrontations with the imposed boundaries, felt anger more than frustration, and have questioned the basis of an unequal society which provides very little breathing space. Together these pieces provide a record of historical struggles and of high levels of courage and determination as they capture the irresistible vibrancy of life.

I owe a personal debt of gratitude to writers, critics, theorists and translators who have so generously given permission for their writing to be used. This anthology simply could not have taken shape without that.

Jasbir Jain

Acknowledgements

The editor and the publisher gratefully acknowledge the permission to use copyright material for the following stories, translations and extracts: "Revenge Herself", the translator Vasanti Sankaranarayanan for the translation, Mahasweta Devi for "Draupadi" and Gayatri Chakraborty Spivak for the translation of "Draupadi", Yasmine Gooneratne for "Masterpiece", Shashi Deshpande for "Hear Me, Sanjaya", Lakshmi Kannan for "Muniyakka", Githa Hariharan for "The Remains of the Feast", Nayantara Sahgal for "Illusion and Reality" and Chandra Talpade Mohanty for "Anthropology and the Third World Woman as 'Native' ". We also thank Katha and the translator Neera Kuckreja Sohoni for permission to use the English translation of Mahadevi Varma's essay "The Hindu Woman's Wifehood", and Urmila Pawar for her essay "My Four Enemies" and Tripti Jain for the translation. Permission for the stories by Lalithambika Antarjanam, Alice Munro and Bessie Head has been requested as has been for the extract from bell hooks. As and when available it'll be acknowledged in subsequent editions. The help given by the American Library in obtaining the transcripts of "Seneca Falls Declaration of Sentiments and Resolutions" is gratefully acknowledged.

Introduction

Patriarchy, at the outset, stands for power and authority. The word has a number of affiliations and goes on to symbolise possession, control and belonging. *Patria* can stretch its meaning to relate to nation. Moreover, women are not the only ones to be oppressed by it: all marginalised categories, whether men or women, get caught in its web of authority. And its arms extend to almost every field – philosophy, law, governance, society itself, and the more modestly constructed family.

The roots of patriarchy lie in the myths of creation and the religious worlds based on them. The initial relationship between the creator and the created world has located itself in the power of man and the subordination of woman. This intent has been camouflaged by other myths – myths of protection, of punishment for transgression, of the power of women, their indispensability and the glory of motherhood. Thus, any questioning of the patriarchal stronghold (and stranglehold) has to contest this domain of belief and begin with the experience of women, their emotional strengths, intellectual abilities, capacity to resist and to endure, to conceptualize, and to transcend the body even as they realise its centrality. An imagined vision of a patriarch may call forth the picture of an old man with a flowing beard, robed in a long gown, and gentle and caring in his attitude. Patriarchs are fabled to have been wise men, men who conserve their energies and their wealth (including their women). But the awe associated with them, their sternness and unforgiving nature, the strong arm of authority would also form part of the aura which is likely to surround the vision. The Patriarch stands for Father Right, the right of ownership over the seed. He is not a person but an institution, a mindset, a practice, a hegemony, and thus an oppressor.

The journey from protector to oppressor is not a sudden one even though the history of development and human progress has accelerated this shift. As men and women have moved from one stage to another, from the nomadic to the agrarian, to industrialism and capitalism, and as means of sustenance and methods of governance have changed, the concepts of purity of lineage and property have also emerged tightening the hold of the patriarch. This journey is marked by a remarkable irony that with the growth in human freedom and 'wisdom', there has been a corresponding shrinking of women's space. In fact it is not only of women but the space of all other marginalised categories that has shrunk. A glaring example is the march of imperialism and the civilizational discourse which accompanied it, and the manner in which it spread its tentacles over half the world. Why is it that development functions like a see-saw? Why is it that the notion of equality has perceived itself as rooted in the male of the species and power has always needed the 'other', the 'powerless' to define itself?

Is the category of gender any different from class, caste or colour? In some measure, yes. The relationship between men and women is one which ordinarily works across other binaries – inside/outside, old/young, rich/poor, physical/emotional, white/black – and has to contend with different kinds of belonging and love. Within marriage the category of desire is a dominant one, and companionship, understanding and children also enter into this relationship. There are then the relationships between fathers and daughters, mothers and sons, which bring into play a whole lot of emotions – known and unknown. Further, the whole notion of respectability, the custodianship of culture, the purity of lineage has come to rest on the female body. In some cultures, conventions like the observance of fasts for the welfare of the husband or the family and restrictions in matters of food devolve on women. This divides their life right through into duty and enjoyment, into the traditional and the modern and creates inner polarities.

The male-centred view of human life which goes on to privilege one gender over another has led to an inability to work toward a holistic development. The discordant notes of conflict and opposition to the other, of want and disease appear to be rooted in the basic concept of power which is one-sided and does not respect other perspectives and needs. It has spilled over into all areas of life: myth and culture, religious practices, physical geography, philosophical and epistemological quests and frameworks, socio-economic constructs, history and art, and above all language – the tool with which we think and communicate. The underprivileged are then challenged to prove themselves and questions are asked: Where is their history? Where are their great achievements? Virginia Woolf has written about this inequality and a whole lot of writers and critics have used this very male-centred language with its inbuilt discriminatory mode to claim some authority for their point of view, which in itself is a major hurdle. Adjectives, verbs, classifications, categorisations all work through either privileging or denigration and idioms and images are heavily loaded. Further they have been internalised as patterns of thought. The basic challenge remains one of making a break through this web of preconceived notions. Subjugation is in itself a verbalised concept – third world, feminization, 'lower' class and similar descriptions, which imprison thought processes. (I have often wondered at the use of the word 'seminal', which is used indiscriminatingly to describe the writings of strong women and to give credibility to their positions). It has not so far been possible to cross this major hurdle of language. Dialects, oral narratives, grandmothers tales and re-readings and reinterpretations are just one tiny step towards giving words new and different meanings, of viewing the world from a side-glance.

Equality, in meaningful terms, in terms of greater freedom and more space for women is a global need. Degrees of oppression may differ, kinds may also differ subject to the difference in other factors: but gender discrimination persists almost in all societies. The dreams of women may differ, their struggles even more so but their need for air to breathe is the same. When one moves across cultures, similar problems can be seen surfacing everywhere. Charlotte Perkins Gilman's suffocation at not being allowed to write is similar to the narrator's juggling with time in 'Revenge Herself', where she knows she can only find time for herself at night. But both the stories work differently. Gilman's narrator tells her own story of the journey toward insanity while Lalithambika Antarajam's writer-narrator shifts the focus on Tatri (a real life person) and allows her to talk about her attack on the hypocritical morality of the high-caste Nambudiris. Again, while Alice Munro's portrayal of old age focuses on the daughters, their dependence, need for freedom and the guilt which they put behind them, Lakshmi Kannan's "Muniyakka" is the old woman's own experience of loneliness. The stories question the whole notion of patriarchal authority, of the subjugation of a woman's life to her sexual functions, the guilt which society induces in them when they demand freedom or think of their own emotional and intellectual needs. Women feel a constant need to contest the hostile environment both within and outside the home. They are viewed primarily as service givers.

The two writers of the "The Yellow Wallpaper" and "Revenge Herself" realise that they have to find ways and means of expressing themselves, their creativity is the burden they carry. But the creativity of the wife in Gooneratne's "Masterpiece" has to work through proxy. There is a total extinction of the woman's creativity as if it was solely a male prerogative. The story also provides us an insight into the falsification of histories, the appropriation of female talent by men, the ascribing of this help to divine categories as well as the truth that talent and creativity do not work on the basis of gender. There is a very sensitive story by Ambai (the pen name of C.S. Lakshmi, a Tamil writer), not included in this volume, but which deserves mention. Titled "Wrestling" it is the narrative of a gifted woman's relationship with her husband, a man not equally talented. He is a musician and gives public performances. She has stilled her creative urge and devotes herself to housewifely duties. She nurtures his feeling of well-being and even praises a not-so-perfect performance, but he would find fault even with the cup of milk she prepares for him with comments such as 'not hot enough', 'not sweet enough'. The sacrifices and the silences which marriage demands require almost a superhuman ability to ignore the self. Simone de Beauvoir in *The Second Sex* writes:

> The category of the *Other* is as primordial as consciousness itself. In the most primitive societies, in the most ancient mythologies, one finds the expression of a duality – that of the self and the other..... The feminine element was at first no more involved in such pairs as Varuna-Mitra, Uranus-Zeus, Sun-Moon and Day-Night than it was in the contrasts between Good and Evil.... Otherness is a fundamental category of human thought.

But, she points out, that when the idea of a Self is constructed, the other ego 'sets up reciprocal claim'. And hence the 'self' and the 'other' can only be relative concepts, not absolute ones. Where gender relations are concerned man defines woman not in herself but as relative to him; she is not regarded as an 'autonomous being' (16-17). This fixedness of norm, whether it be a gendered one or a politico-geographical one – as one perceives in the continued dominance of Eurocentric/Westcentric normative measures, ideas and ideologies – is in itself a manifestation of patriarchal values. When women question power they also question the very idea of an 'absolute' superiority. The fluctuation perhaps needs to be no longer between centre and margin, but a total decentralization, a multiplicity of affiliations and relationships. When women challenge patriarchy, they come up against biology, experimental psychology, anthropology, history and the concept of productivity. Both culture and fundamentalism are rooted in this external world which seeks to construct femininity, virtue and morality, circumscribe a woman's social role, prescribe dress code and control her body. In fact throughout history, one finds an over concern with the female body, which both attracts and threatens the male. It is on this basis that segregation, purdah and exclusion are practiced; the female blood is treated as impure, her role in procreation underplayed and her strengths described as domestic. How do women dethrone this control? Are barrenness and a single state also modes of rebellion? If dualities are imprisoning and monism is limiting, then is it a multiplicity of attitudes, approaches, values, structures which can provide for some space for the individual irrespective of gender?

The romantic impulse is also partly responsible for holding the woman to ransom, for making her a prisoner of her own self. It is difficult to say as to where it originates – in the socio-religious view of woman as someone who can seduce, tempt and attract the male, or in the poetic view of undying love, of woman waiting for her demon lover, or in the chemistry of the body. Perhaps it is the idea of being loved. This romantic view looks at woman as a beautiful being, capable of surrender both physically and emotionally, and it goes on to build a notion of female heroism which is based on sacrifice and self-abnegation. This romantic image is more solidly vested in the socio-cultural environment than in the person of woman herself and in contemporary times has yielded place to an image of beauty and desirability created by the cosmetic medicine industry where the body is shaped according to the demands of fashion. The world of commerce does not necessarily address itself to any aesthetic sense of beauty but is more interested in creating a market for the various products which are waiting to be sold. Capitalism is the modern face of patriarchy.

The issue is not whether single sex societies are desirable or possible. Such views have generated their own nightmares and dystopias. Charlotte Perkins Gilman's *Herland* (1915), Margaret Atwood's *The Handmaid's Tale* (1987) and Suniti Namjoshi's *Mothers of Maya Diip* (1989) are some of these and they portray societies which are imbalanced and dehumanized. The question rather is the *relationship* between the dualities and the need to free them from any unequal slotting. There is also a need to recognise the diversities and multiplicities as equal presences despite the differences.

Man has not only been viewed as the 'master' but also as the protector and the bread earner, a belief, which in large measure, is a myth. Epics and folk tales alike throw up examples of how women have been abandoned or left unprotected either because of the turn of events or because of male rejection, persecution or authority.

There are also sufficient examples in real life, almost in every society, of women struggling to support their families – orphaned women, single or widowed women, abandoned wives, persecuted or rejected women, and those who support sick husbands and many who earn the bread while the men spend their hard earned money in drink or self-indulgence. These are realities and compel one to discern between the prevalent myth and its social face.

But this myth has also constructed its own idea of masculinity, of men as strong, infallible creatures, as those who have a right to authority, respect and dignity. Bessie Head's 'Property' allows the reader to understand the falsity of such a construction of masculinity which denies a man the right to be sensitive and considerate. The husband is seen to be effeminate and his wife would rather have him aggressive and demanding. Similarly, non-aggressive cultures are also devalued as imperialism has compelled us to admit. Between the aggressive and the non-aggressive, it is the right to be human and the right to relate to others which are being squeezed out of existence. Feminism therefore is a position which requires a reconstruction of what we consider 'values'. Not a fixed notion of 'morality' or of right and wrong, good and evil, but values which value emotions, relationships, which are based on non-greed and non-appropriation and are rooted in a sense of respect for self as well as for the other. And these are the values which seem so difficult to achieve, so much out of reach, despite the long strides the human race believes itself to have taken towards the idea of progress!

Women have struggled both for a visibility and a voice – a visibility in terms of being seen and counted to participate and share. The dominate epistemological frameworks do not recognize them, and western thought does not necessarily pay heed to the culture of marginalised groups. Foucault, who has otherwise gone on to consider the idea of freedom, the rise of madness, the strengthening of power and even the nature of sexuality, has no place in it for non-western societies. Every time the non-west wishes to make a point, it has to contend with the definition which begins with a negation – 'non', a definition which begins through separation. This, in itself, is humiliating and makes one angry. Patriarchal structures will sooner or later have to understand this anger and respond constructively to it.

The present confrontation between Islamic and non-Islamic civilizations has also been brought into existence by two equally aggressive systems. The third which represents a 'sane' voice is struggling hard to survive, but it does prove that polarities are no longer valuable. The time has come to move outside polarities and oppositional positions.

Gayatri Spivak has defined feminism as the blurring of boundaries between the public and the private space. The Indian counterpart to this is the myth of the 'home and the world'. But these boundaries do not reflect the actual reality: it may be possible to enclose spaces but it is not possible to demarcate influences, thoughts, ideas and consequences, both of belief and action. Women have challenged these boundaries by describing the sexual character of women and making their strengths the basis of the claim for political rights (like Mary Wollstonecraft). Their main battle has been, in the first instance, for political participation. This battle for suffrage continued in different ways all over the world gradually winning small concessions. Simone de Beauvoir delineates the history of these struggles in the western hemisphere in the extract from *The Second Sex.* The parallels between class and gender discriminations are pointed out as are the manner in which women moved into employment outside the home.

In Mahadevi Varma's piece 'The Hindu Woman's Wifehood', a piece written in the 1930s and written nearly half-a-century after Pandita Ramabai Saraswati's work *The High Caste Hindu Woman,* the shackles of the religious tradition and law are delineated. Together they also compel one to note the slow pace of social change, for which the political forces can be held responsible. The pull towards tradition took place because Hindu society was working (i) within an oppositional discourse in its resistance to the culture of the imperial rulers, and (ii) gradually progressing toward a monistic view of Indian culture. How can women's struggles be the same across the world when political constructs are different? Thus over the layer of commonalty is the layer of difference.

Education which is perceived as an agency of social change is also in the hands of the power-wielders, controlled by their money power, and the lead in matters of intellectual tradition which they have gained is difficult to surmount. Virginia Woolf demonstrates how by depriving women of equal participation in socio-political affairs, by depriving them of equal opportunities of growth, society has blocked its own potential for constructive possibilities. In "My Four Enemies", Urmila Pawar gives a clear example of how education has enabled her to work for personal dignity and freedom. She has also gone on to problematise the gender dimensions of subordination. Nayantara Sahgal and bell hooks challenge the notion of normative standards of evaluation as well as of conceptualization while Chandra Talpade Mohanty works out new approaches to gender positions putting race, colour and class behind her and making a distinction between solidarity and coalition.

Together the essays and short stories in this collection articulate women's experience of their life in a patriarchal society and their attempts to work toward visibility and cohesion. Every such attempt is also a way of 'reading' the past, controlling the present and shaping the future. These women have taken some positions which are akin to steering the course of the discourse. These pieces express a way of 'knowing' and of learning 'how to know'. They demonstrate the intricate linkages between the different aspects of human life and hence the myopia of limiting women to any single perspective. Birth, education, relationships, marriage, wifehood, motherhood and citizenship are all of a pattern. Women as producers of goods, of knowledge, of posterity, as carriers of tradition and agents of change, refuse to be passive objects of desire or of subordination. In fact sex and sexuality both have come in for a complete reworking in the process, it is not only society but art as well which has had to accommodate the change in women's self-perception. A new kind of literary realism is evident in the writing of marginalised categories – women, blacks, natives, tribals and dalits – primarily because the bases of their knowledge are different from the elitist, western, patriarchal power structures. Their phenomenological experiences are different. Women have been at work in various ways in small measures and in large measures. They have spoken up, agitated, faced excommunication and social ostracism, and also, died in protest. They are still at work, still hope to create harmony out of this confrontation and change the definition and function of power.

Fictional Representations

Kate Chopin
(1850-1904)

Kate Chopin is well known as the writer of *The Awakening* (1899), the publication of which brought her a great deal of criticism and pushed her into obscurity. Ironically, it has gone on to become one of the best known works for feminist studies, as the heroine Edna Pontellier progresses from the almost passive role of a wife and mother to one of an aware woman and a full-blooming of herself. Christina Ker has referred to Chopin as a writer 'ahead of her time'.

Born of an immigrant Irishfather, Thomas O'Flaherty and a French-American mother, Eliza Faris, Kate was their youngest child. At age five, she lost her father and subsequently grew up in a house full of women – her widowed mother, her widowed grand-mother and her widowed great grandmother. No part of her socialization stressed the need for female subordination.

Her career as a writer began fairly late in life, at the age of 39, when she had behind her a married life of twelve years, her husband Oscar Chopin, whom she had married in 1870, having died suddenly in 1882. She was also the mother of six children. Her first collection of stories *Wiser Than a God* appeared in 1889, followed by the novel *At Fault* (1890), and another collection *Bayou Folk* (1894).

"The Story an Hour" is remarkable for its compressed narrative, the human self's ambivalence where loss and freedom are concerned, the interpretation of 'facts' by the observers, an interpretation which does not take account of the ambivalence. How much difference is there between shock and joy? The narrative reveals the impact of Guy de Maupassant, a writer whose work Chopin admired. The protagonist of the narrative comments upon the institution of marriage, not directly but obliquely, through her response to the news of her husband's death.

The Story of an Hour

Knowing that Mrs. Mallard was afflicted with heart trouble, great care was taken to break to her as gently as possible the news of her husband's death.

It was her sister Josephine who told her in broken sentences, veiled hints that revealed in half concealing. Her husband's friend Richards was there too, near her. It was he who had been in the newspaper office when intelligence of the railroad disaster was received with Brently Mallard's name leading the list of "killed". He had only taken the time to assure himself of its truth by a second telegram and had hastened to forestall any less careful, less tender friend in bearing the sad message.

She did not hear the story as many women have heard the same, with a paralyzed inability to accept its significance. She wept at once, with sudden, wild abandonment in her sister's arms. When the storm of grief had spent itself she went away to her room alone. She would have no one follow her.

There stood, facing the open window, a comfortable roomy armchair. Into this she sank, pressed down by a physical exhaustion that haunted her body and seemed to reach into her soul.

She could see in the open square before her house the tops of trees that were all aquiver with the new spring life. The delicious breath of rain was in the air. In the street below a peddler was crying his wares. The routes of a distant song which some one was singing reached her faintly, and countless sparrows were twittering in the eaves.

There were patches of blue sky showing here and there through two clouds that had met and piled one above the other in the west facing her window.

She sat with her head thrown back upon the cushion of the chair, quite motionless, except when a sob came up into her throat and shook her, as a child who had cried itself to sleep continues to sob in its dreams.

She was young, with a fair, calm face, whose lines bespoke repression and even a certain strength. But now there was a dull stare in her eyes whose gaze was fixed away off yonder on one of those patches of blue sky. It was not a glance of reflection, but rather indicated a suspension of intelligent thought.

There was something coming to her and she was waiting for it, fearfully. What was it? She did not know; it was too subtle and elusive to name. But she felt it, creeping out of the sky, reaching toward her through the sounds, the scents, the color that filled the air.

Now her bosom rose and fell tumultuously. She was beginning to recognize this thing that was approaching to possess her, and she was striving to beat it back with her will – as powerless as her two white slender hands would have been.

When she abandoned herself a little whispered word escaped her slightly parted lips. She said it over and over under her breath: "free, free free!" The vacant stare and the look of terror that had followed it went from her eyes. They stayed keen and bright. Her pulses beat fast, and the coursing blood warmed and relaxed every inch of her body.

She did not stop to ask if it were or were not a monstrous joy that held her. A clear and exalted perception enabled her to dismiss the suggestion as trivial.

She knew that she would weep again when she saw the kind, tender hands folded in death; the face that had never looked save with love upon her, fixed and gray and dead. But she saw beyond that bitter moment a long procession of years to come that would belong to her absolutely. And she opened and spread her arms out to them in welcome.

There would be no one to live for her during those coming years; she would live for herself. There would be no powerful will bending hers in that blind persistence with which men and women believe they have a right to impose a private will upon a fellow creature. A kind intention or a cruel intention made the act seem no less a crime as she looked upon it in that brief moment of illumination.

And yet she had loved him – sometimes. Often she had not. What did it matter! What could love, the unsolved mystery, count for in face of this possession of self-assertion which she suddenly recognized as the strongest impulse of her being.

"Free! Body and soul free!" she kept whispering.

Josephine was kneeling before the closed door with her lips to the keyhole, imploring for admission. "Louise, open the door! I beg; open the door – you will make yourself ill. What are you doing Louise? For heaven's sake open the door."

"Go away I am not making myself ill." No; she was drinking in a very elixir of life through that open window.

Her fancy was running riot along those days ahead of her. Spring days, and summer days, and all sorts of days that would be her own. She breathed a quick prayer that life might be long. It was only yesterday she had thought with a shudder that life might be long.

She arose at length and opened the door to her sister's importunities. There was a feverish triumph in her eyes and she carried herself unwittingly like a goddess of Victory. She clasped her sister's waist, and together they descended the stairs. Richards stood waiting for them at the bottom.

Some one was opening the front door with a latchkey. It was Brently Mallard who entered, a little travel-stained, composedly carrying his gapsack and umbrella. He had been far from the scene of accident, and did not even know there had been one. He stood amazed at Josephine's piercing cry; at Richards' quick motion to screen him from the view of his wife.

But Richards was too late.

When the doctors came they said she had died of heart disease – of joy that kills.

Charlotte Perkins Gilman
(1860-1935)

Charlotte Perkins Gilman grew up in a family of women activists. Her great aunts were all women who had made a mark in their chosen field of activism – Harriet Beecher Stowe, the well-known, author of Uncle Tom's Cabin, Catherine Beecher, an educationist who wanted to bring about a change in the social and domestic roles for women, and Isabella Beecher Stowe who was a suffragist.

Gilman's work has received a recognition from the upsurge of feminist thought. Prior to that the *Penguin Companion to Literature*, Vol. 3, 1971, fails to list her as a writer worth mentioning. "The Yellow Wallpaper" is one of her best known stories. Written in 1890, it is semi-autobiographical. Besides stories, she also wrote a full-length feminist utopia *Herland* (1915) and a socio-economic analysis of women's role in *Women and Economics* (1898).

Gilman's father had deserted her mother soon after Charlotte's birth and the memories of her mother's unhappiness lingered in her mind. This fact, however, did not deter the daughter from getting married in 1884. Nevertheless she sank into a postnatal depression after the birth of their first child and a rest cure was recommended – a rest cure which seemed to control and curtail her natural instincts. This experience forms the basis of "The Yellow Wallpaper". After a ten-year marriage of sorts, the couple went in for a divorce, which surprisingly was not based on any criticism of the partner. She married again in 1900, six years after her divorce. In 1935, Gilman committed suicide a year after she had been widowed.

The "Yellow Wallpaper" is a very sensitive story which critiques the 'caring' ways of patriarchy, ways which constitute a rule of imposition and deny both choice and creativity. As the narrative goes on to describe a young woman's mental breakdown, one begins to realise the power of the external forces which lead women to madness. Neither her husband, nor her brother are willing to concede to her wishes. Their love and care stifles her and forces her to seek escape in insanity.

The Yellow Wallpaper

It is very seldom that mere ordinary people like John and I secure ancestral halls for the summer.

A colonial mansion, a hereditary estate, I would say a haunted house, and reach the height of romantic felicity – but that would be asking too much of fate!

Still I would proudly declare that there is something queer about it. Else, why should it be let so cheaply? And why have stood so long untenanted?

John laughs at me of course, but one expects that in marriage. John is practical in the extreme. He has no patience with faith, an intense horror of superstition, and he scoffs openly at any talk of things not to be felt and seen and put down in figures.

John is a physician, and *perhaps* – (I wouldn't say it to a living soul of course, but this is dead paper and a great relief to my mind–) *perhaps* that is one reason I do not get well faster.

You see, he does not believe I am sick!

And what can one do?

If a physician of high standing and one's own husband, assures friends and relatives that there is really nothing the matter with one but temporary nervous depression – a slight hysterical tendency – what is one to do?

My brother is also a physician and also of high standing, and he says the same thing.

So I take phosphates or phosphites – whichever it is, and tonics and journeys, and air, and exercise, and am absolutely forbidden to "work" until I am well again.

Personally, I disagree with their ideas.

Personally I believe that congenial work, with excitement and change, would do me good.

But what is one to do?

I did write for a while in spite of them; but it *does* exhaust me a good deal – having to be so sly about it, or else meet heavy opposition.

I sometimes fancy that in my condition if I had less opposition and more society and stimulus – but John says the very worst thing I can do is to think about my condition and I confess it always makes me feel bad.

So I will let it alone and write about the house.

The most beautiful place! It is quite alone, standing well back from the road and quite three miles from the village. It makes me think of English places that you read about, for there are hedges and walls and gates that lock, and lots of separate little houses for the gardeners and people.

There is a *delicious* garden, I never saw such a garden – large and shady, full of box-bordered paths, and lined with long grape-covered arbors with seats under them.

There were greenhouses too, but they are all broken now.

There was some legal trouble, I believe, something about the heirs and co-heirs; anyhow it has been empty for years and years.

That spoils my ghostliness, I am afraid but I don't care – there is something strange about the house – I can feel it.

I even said so to John one moonlit evening but he said what I felt was a *draught*, and shut the window.

I get unreasonably angry with John sometimes. I'm sure I never used to be so sensitive. I think it is due to this nervous condition.

But John says if I feel so, I shall neglect proper self-control; so I take pains to control myself – before him at least, and that makes me very tired.

I don't like our room a bit. I wanted one downstairs that opened on the piazza and had roses all over the windows, and such pretty old-fashioned chintz hangings! but John wouldn't hear of it.

He said there was only one window and not room for two beds, and no near room for him if he took another.

He is very careful and loving, hardly lets me stir without special direction.

I have a schedule prescription for each hour in the day; he takes every care of me, and I feel basely ungrateful not to value it more.

He said we came here solely on my account, that I was to have perfect rest, and all the air I could get. "Your exercise depends on your strength, my dear" said he, "and your food somewhat on your appetite; but air you can absorb all the time." So we took the nursery at the top of the house.

It is a big, airy room, the whole floor nearly, with windows that look all ways, and air and sunlight galore. It was nursery first, and then playroom and gymnasium, I should judge, for the windows are barred for little children, and there are rings and things in the walls. The paint and paper as if a boy's school had used it. It is stripped off – the paper – in great patches all around the head of my bed, about as far as I can reach, and in a great place on the other side of the room low down. I never saw a worse paper in my life.

One of those sprawling, flamboyant patterns, committing every artistic sin.

It is dull enough to confuse the eye in following, pronounced enough to constantly irritate and provoke study, and when you follow the lame uncertain curves for a little distance they suddenly commit suicide – plunge off at outrageous angles, destroy themselves in unheard of contradictions.

The color is repellant, almost revolting; a smoldering unclean yellow, strangely faded by the slow-turning sunlight.

It is a dull yet lurid orange in some places, a sickly sulphur tint in others.

No wonder the children hated it! I should hate it myself if I had to live in this room long.

There comes John and I must put this away, – he hates to have me write a word.

We have been here two weeks, and I haven't felt like writing before since that first day.

I am sitting by the window now, up in this atrocious nursery, and there is nothing to hinder my writing as much as I please save lack of strength.

John is away all day, and even some nights, when his cases are serious.

I am glad my case is not serious!

But these nervous troubles are dreadfully depressing.

John does not know how much I really suffer. He knows there is no reason to suffer, and that satisfies him. Of course it is only nervousness. It does weigh on me so not to do my duty in any way.

I meant to be such a help to John such a real rest and comfort, and here I am a comparative burden already!

Nobody would believe what an effort it is just to do what little I am able, – to dress and entertain, and order things. It is fortunate. Mary is so good with the baby. Such a dear baby!

And yet I *cannot* be with him, it makes me so nervous.

I suppose John never was nervous in his life. He laughs at me so about this wallpaper!

At first he meant to re-paper the room, but afterwards he said that I was letting it get the better of me and that nothing was worse for a nervous patient than to give way to such fancies. He said that after the wallpaper was changed it would be heavy bedstead, and then the barred windows and then that gate at the head of the stairs and so on.

"You know the place is doing you good" he said "and really, dear, I don't care to renovate the house just for a three months rental."

"Then do let us go downstairs" I said, "there are such pretty rooms there!"

Then he took me in his arms and called me a blessed little goose, and said he would go down cellar if I wished, and have it white-washed into the bargain!

But he is right enough about the beds and windows and things. It is as airy and comfortable a room as anyone need wish, and of course I wouldn't be so silly as to make him uncomfortable just for a whim.

I am really getting quite fond of the big room all but that horrid paper.

Out of one window I can see the garden, those mysterious deep-shaded arbors, the riotous old fashioned flowers and bushes, the gnarly trees.

Out of another I get a lovely view of the bay and a little private wharf that belongs to the estate. There is a beautiful shaded lane that runs down there from the house. I always fancy I see people walking in these numerous paths and arbors, but John has cautioned me not to give way to fancy in the least. He says that with my imaginative power and habit of story-making, a nervous weakness like mine is sure to lead to all manner of excited fancies, and that I ought to use my will and good sense to check the tendency. So I try.

I think sometimes that if I were only well enough to write a little it would relieve the pressure of ideas and rest me.

But I find I get pretty tired when I try.

It is so discouraging not to have any advice and companionship about my work. When I get really well, John says we will ask Cousin Henry and Julia down for a long visit; but he says he would as soon put fireworks in my pillowcase as to let me have those stimulating people about now.

I wish I could get well faster. But I mustn't think about that.

This paper looks to me if it *knew* what a vicious influence it had!

There is a recurrent spot where the pattern lolls like broken neck, and two bulbous eyes stare at you upside down.

I get positively angry with the impertinence of it and the everlastingness. Up and down and sideways they crawl, and those absurd unblinking eyes are everywhere. There is one place where two breadths didn't match; and the eyes go all up and down the line, one a little higher than the other.

I never saw so much expression in an inanimate thing before, and we all know how much expression inanimate things have! I used to lie awake as a child, and get more entertainment and terror out of blank walls and plain furniture than most children could find in a toy store.

I remember what a kindly wink the knobs of our big old bureau used to have; and there was one chair that always seemed like a strong friend.

I used to feel that if any of the other things looked too fierce I could always hop into that chair and be safe.

The furniture in this room is no worse than inharmonious, however, for we had to bring it all from downstairs. I suppose when this was used as a play room they had to take the nursery things out, and no wonder! For I never saw such ravages as the children have made here.

The wallpaper, as I said before, is torn off in spots, and it sticketh closer than a brother – they must have had perseverance as well as hatred. Then the floor is scratched and gouged and splintered, the plaster itself is dug out here and there and this great heavy bed which is all we found in the room looks as if it had been through the wars. But I don't mind it a bit – only the paper.

There comes John's sister. Such a dear girl as she is and so careful of me! I mustn't let her find me writing.

She is a perfect – an enthusiastic – housekeeper and hopes for no better profession. I verily believe she thinks it is the writing which made me sick!

But I can write when she is out and see her a long way off from these windows.

There is one that commands the road, a lovely shaded winding road, and one that just looks off over the country. A lovely country too, full of great elms and velvet meadows.

This wallpaper has a kind of sub pattern in a different shade, a particularly irritating one, for you can only see it in certain lights, and not clearly then. But in the places where it isn't faded, and when the sun is just so, I can see a strange provoking form less sort of figure that seems to skulk about behind that silly and conspicuous front design.

There's sister on the stairs!

Well the Fourth of July is over! The people are all gone and I am tired out.

John thought it might do me good to see a little company so we just had Mother and Nellie and the children down for a week.

Of course I didn't do a thing – Jennie sees to everything now. But it tired me all the same. John says if I don't pick up faster he shall send me to Weir Mitchell in the Fall.

But I don't want to go there at all. I had a friend who was in his hands once and she says he is just like John and my brother, only more so!

Besides it is such an undertaking to go so far. I don't feel as if it were worth while to turn my hand over for anything and I'm getting dreadfully and querulous. I cry at nothing and cry most of the time. Of course I don't when John is here or anybody else but when I am alone.

And I am alone a good deal just now. John is kept in town very often by serious cases and Jennie is good and lets me alone when I want her to. So I walk a little in the garden or down that lovely lane sit on the porch under the roses, and lie down up here a good deal.

I'm getting really fond of the room in spite of the wallpaper.

Perhaps *because* of the wallpaper! It dwells in my mind so!

I lie here on this great immovable bed – it's nailed down. I believe – and follow that pattern about by the hour. It is as good as gymnastics. I assure you.

I start, we'll say, at the bottom down in the corner over there where it hasn't been touched and I determine for the thousandth time, that I will follow that pointless pattern to some sort of a conclusion.

I know a little of the principles of design and I know this thing was not arranged on any laws of radiation, or alternation, or repetition, or symmetry or anything else that I ever heard of. It is repeated, of course, by the breadths, but not otherwise.

Looked at in one way each breadth stands alone, the bloated curves and flourishes – a kind of 'debased Romanesque' with *delirium tremens* – go waddling up and down in isolated columns of fatuity.

But, on the other hand, they connect diagonally, and the sprawling outlines run off in great slanting waves of optic horror, like a lot of wallowing sea-weeds in full chase.

The whole thing goes horizontally too, at least it seems so, and I exhaust myself in trying to distinguish the order of its going in that direction. They have used a horizontal breadth for a border and that adds wonderfully to the confusion.

There is one end of the room where it is almost intact and there when the cross lights fade and the low sun shines directly on it, I can almost fancy radiation after all, – the interminable grotesques seem to form around a common center and rush off in headlong plunges of equal distraction.

It makes me tired to follow it. I will take a nap I guess.

I don't know why I should write this.

I don't want to.

I don't feel able.

And I know John would think it absurd. But I must say what I feel and think in some way – it is such a relief!

But the effort is getting to be greater than the relief.

Half the time now I am lazy awfully lazy, and lie down ever so much.

John says I musn't lose any strength and has me take cod liver oil and lots of tonics and things, to say nothing of ale and wine and rare meat.

Dear John! He loves me very dearly and hates to have me sick. I tried to have a real earnest reasonable talk with him the other day and tell him how I wish he would let me go and make a visit to Cousin Henry and Julia.

But he said I wasn't able to go, nor able to stand it after I got there and I did not make out a very good case for myself for I was crying before I had finished.

It is getting to be a great effort for me to think straight. Just this nervous weakness I suppose.

And dear John gathered me up in his strong arms and just carried me up stairs and laid me on the bed and sat by me and read to me till it tired my head.

He said I was his darling and his comfort and all he had and that I must take care of myself for his sake and keep well.

He says no one but myself can help me out of it that I must use my will and self-control and not let any silly fancies run away with me.

There's one comfort, the baby is well and happy, and does not have to occupy this nursery with the horrid wallpaper. If I had not used it that blessed child would have!

What a fortunate escape!

Why I wouldn't have a child of mine, an impressionable little thing, live in such a room for worlds.

I never thought of it before, but it is lucky that John kept me here after all, I can stand it so much easier than a baby you see!

Of course I never mention it to them any more – I am too wise – but I keep watch of it all the same.

There are things in that paper that nobody knows but me or ever will. Behind that outside pattern the dim shapes get clearer every day. It is always the same shape only very numerous.

And it's like a woman stooping down and creeping about behind that pattern. I don't like it a bit. I wonder – I begin to think – I wish John would take me from here!

It is so hard to talk with John about my case, because he is so wise, and because he loves me so.

But I tried it last night.

It was moonlight. The moon shines in all round just as the sun does.

I hate to see it sometimes, it creeps so slowly, and always come in by one window or another.

John was asleep and I hated to waken him so I kept still and watched the moonlight on that undulating wallpaper till it made me creepy.

The faint figure behind seemed to shake the pattern, just as if she wanted to get out.

I got up softly and went to feel and see if the paper *did* move and when I came back John was awake.

"What is it, little girl?" He said. "Don't go walking about like that – you'll get cold."

I thought it was a good time to talk so I told him that I really was not gaining here and that I wished he would take me away.

"Why darling!" said he, "our lease will be up in three weeks and I can't see how to leave before.

"The repairs are not done at home and I can't possibly leave town just now. Of course if you were in any danger I could and would but you really are better dear whether you can see it or not. I am a doctor dear, and I know. You are gaining flesh and color your appetite is better, I feel really much easier about you".

"I don't weigh a bit more," said I "nor as much and my appetite may be better in the evening when you are here but it is worse in the morning when you are away."

"Bless her little heart!" said he with a big hug, "she shall be as sick as she pleases! But now let's improve the shining hours by going to sleep and talk about it in the morning!"

"And you won't go away?" I asked gloomily.

"Why, how can I dear? It is only three weeks more and then we will take a nice little trip of a few days while Jennie is getting the house ready. Really dear you are better!"

"Better in body perhaps –" I began and stopped short, for he sat up straight and looked at me with such a stern, reproachful look that I could not say another word.

"My darling," said he, "I beg of you for my sake and our child's sake as well as for your own that you will never for one instant let that idea enter your mind. There is nothing so dangerous so fascinating to a temperament like yours. It is a false and foolish fancy. Can you not trust me as a physician when I tell you so?"

So of course I said no more on that score and he went to sleep before long.

He thought I was asleep first, but I wasn't, I lay there for hours trying to decide whether the front pattern and the back pattern really did move together or separately.

On a pattern like this, by daylight, there is a certain lack of sequence, a defiance of law, that is a constant irritant to a normal mind.

The color is hideous enough and unreliable enough and infuriating enough but the pattern is torturing.

You think you have mastered it, but just as you get well under-way in following it, it turns a back-somersault and there you are! It slaps you in the face, knocks you down, and tramples on you. It is like a bad dream. The outside pattern is a florid arabesque reminding one of a fungus. If you can imagine a toadstool in joints, an interminable string of toadstools, budding and sprouting in endless convolutions – why, that is something like it.

That is, sometimes!

There is one marked peculiarity about this paper, a thing nobody seems to notice but myself and that is that it changes as the light changes.

When the sun shoots in through the east window – I always watch for that first long straight ray – it changes so quickly that I never can quite believe it.

That is why I watch it always.

By moonlight – the moon shines in all night when there is a moon – I wouldn't know it was the same paper.

At night in any kind of light, in twilight, candlelight, lamplight, and worst of all by moonlight – it becomes bars! The outside pattern, I mean, and the woman behind is as plain as can be.

I didn't realize for a long time what the thing was that showed behind, that dim sub-pattern but now I am quite sure it is a woman.

By daylight she is subdued, quiet. I fancy, it is the pattern that keeps her so still. It is so puzzling. It keeps me quiet by the hour.

I lie down ever so much now John says it is good for me, and to sleep all I can.

Indeed he started the habit by making me lie down for an hour after each meal.

It is a very bad habit I am convinced for you see I don't sleep!

And that cultivates deceit for I don't tell them I'm awake – O no!

The fact is I am getting a little afraid of John.

He seems very queer sometimes. And even Jennie has an inexplicable look.

It strikes me occasionally just as scientific hypothesis – that perhaps it is the paper!

I have watched John when he didn't know I was looking – and come into the room suddenly on the most innocent excuses and I've caught him several times *looking at the paper*! And Jennie too. I caught Jennie with her hand on it once.

She didn't know I was in the room, and when I asked her in a quiet, a very quiet voice with the most restrained manner possible, what she was doing with the paper – she turned around as if she had been caught stealing and looked quite angry – asked me why I should frighten her so!

Then she said that the paper stained everything it touched that she had found yellow smooches on all my clothes and John's and she wished we would be more careful.

Did not that sound innocent? But I know she was studying that pattern, and I am determined that nobody shall find it out but myself!

Life is very much more exciting now than it used to be. You see I have something more to expect, to look forward to, to watch. I really do eat better, and am much more quiet than I was.

John is so pleased to see me improve. He laughed a little the other day and said I seemed to be flourishing in spite of my wallpaper.

I turned it off with a laugh. I had no intention of telling him it was *because* of the wallpaper he would make fun of me. He might even take me away.

I don't want to leave now until I have found it out. There is a week more, and I think that will be enough.

I'm feeling ever so much better! I don't sleep much at night, for it is so interesting to watch developments; but I sleep a good deal in the daytime.

In the daytime it is tiresome and perplexing.

There are always new shoots on the fungus, and new shades of yellow all over it. I cannot keep count of them, though I have tried conscientiously.

It is the strangest yellow, that paper. A sickly penetrating suggestive yellow. It make me think of all the yellow things I ever saw – not beautiful ones like butter-cups but old foul, bad yellow things.

But there is something else about that paper – the smell!

I noticed it the moment we came into the room, but with so much air and sun it was not bad. Now we have a had a week of fog and rain and whether the windows are open or not the smell is here.

It creeps all over the house.

I find it hovering in the dining room, skulking in the parlor, hiding in the hall, lying in wait for me on the stairs.

It gets into my hair.

Even when I go to ride, if I turn my head suddenly and surprise it – there is that smell!

Such a peculiar odor too! I have spent hours in trying to analyze it, to find what it smelled like. It is not bad – at first, and very gentle, but quite the subtlest most enduring odor I ever met.

In this damp weather it is awful, I wake up in the night and find it hanging over me.

It used to disturb me at first. I thought seriously of burning the house – to reach the smell.

But now I am used to it. The only thing I can think of that is like is the *color* of the paper. A yellow smell.

There is a very funny mark on this wall, low down near the mop-board. A streak that runs all round the room. It goes behind every piece of furniture except the bed; a long straight even smooch as if it had been rubbed over and over.

I wonder how it was done and who did it and what they did it for. Round and round and round – round and round and round – it makes me dizzy!

I really have discovered something at last. Through watching so much at night when it changes so I have finally found out.

The front pattern *does* move – and no wonder! The woman behind shakes it.

Sometimes I think there are a great many women behind, and sometimes only one, and she crawls around fast. And her crawling shakes it all over.

Then in the very bright spots she keeps still, and in very shady spots she just takes hold of the bars and shakes them hard.

And she is all the time trying to climb through. But nobody could climb through that pattern, it strangles so. I think that is why it has so many heads. They got through and then the pattern strangles them off and turns them upside down and makes their eyes white!

If those heads were covered or taken off it would not be half so bad.

I think that woman gets out in the daytime!

And I'll tell you why – privately – I've seen her! I can see her out of every one of my windows!

It is the same woman. I know, for she is always creeping and most women do not creep by daylight.

I see her in that long shaded lane, creeping up and down. I see her in those dark grape arbors, creeping all around the garden.

I see her on that long road under the trees, creeping along, and when a carriage comes she hides under the blackberry vines.

I don't blame her a bit. It must be very unpleasant to be caught creeping by daylight! I always lock the door when I creep by daylight. I can't do it at night for I know John would suspect something at once. And John is so queer now that I don't want to irritate him. I wish he would take another room! Besides, I don't want anybody to get that woman out at night but myself.

I often wonder if I could see her out of all the windows at once. But, turn as fast as I can, I can only see out of one at a time.

And though I always see her she *may* be able to creep faster than I can turn.

I have watched her sometimes away off in the open country, creeping as fast as a cloud shadow in a high wind.

If only that top pattern could be gotten off from the under one! I mean to try tearing it, little by little.

I have found out another funny thing but I shan't tell it this time. It does not do to trust people too much.

There are only two more days to get this paper off, and I believe John is beginning to notice. I don't like the look in his eyes.

And I heard him ask Jennie a lot of professional questions about me. She had a very good report to give.

She said I slept a good deal in the daytime. John knows I don't sleep very well at night, for all I'm so quiet! He asked me all sorts of questions too and pretended to be very loving and kind.

As if I couldn't see through him.

Still, I don't wonder he acts so, sleeping under this paper for three months.

It only interests me, but I feel sure John and Jennie are secretly affected by it.

Hurrah! This is the last day but it is enough. John had to stay in town overnight and won't be out till this evening.

Jennie wanted to sleep with me – the sly thing – but I told her I should undoubtedly rest better for a night all alone.

That was clever, for really I wasn't alone a bit! As soon as it was moonlight and that poor thing began to crawl and shake the pattern, I got up and ran to help her.

I pulled and she shook, I shook and she pulled, and before morning we had peeled off yards of that paper.

A strip about as high as my head and half around the room.

And then when the sun came and that awful pattern began to laugh at me I declared I would finish it today!

We go away tomorrow and they are moving all my furniture down again to leave things as they were before.

Jennie looked at the wall in amazement, but I told her merrily that I did it out of pure spite at the vicious thing.

She laughed and said she wouldn't mind doing it herself, but I must not get tired. How she betrayed herself that time.

But I am here and no person touches this paper but me – not *alive*!

She tried to get me out of the room – it was too patent! But I said it was so quiet and empty and clean now that I believed I would lie down again and sleep all I could and not to wake me even for dinner – I would call when I woke.

So now she is gone, and the servants are gone and the things are gone and there is nothing left but that great bedstead nailed down with the canvas mattress we found on it.

We shall sleep downstairs tonight and take the boat home tomorrow.

I quite enjoy the room, now it is bare again.

How those children did tear about here! This bedstead is fairly gnawed.

But I must get to work.

I have locked the door and thrown the key down into the front path.

I don't want to go out, and I don't want to have anybody come in until John comes. I want to astonish him.

I've got a rope up here that even Jennie did not find. If that woman does get out and tries to get away, I can tie her!

But I forgot I couldn't reach far without anything to stand on!

This bed will *not* move.

I tried to lift or push it till I was lame, and then I got so angry I bit off a little piece at one corner – but it hurt my teeth.

Then I peeled off all the paper I could reach standing on the floor. It sticks horribly. And the pattern just enjoys it! All those strangled heads and bulbous eyes and waddling fungus growths just shriek with derision!

I am getting angry enough to do something desperate. To jump out the window would be admirable exercise, but the bars are too strong even to try. Besides I wouldn't do it. Of course not. I know well enough that a step like that is improper and might be misconstrued.

I don't like top look out of the windows even – there are so many of those creeping women, and they creep so fast.

I wonder if they all came out of that wallpaper as I did? But I am securely fastened now by my well-hidden rope – you don't get *me* out in the road there.

It is so pleasant to be out in this great room and creep around as I please!

I don't want to go outside. I won't, even if Jennie asks me to. For outside you have to creep on the ground and everything is green instead of yellow.

But here I can creep smoothly on the floor and my shoulder just fits in that long smooch around the wall, so I cannot lose my way.

Why there's John at the door!

It is no use, young man, you can't open it!

How he does call and pound?

Now he's crying for an ax!

It would be a shame to break that beautiful strong door.

"John dear" said I in the gentlest voice-"The key is down by the front steps under a plantain leaf".

That silenced him for a few moments.

Then he said – very quietly indeed-"Open the door, my darling".

"I can't", said I. "The key is down by the front steps under a plantain leaf!"

And then I said it again several times very gently and slowly.

I said it so often that he had to go and see, and he got it of course and came in.

He stopped short by the door. "What is the matter?" he cried. "For God's sake what are you doing?"

I kept on creeping just the same, but I looked at him over my shoulder.

"I've got out at last," said I. "in spite of you and Jane. And I've pulled off most of the paper so you can't put me back."

Now why should that man have fainted?

But he did and right across my path by the wall so that I had to creep over him every time.

Rokeya Sakhawat Hossain

(1880-1932)

Rokeya Sakhawat Hossain was an educationist and a social reformer. Critics have described her as a "tireless activist' for the women's cause. In an age when Muslim women were not encouraged to learn Bengali, she wrote in Bengali and a great part of her work, in the form of essays, appeared in contemporary magazines.

Born in a small village of Bengal in undivided India, (now the village is in Bangladesh), Rokeya married at the age of 18, a widower who was much senior to her in age. Her husband however encouraged her and took interest in her social activism and set aside a sum of money with which she opened a school for girls.

While the Hindus in Bengal had initiated several progressive steps to encourage social participation of women, the Muslims were a little wary of modernist ways. The practice of purdah was in itself a major hindrance to any notion of a change in women's roles. Rokeya wrote a series of articles describing the condition of *purdahnashins* and the disadvantages of 'purdah'. These were brought together in a book *Avarodhbasini* which has subsequently been translated into English by Roushan Jahan as *Inside Seclusion: The Avarodhbasini of Rokeya Sakhawat Hossain* (Dacca: Women for Women, 1981).

"Sultana's Dream", originally written in English, is a fantasy, an imagined society where women are in control and men have been relegated to secondary roles. This reversal has also brought about a change in the value structures. Feminine values of team work and tolerance have supplanted masculine aggression and the need for power. Women learn to use their imagination and confront their enemies through the use of intelligence and learning. Their ability to harness nature for their own protection is another dimension of the utopian vision.

Sultana's Dream

One evening I was lounging in an easy chair in my bedroom and thinking lazily of the condition of Indian womanhood. I am not sure whether I dozed off or not. But, as far as I remember, I was wide awake. I saw the moonlit sky sparkling with thousands of diamondlike stars, very distinctly.

All of a sudden a lady stood before me; how she came in, I do not know. I took her for my friend, Sister Sara.

"Good morning," said Sister Sara. I smiled inwardly as I knew it was not morning, but starry night. However, I replied to her, saying, "How do you do?"

"I am all right, thank you. Will you please come out and have a look at our garden?"

I looked again at the moon through the open window, and thought there was no harm in going out at that time. The men-servants outside were fast asleep just then, and I could have a pleasant walk with Sister Sara.

I used to take my walks with Sister Sara, when we were at Darjeeling. Many a time did we walk hand in hand and talk light-heartedly in the Botanical gardens there. I fancied Sister Sara had probably come to take me to some such garden, and I readily accepted her offer and went out with her.

When walking I found to my surprise that it was a fine morning. The town was fully awake and the streets alive with bustling crowds. I felt very shy, since I was walking in the street in broad daylight, but there was not a single man visible.

Some of the passers-by made jokes at me. Though I could not understand their language, yet I felt sure they were joking. I asked my friend, "What do they say?"

"The women say that you look very mannish."

"Mannish?" said I, "What do they mean by that?"

"They mean that you are shy and timid like men."

"Shy and timid like men?" It was really a joke. I became very nervous, when I found that my companion was not Sister Sara, but a stranger. Oh, what a fool had I been to mistake this lady for my dear old friend, Sister Sara.

She felt my fingers tremble in her hand, as we were walking hand in hand.

"What is the matter, dear, dear?" she said affectionately.

"I feel somewhat awkward," I said in a rather apologising tone, "as being a *purdahnashin* woman, I am not accustomed to walking about unveiled."

"You need not be afraid of coming across a man here. This is Ladyland, free from sin and harm. Virtue herself reigns here."

By and by I was enjoying the scenery. Really it was very grand. I mistook a patch of green grass for a velvet cushion. Feeling as if I were walking on a soft carpet, I looked down and found the path covered with moss and flowers.

"How nice it is," said I.

"Do you like it?" asked Sister Sara. (I continued calling her "Sister Sara," and she kept calling me by my name.)

"Yes, very much; but I do not like to tread on the tender and sweet flowers."

"Never mind, dear Sultana. Your treading will not harm them; they are street flowers."

"The whole place looks like a garden," said I admiringly. "You have arranged every plant so skilfully."

"Your Calcutta could become a nicer garden than this, if only your countrymen wanted to make it so."

"They would think it useless to give so much attention to horticulture, while they have so many other things to do."

"They could not find a better excuse," said she with [a] smile.

I became very curious to know where the men were. I met more than a hundred women while walking there, but not a single man.

"Where are the men?" I asked her.

"In their proper places, where they ought to be."

"Pray let me know what you mean by 'their proper places.' "

"O, I see my mistake, you cannot know our customs, as you were never here before. We shut our men indoors."

"Just as we are kept in the Zenana?"

"Exactly so."

"How funny," I burst into a laugh. Sister Sara laughed too.

"But dear Sultana, how unfair it is to shut in the harmless women and let loose the men."

"Why? It is not safe for us to come out of the zenana, as we are naturally weak."

"Yes, it is not safe so long as there are men about the streets, nor is it so when a wild animal enters a marketplace."

"Of course not."

"Suppose, some lunatics escape from the asylum and begin to do all sorts of mischief to men, horses and other creatures, in that case what will your countrymen do?"

"They will try to capture them and put them back into their asylum."

"Thank you! And you do not think it wise to keep sane people inside an asylum and let loose the insane?"

"Of course not!" said I laughing lightly.

"As a matter of fact, in your country this very thing is done! Men, who do or at least are capable of doing no end of mischief, are let loose and the innocent women shut up in the zenana! How can you trust those untrained men out of doors?"

"We have no hand or voice in the management of our social affairs. In India man is lord and master. He has taken to himself all powers and privileges and shut up the women in the zenana."

"Why do you allow yourselves to be shut up?"

"Because it cannot be helped as they are stronger than women."

"A lion is stronger than a man, but it does not enable him to dominate the human race. You have neglected the duty you owe to yourselves and you have lost your natural rights by shutting your eyes to your own interests."

"But my dear sister Sara, if we do everything by ourselves, what will the men do then?"

"They should not do anything, excuse me; they are fit for nothing. Only catch them and put them into the zenana."

"But would it be very easy to catch and put them inside the four walls?" said I. "And even if this were done, would all their business – political and commercial – also go with them into the zenana!"

Sister Sara made no reply. She only smiled sweetly. Perhaps she thought it useless to argue with one who was no better than a frog in a well.

By this time we reached Sister Sara's house. It was situated in a beautiful heart-shaped garden. It was a bungalow with a corrugated iron roof. It was cooler and nicer than any of our rich buildings. I cannot describe how neat and how nicely furnished and how tastefully decorated it was.

We sat side by side. She brought out of the parlour a piece of embroidery work and began putting on a fresh design.

"Do you know how to knit and do needlework?"

"Yes; we have nothing else to do in our zenana."

"But we do not trust our zenana members with embroidery!" she said laughing, "as a man has not patience enough to pass thread through a needlehole even!"

"Have you done all this work yourself?" I asked her pointing to the various pieces of embroidered teapoy cloths.

"Yes."

"How can you find time to do all these? You have to do the office work as well? Have you not?"

"Yes. I do not stick to the laboratory all day long. I finish my work in two hours."

"In two hours! How do you manage? In our land the officers, magistrates for instance, work seven hours daily."

"I have seen some of them doing their work. Do you think they work all the seven hours?"

"Certainly they do!"

"No, dear Sultana, they do not. They dawdle away their time in smoking. Some smoke two or three cheroots during the office time. They talk much about their work, but do little. Suppose one cheroot takes half an hour to burn off, and a man smokes twelve cheroots daily; then you see, he wastes six hours every day in sheer smoking."

We talked on various subjects; and I learned that they were not subject to any kind of epidemic disease – nor did they suffer from mosquito-bites as we do. I was very much astonished to hear that in Ladyland no one died in youth except by rare accident.

"Will you care to see our kitchen?" she asked me.

"With pleasure," said 1, and we went to see it. Of course the men had been asked to clear off when I was going there. The kitchen was situated in a beautiful vegetable garden. Every creeper, every tomato plant was itself an ornament. I found no smoke, nor any chimney either in the kitchen, – it was clean and bright; the windows were decorated with flower garlands. There was no sign of coal or fire.

"How do you cook?" I asked.

"With solar heat," she said, at the same time showing me the pipe, through which passed the concentrated sunlight and heat. And she cooked something then and there to show me the process.

"How did you manage to gather and store up the sun heat?" I asked her in amazement.

"Let me tell you a little of our past history then. Thirty years ago, when our present Queen was thirteen years old, she inherited the throne. She was Queen in name only, the Prime Minister really ruling the country.

"Our good Queen liked science very much. She circulated an order that all the women in her country should be educated. Accordingly a number of girls' schools were founded and supported by the Government. Education was spread far and wide among women. And early marriage also was stopped. No woman was to be allowed to marry before she was twenty-one. I must tell you that, before this change we had been kept in strict-purdah."

"How the tables are turned," I interposed with a laugh.

"But the seclusion is the same, she said. "In a few years we had separate universities, where no men were admitted.

"In the capital, where our Queen lives, there are two universities. One of these invented a wonderful balloon, to which they attached a number of pipes. By means of this captive balloon which they managed to keep afloat above the cloud-land, they could draw as much water from the atmosphere as they pleased. As the water was incessantly being drawn by the University people, no cloud gathered and the ingenious lady Principal stopped rain and storms thereby."

"Really! Now I understand why there is no mud here!" said I. But I could not understand how it was possible to accumulate water in the pipes. She explained to me how it was done; but I was unable to understand her, as my scientific knowledge was very limited. However, she went on, –

"When the other university came to know of this, they became exceedingly jealous and tried to do something more extraordinary still. They invented an instrument by which they could collect as much sun heat as they wanted. And they kept the heat stored up to be distributed among others as required.

"While the women were engaged in scientific researches, the men of this country were busy increasing their military power. When they came to know that the female universities were able to draw water from the atmosphere and collect heat from the sun, they only laughed at the members of the universities and called the whole thing 'a sentimental nightmare'!"

"Your achievements are very wonderful indeed! But tell me, how you managed to put the men of your country into the zenana. Did you entrap them first?"

"No."

"It is not likely that they would surrender their free and open air life of their own accord and confine themselves within the four walls of the zenana! They must have been overpowered."

"Yes, they have been!"

"By whom?, by some lady-warriors, I suppose?"

"No, not by arms."

"Yes, it cannot be so. Men's arms are stronger than women's."

"Then?"

"By brain."

"Even their brains are bigger and heavier than women's. Are they not?"

"Yes, but what of that? An elephant also has got a bigger and heavier brain than a man has. Yet men can enchain elephants and employ them, according to their own wishes."

"Well said, but tell me please, how it all actually happened. I am dying to know it!"

"Women's brains are somewhat quicker than men's. Ten years ago, when the military officers called our scientific discoveries 'a sentimental nightmare,' some of the young ladies wanted to say something in reply to those remarks. But both the Lady Principals restrained them and said, they should reply, not by word, but by deed, if ever they got the opportunity. And they had not long to wait for that opportunity."

"How marvellous!" I heartily clapped my hands.

"And now the proud gentlemen are dreaming sentimental dreams themselves.

"Soon afterwards certain persons came from a neighbouring country and took shelter in ours. They were in trouble having committed some political offence. The King who cared more for power than for good government asked our kind-hearted Queen to hand them over to his officers. She refused, as it was against her principle to turn out refugees. For this refusal the King declared war against our country.

"Our military officers sprang to their feet at once and marched out to meet the enemy.

"The enemy however, was too strong for them. Our soldiers fought bravely, no doubt. But in spite of all their bravery the foreign army advanced step by step to invade our country.

"Nearly all the men had gone out to fight; even a boy of sixteen was not left home. Most of our warriors were killed, the rest driven back and the enemy came within twenty-five miles of the capital.

"A meeting of a number of wise ladies was held at the Queen's palace to advise [as] to what should be done to save the land.

"Some proposed to fight like soldiers; others objected and said that women were not trained to fight with swords and guns; nor were they accustomed to fighting with any weapons. A third party regretfully remarked that they were hopelessly weak of body.

'If you cannot save your country for lack of physical strength,' said the Queen, 'try to do so by brain power.'

"There was a dead silence for a few minutes. Her Royal Highness said again, 'I must commit suicide if the land and my honour are lost.'

"Then the Lady Principal of the second University, (who had collected sun-heat), who had been silently thinking during the consultation, remarked that they were all but lost; and there was little hope left for them. There was however, one plan which she would like to try, and this would be her first and last effort; if she failed in this, there would be nothing left but to commit suicide. All present solemnly vowed that they would never allow themselves to be enslaved, no matter what happened.

"The Queen thanked them heartily, and asked the Lady Principal to try her plan.

"The Lady Principal rose again and said, 'before we go out the men must enter the zenanas. I make this prayer for the sake of purdah.' 'Yes, of course,' replied Her Royal Highness.

"On the following day the Queen called upon all men to retire into zenanas for the sake of honour and liberty.

"Wounded and tired as they were, they took that order rather for a boon! They bowed low and entered the zenanas without uttering a single word of protest. They were sure that there was no hope for this country at all.

"Then the Lady Principal with her two thousand students marched to the battlefield, and arriving there directed all the rays of the concentrated sunlight and heat towards the enemy.

"The heat and light were too much for them to bear. They all ran away panic-stricken, not knowing in their bewilderment how to counteract that scorching heat. When they fled away leaving their guns and other ammunitions of war, they were burnt down by means of the same sun-heat.

"Since then no one has tried to invade our country any more."

"And since then your countrymen never tried to come out of the zenana?"

"Yes, they wanted to be free. Some of the Police Commissioners and District Magistrates sent word to the Queen to the effect that the Military Officers certainly deserved to be imprisoned for their failure; but they never neglected their duty and therefore they should not be punished and they prayed to be restored to their respective offices.

"Her Royal Highness sent them a circular letter intimating to them that if their services should ever be needed they would be sent for, and that in the meanwhile they should remain where they were.

"Now that they are accustomed to the purdah system and have ceased to grumble at their seclusion, we call the system 'Murdana' instead of 'zenana.' "

"But how do you manage," I asked Sister Sara, "to do without the Police or Magistrates in case of theft or murder?"

"Since the 'Murdana' system has been established, there has been no more crime or sin; therefore we do not require a Policeman to find out a culprit, nor do we want a Magistrate to try a criminal case."

"That is very good, indeed. I suppose if there were any dishonest person, you could very easily chastise her. As you gained a decisive victory without shedding a single drop of blood, you could drive off crime and criminals too without much difficulty!"

"Now, dear Sultana, will you sit here or come to my parlour?" she asked me.

"Your kitchen is not inferior to a queen's boudoir!" I replied with a pleasant smile, "but we must leave it now; for the gentlemen may be cursing me for keeping them away from their duties in the kitchen so long." We both laughed heartily.

"How my friends at home will be amused and amazed, when I go back and tell them that in the far-off Ladyland, ladies rule over the country and control all social matters, while gentlemen are kept in the Murdanas to mind babies, to cook and to do all sorts of domestic work; and that cooking is so easy a thing that it is simply a pleasure to cook!"

"Yes, tell them about all that you see here."

"Please let me know, how you carry on land cultivation and how you plough the land and do other hard manual work."

"Our fields are tilled by means of electricity, which supplies motive power for other hard work as well and we employ it for our aerial conveyances too. We have no railroad nor any paved streets here."

"Therefore neither street nor railway accidents occur here," said I. "Do not you ever suffer from want of rainwater?" I asked.

"Never since the 'water balloon' has been set up. You see the big balloon and pipes attached thereto. By their aid we can draw as much rainwater as we require. Nor do we ever suffer from flood or thunderstorms. We are all very busy making nature yield as much as she can. We do not find time to quarrel with one another as we never sit idle. Our noble Queen is exceedingly fond of Botany; it is her ambition to convert the whole country into one grand garden."

"The idea is excellent. What is your chief food?"

"Fruits."

"How do you keep your country cool in hot weather? We regard the rainfall in summer as a blessing from heaven."

"When the heat becomes unbearable, we sprinkle the ground with plentiful showers drawn from the artificial fountains. And in cold weather we keep our room warm with sun-heat."

She showed me her bathroom, the roof of which was removable. She could enjoy a shower bath whenever she liked, by simply removing the roof (which was like the lid of a box) and turning on the tap of the shower pipe.

"You are a lucky people!" ejaculated I. "You know no want. What is your religion, may I ask?"

"Our religion is based on Love and Truth. It is our religious duty to love one another and to be absolutely truthful. If any person lies, she or he is – ."

"Punished with death?"

"No; not with death. We do not take pleasure in killing a creature of God, – specially a human being. The liar is asked to leave this land for good and never to come to it again."

"Is an offender never forgiven?"

"Yes, if that person repents sincerely."

"Are you not allowed to see any men, except your own relations?"

"No one except sacred relations."

"Our circle of sacred relations is very limited to, even first cousins are not sacred."

"But ours is very large; a distant cousin is as sacred as a brother."

"That is very good. I see Purity itself reigns over your land. I should like to see the good Queen, who is so sagacious and farsighted and who has made all these rules."

"All right," said Sister Sara.

Then she screwed a couple of seats on to a square piece of plank. To this plank she attached two smooth and well-polished balls. When I asked her what the balls were for, she said, they were hydrogen balls and they were used to overcome the force of gravity. The balls were of different capacities to be used according to the different weights desired to be overcome. She then fastened to the air-car two wing-like blades, which, she said, were worked by electricity. After we were comfortably seated she touched a knob and the blades began to whirl, moving faster and faster every moment. At first we were raised to the height of about six or seven feet and then off we flew. And before I could realize that we had commenced moving, we reached the Garden of the Queen.

My friend lowered the air-car by reversing the action of the machine, and when the car touched the ground the machine was stopped and we got out.

I had seen from the air-car the Queen walking on a garden path with her little daughter (who was four years old) and her maids of honour.

"Halloo! you here!" cried the Queen addressing Sister Sara. I was introduced to Her Royal Highness and was received by her cordially without any ceremony.

I was very much delighted to make her acquaintance. In [the] course of the conversation I had with her, the Queen told me that she had no objection to permitting her subjects to trade with other countries. "But," she continued, "no trade was possible with countries where the women were kept in the zenanas and so unable to come and trade with us. Men, we find, are rather of lower morals and so we do not like dealing with them. We do not covet other people's land, we do not fight for a piece of diamond though it may be a thousand-fold brighter than the Koh-i-Noor, nor do we grudge a ruler his Peacock Throne. We dive deep into the ocean of knowledge and try to find out the precious gems, which Nature has kept in store for us. We enjoy Nature's gifts as much as we can."

After taking leave of the Queen, I visited the famous universities, and was shown over some of their manufactories, laboratories and observatories.

After visiting the above places of interest we got again into the air-car, but as soon as it began moving I somehow slipped down and the fall startled me out of my dream. And on opening my eyes, I found myself in my own bedroom still lounging in the easy-chair.

Katherine Mansfield
(1888-1923)

Katherine Mansfield, a New Zealander, moved to England, first for the purposes of study (1903-1906), and later to opt out of the restrictive family environment. Her father, a well established banker, failed to notice his daughter's talent. A contemporary of Virginia Woolf, Katherine Mansfield was, like Woolf, sensitive to the nuances of language and to the experience of women. She published several short story collections during her lifetime, of which the two better known ones are: *Bliss and Other Stories* (1920), *The Garden Party and Other Stories* (1922). Her stories vary in length right from brief sketches to short novels. Some of them work through many generations, and are finely crafted like music pieces. She herself was an accomplished violincelloist who had been unable to pursue a career in music.

Like Gilman and Virginia Woolf, Mansfield too went through a spell of mental illness. She died in 1923 a year after she had entered a nursing home.

"The Late Colonel's Daughters" is a story which lives through the aftermath of the dictatorial father's death and with gentle irony describes the feelings of insecurity and fear which still inhabit the house as well as the lives of the daughters. The old man had never really allowed the girls any space for self-expression. Even their housekeeping reflects their timidity and the dead man's nurse also frightens them into pretension. The story has its comic side despite which it comes through as an exposition of the sad life of the two women who do not know the meaning of freedom and continue to be afraid of the ghosts of the past.

The Daughters of the Late Colonel

I

The week after was one of the busiest weeks of their lives. Even when they went to bed it was only their bodies that lay down and rested; their minds went on, thinking things out, talking things over, wondering, deciding, trying to remember where...

Constantia lay like a statue, her hands by her sides, her feet just overlapping each other, the sheet up to her chin. She stared at the ceiling.

'Do you think father would mind if we gave his top-hat to the porter?'

'The porter?' snapped Josephine. 'Why ever the porter? What a very extraordinary idea!'

'Because,' said Constantia slowly, 'he must often have to go to funerals. And I noticed at – at the cemetery that he only had a bowler.' She paused. 'I thought then how very much he'd appreciate a top-hat. We ought to give him a present, too. He was always very nice to father.'

'But,' cried Josephine, flouncing on her pillow and staring across the dark at Constantia, 'father's head!' And suddenly, for one awful moment, she nearly giggled. Not, of course, that she felt in the least like giggling. It must have been habit. Years ago, when they had stayed awake at night talking, their beds had simply heaved. And now the porter's head, disappearing, popped out, like a candle, under father's hat ... The giggle mounted, mounted; she clenched her hands; she fought it down; she frowned fiercely at the dark and said, Remember,' terribly sternly.

'We can decide tomorrow,' she said.

Constantia had noticed nothing; she sighed.

'Do you think we ought to have our dressing-gowns dyed as well?'

'Black?' almost shrieked Josephine.

'Well, what else?' said Constantia. "I was thinking – it doesn't seem quite sincere, in a way, to wear black out of doors and when we're fully dressed, and then when we're at home –'

'But nobody sees us,' said Josephine. She gave the bed-clothes such a twitch that both her feet became uncovered and she had to creep up the pillows to get them well under again.

'Kate does,' said Constantia. 'And the postman very well might.'

Josephine thought of her dark-red slippers, which matched her dressing-gown, and of Constantia's favourite indefinite green ones which went with hers. Black! Two black dressing-gowns and two pairs of black woolly slippers, creeping off to the bathroom like black cats.

'I don't think it's absolutely necessary,' said she.

Silence. Then Constantia said, "We shall have to post the papers with the notice in them tomorrow to catch the Ceylon mail... How many letters have we had up till now?'

'Twenty-three.'

Josephine had replied to them all, and twenty-three times when she came to 'We miss our dear father so much' she had broken down and had to use her handkerchief, and on some of them even to soak up a very light-blue tear with an edge of blotting-paper. Strange! She couldn't have put it on – but twenty-three times. Even now, though, when she said over to herself sadly, 'We miss our dear father *so* much,' she could have cried if she'd wanted to.

'Have you got enough stamps?' came from Constantia.

'Oh, how can I tell?' said Josephine crossly. 'What's the good of asking me that now?'

'I was just wondering,' said Constantia mildly.

Silence again. There came a little rustle, a scurry, a hop.

'A mouse,' said Constantia.

'It can't be a mouse because three aren't any crumbs,' said Josephine.

'But it doesn't know there aren't,' said Constantia.

A spasm of pity squeezed her heart. Poor little thing! She wished she'd left a tiny piece of biscuit on the dressing-table. It was awful to think of it not finding anything. What would it do?

'I can't think how they manage to live at all,' she said slowly.

'Who?' demanded Josephine.

And Constantia said more loudly than she meant to, 'Mice.'

Josephine was furious. 'Oh, what nonsense, Con!' she said. 'What have mice got to do with it? You're asleep.'

'I don't think I am,' said Constantia. She shut her eyes to make sure. She was.

Josephine arched her spine, pulled up her knee, folded her arms so that her fists came under her ears, and pressed her cheek hard against the pillow.

II

Another thing which complicated matters was they had Nurse Andrews staying on with them that week. It was their own fault; they had asked her. It was Josephine's idea. On the morning – well, on the last morning, when the doctor had gone, Josephine had said to Constantia, 'Don't you think it would be rather nice if we asked Nurse Andrews to stay on for a week as our guest?'

'Very nice,' said Constantia.

'I thought,' went on Josephine quickly, 'I should just say this afternoon, after I've paid her, "My sister and I would be very pleased, after all you've done for us, Nurse Andrews, if you would stay on for a week as our guest." I'd have to put that in about being our guest in case –'

'Oh, but she could hardly expect to be paid!' cried Constantia.

'One never knows,' said Josephine sagely.

Nurse Andrews had, of course, jumped at the idea. But it was a bother. It meant they had to have regular sit-down meals at the proper times, whereas if they'd been alone they could just have asked Kate if she wouldn't have minded bringing them a tray wherever they were. And meal-times now that the strain was over were rather a trial.

Nurse Andrews was simply fearful about butter. Really they couldn't help feeling that about butter, at least, she took advantage of their kindness. And she had that maddening habit of asking for just an inch more bread to finish what she had on her plate, and then, at the last mouthful, absent-mindedly – of course it wasn't absent-mindedly – taking another helping. Josephine got very red when this happened, and she fastened her small, bead-like eyes on the tablecloth as if she saw a minute strange insect creeping through the web of it. But Constantia's long, pale face lengthened and set, and she gazed away – away – far over the desert, to where that line of camels unwound like a thread of wool...

'When I was with Lady Tukes,' said Nurse Andrews, 'she had such a dainty little contrayvance for the buttah. It was a silvah Cupid balanced on the – on he bordah of a glass dish, holding a tayny fork. And when you wanted some buttah you simply pressed his foot and he bent down and speared you a piece. It was quite a gayme.'

Josephine could hardly bear that. But 'I think those things are very extravagant' was all she said.

'But whey?' asked Nurse Andrews, beaming through her eyeglasses. 'No one, surely, would take more buttah than one wanted – would one?'

'Ring, Con,' cried Josephine. She couldn't trust herself to reply.

And proud young Kate, the enchanted princess, came in to see what the old tabbies wanted now. She snatched away their plates of mock something or other and slapped down a white, terrified blancmange.

'Jam, please, Kate,' said Josephine kindly.

Kate knelt and burst open the sideboard, lifted the lid of the jam-pot, saw it was empty, put it on the table, and stalked off.

'I'm afraid,' said Nurse Andrews a moment later, 'there isn't any.'

'Oh, what a bother!' said Josephine. She bit her lip. 'What had we better do?'

Constantia looked dubious. 'We can't disturb Kate again,' she said softly.

Nurse Andrews waited, smiling at them both. Her eyes wandered, spying at everything behind her eyeglasses. Constantia in despair went back to her camels. Josephine frowned heavily –

concentrated. If it hadn't been for this idiotic woman she and Con would, of course, have eaten their blancmange without. Suddenly the idea came.

'I know,' she said. 'Marmalade. There's some marmalade in the sideboard. Get it, Con.'

'I hope,' laughed Nurse Andrews – and her laugh was like a spoon tinkling against a medicine-glass – 'I hope it's not very bittah marmalayde.'

III

But, after all, it was not long now, and then she'd be gone for good. And there was no getting over the fact that she had been very kind to father. She had nursed him day and night at the end. Indeed, both Constantia and Josephine felt privately she had rather overdone the not leaving him at the very last. For when they had gone in to say good-bye Nurse Andrews had sat beside his bed the whole time, holding his wrist and pretending to look at her watch. It couldn't have been necessary. It was so tactless, too. Supposing father had wanted to say something – something private to them. Not that he had. Oh, far from it! He lay there, purple, a dark, angry purple in the face, and never even looked at them when they came in. Then, as they were standing there, wondering what to do, he had suddenly opened one eye. Oh, what a difference it would have made, what a difference to their memory of him, how much easier to tell people about it, if he had only opened both! But no – one eye only. It glared at them a moment and then ... went out.

IV

It had made it very awkward for them when Mr Farolles, of St John', called the same afternoon.

'The end was quite peaceful, I trust?' were the first words he said as he glided towards them through the dark drawing-room.

'Quite,' said Josephine faintly. They both hung their heads. Both of them felt certain that eye wasn't at all a peaceful eye.

'Won't you sit down?' said Josephine.

'Thank you, Miss Pinner,' said Mr Farolles gratefully. He folded his coat-tails and began to lower himself into father's arm-chair, but just as he touched it he almost sprang up and slid into the next chair instead.

He coughed. Josephine clasped her hands; Constantia looked vague.

'I want you to feel, Miss Pinner,' said Mr Farolles, 'and you, Miss Constantia, that I'm trying to be helpful. I want to be helpful to you both, if you will let me. These are the times,' said Mr Farolles, very simply and earnestly, 'when God means us to be helpful to one another.'

'Thank you very much, Mr Farolles,' said Josephine and Constantia.

'Not at all,' said Mr Farolles gently. He drew his kid gloves through his fingers and leaned forward. 'And if either of you would like Communion, either or both of you, here *and* now, you have only to tell me. A little Communion is often very help – a great comfort,' he added tenderly.

But the idea of a little Communion terrified them. What! In the drawing-room by themselves – with no – no altar or anything! The piano would be much too high, thought Constantia, and Mr Farolles could not possibly lean over it with the chalice. And Kate would be sure to come bursting in and interrupt them, thought Josephine. And supposing the bell rang in the middle? It might be somebody important – about their mourning. Would they get up reverently and go out, or would they have to wait...in torture?

'Perhaps you will send round a note by your good Kate if you would care for it later,' said Mr Farolles.

'Oh yes, thank you very much!' they both said.

Mr Farolles got up and took his black straw hat from the round table.

'And about the funeral,' he said softly. 'I may arrange that – as your dear father's old friend and yours, Miss Pinner – and Miss Constantia?'

Josephine and Constantia got up too.

'I should like it to be quite simple,' and Josephine firmly, 'and not too expensive. At the same time, I should like-'

'A good one that will last,' thought dreamy Constantia, as if Josephine were buying a night-gown. But, of course, Josephine didn't say that. 'One suitable to our father's position.' She was very nervous.

'I'll run round to our good friend Mr. Knight,' said Mr Farolles soothingly. 'I will ask him to come and see you. I am sure you will find him very helpful indeed.'

V

Well, at any rate, all that part of it was over, though neither of them could possibly believe that father was never coming back. Josephine had had a moment of absolute terror at the cemetery, while the coffin was lowered, to think that she and Constantia had done this thing without asking his permission. What would father say when he found out? For he was bound to find out sooner or later. He always did. 'Buried. You two girls had me *buried!*' She heard his stick thumping. Oh, what would they say? What possible excuse could they make? It sounded such an appallingly heartless thing to do. Such a wicked advantage to take of a person because he happened to be helpless at the moment. The other people seemed to treat it all as a matter of course. They were strangers; they couldn't be expected to understand that father was the very last person for such a thing to happen to. No, the entire blame for it all would fall on her and Constantia. And the expense, she thought, stepping into the tight-buttoned cab. When she had to show him the bills. What would he say then?

She heard him absolutely roaring. 'And do you expect me to pay for this gimcrack excursion of yours?'

'Oh,' groaned poor Josephine aloud, 'we shouldn't have done it, Con!'

And Constantia, pale as a lemon in all that blackness, said in a frightened whisper, 'Done what, Jug?'

'Let them bu-bury father like that,' said Josephine, breaking down and crying into her new, queer-smelling mourning handkerchief.

'But what else could we have done?' asked Constantia wonderingly. 'We couldn't have kept him, Jug – we couldn't have kept him unburied. At any rate, not in a flat that size.'

Josephine blew her nose; the cab was dreadfully stuffy.

'I don't know,' she said forlornly. 'It is all so dreadful. I feel we ought to have tried to, just for a time at least. To make perfectly sure. One thing's certain' – and her tears sprang out again – 'father will never forgive us for this – never!'

VI

Father would never forgive them. That was what they felt more than ever when, two mornings later, they went into his room to go through his things. They had discussed it quite calmly. It was even down on Josephine's list of things to be done. *Go through father's things and settle about them.* But that was a very different matter from saying after breakfast:

'Well, arc you ready, Con?'

'Yes, Jug – when you are.'

'Then I think we'd better get it over.'

It was dark in the hall. It been a rule for years never to disturb father in the morning, whatever happened. And now they were going to open the door without knocking even... Constantia's eyes were enormous at the idea; Josephine felt weak in the knees.

'You – you go first,' she gasped, pushing Constantia.

But Constantia said, as she always had said on those occasions, 'No, Jug, that's not fair. You're eldest.'

Josephine was just gong to say – what at other times she wouldn't have owned to for the world – what she kept for her very last weapon, 'But you're tallest,' when they noticed that the kitchen door was open, and there stood Kate...

'Very stiff,' said Josephine, grasping the door-handle and doing her best to turn it. As if anything ever deceived Kate!

It couldn't be helped. That girl was ... Then the door was shut behind them, but – but they weren't in father's room at all. They might have suddenly walked through the wall by mistake into a different flat altogether. Was the door just behind them? They were too frightened to look. Josephine knew that if it was it was holding itself tight shut; Constantia felt that, like the doors in dreams, it hadn't any handle at all. It was the coldness which made it so awful. Or the whiteness – which? Everything was covered. The blinds were down, a cloth hung over the mirror, a sheet hid the bed; a huge fan of white paper filled the fire-place. Constantia timidly put out her hand; she almost expected a snowflake to fall. Josephine felt a queer tingling in her nose, as if her nose was freezing. Then a cab klop-klopped over the cobbles below, and the quiet seemed to shake into little pieces.

'I had better pull up a blind,' said Josephine bravely.

'Yes, it might be a good idea,' whispered Constantia.

They only gave the blind a touch, but it flew up and the cord flew after, rolling the blind-stick, the little tassel tapped as if trying to get free. That was too much for Constantia.

'Don't you think – don't you think we might put it off for another day?' she whispered.

'Why?' snapped Josephine, feeling, as usual, much better now that she knew for certain that Constantia was terrified, 'it's got to be done. but I do wish you wouldn't whisper. Con.'

'I didn't know I was whispering,' whispered Constantia.

'And why do you keep on staring at the bed?' said Josephine, raising her voice almost defiantly. 'There's nothing *on* the bed.'

'Oh, Jug, don't say so!' said poor Connie. 'At any rate, not so loudly.'

Josephine felt herself that she had gone too far. She took a wide swerve over to the chest of drawers, put out her hand, but quickly drew it back again.

'Connie!' she gasped, and she wheeled round and leaned with her back against the chest of drawers.

'Oh, Jug – what?'

Josephine could only glare. She had the most extraordinary feeling that she had just escaped something simply awful. But how could she explain to Constantia that father was in the chest of drawers? He was in the top drawer with his handkerchiefs and neckties, or in the next with his shirts and pyjamas, or in the lowest of all with his suits. He was watching there, hidden away – just behind the door-handle – ready to spring.

She pulled a funny old-fashioned face at Constantia, just as she used to in the old days when she was going to cry.

'I can't open,' she nearly wailed.

'No, don't, Jug,' whispered Constantia earnestly. 'It's much better not to. Don't let's open anything. At any rate, not for a long time.'

'But – but it seems so weak,' said Josephine, breaking down.

'But why not be weak for once, Jug?' argued Constantia, whispering quite fiercely. 'If it is weak.' And her pale stare flew from the locked writing-table – so safe – to the huge glittering wardrobe, and she began to breathe in a queer, panting way. 'Why shouldn't we be weak for once in our lives, Jug? It's quite excusable. Let's be weak – be weak, Jug. It's much nicer to be weak than to be strong.'

And then she did one of those amazingly bold things that she'd done about twice before in their lives; she marched over to the wardrobe, turned the key, and took it out of the lock. Took it out of the lock and held it up to Josephine, showing Josephine by her extraordinary smile that she knew what she'd done – she'd risked deliberately father being in there among his overcoats.

If the huge wardrobe had lurched forward, had crashed down on Constantia, Josephine wouldn't have been surprised. On the contrary, she would have thought it the only suitable thing to happen. But nothing happened. Only the room seemed quieter than ever, and bigger flakes of cold air fell on Josephine's shoulders and knee. She began to shiver.

'Come, Jug,' said Constantia, still with that awful callous smile; and Josephine followed just as she had that last time, when Constantia had pushed Benny into the round pond.

VII

But the strain told on them when they were back in the dining-room. They sat down, very shaky, and looked at each other.

'I don't feel I can settle to anything,' said Josephine, 'until I've had something. Do you think we could ask Kate for two cups of hot water?'

'I really don't see why we shouldn't,' and Constantia carefully. She was quite normal again. 'I won't ring. I'll go to the kitchen door and ask her.'

'Yes, do,' said Josephine, sinking down into a chair. 'Tell her, just two cups, Con, nothing else – on a tray.'

'She needn't even put the jug on, need she?' said Constantia, as though Kate might very well complain if the jug had been there.

'Oh no, certainly not! The jug's not at all necessary. She can pour it direct out of the kettle,' cried Josephine, feeling that would be a labour-saving indeed.

Their cold lips quivered at the greenish brims. Josephine curved her small red hands round the cup; Constantia sat up and blew on the wavy steam, making it flutter from one side to the other.

'Speaking of Benny,' said Josephine.

And though Benny hadn't been mentioned Constantia immediately looked as though he had.

'He'll expect us to send him something of father's, of course. But it's so difficult to know what to send to Ceylon.'

'You mean things get unstuck so on the voyage,' murmured Constantia.

'No, lost,' said Josephine sharply. 'You know there's no post. Only runners.'

Both paused to watch a black man in white linen drawers running through the pale fields for dear life, with a large brown-paper parcel in his hands. Josephine's black man was tiny; he scurried along glistening like an ant. but there was something blind and tireless about Constantia's tall, thin fellow, which made him, she decided, a very unpleasant person indeed ... On the veranda, dressed all in white and wearing a cork helmet, stood Benny. His right hand shook up and down, as father's did when he was impatient. And behind him, not in the least interested, sat Hilda, the unknown sister-in-law. She swung in a cane rocker and flicked over the leaves of the *Tatler.*

'I think his watch would be the most suitable present,' said Josephine.

Constantia looked up; she seemed surprised.

'Oh, would you trust a gold watch to a native?'

'But, of course, I'd disguise it,' said Josephine. 'No one would know it was a watch.' She liked he idea of having to make a parcel such a curious shape that no one could possibly guess what it was. She even thought for a moment of hiding the watch in a narrow cardboard corset-box that she'd kept by her for a long time, waiting for it to come in for something. It was such beautiful, firm cardboard. But, no, it wouldn't be appropriate for this occasion. It had lettering on it: *Medium Women's* 28. *Extra Firm Busks*. It would be almost too much of a surprise for Benny to open that and find father's watch inside.

'And, of course, it isn't as though it would be going ticking, I mean,' said Constantia, who was still thinking of the native love of jewellery. 'At least,' she added, 'it would be very strange if after all that time it was.'

VIII

Josephine made no reply. She had flown off one of her tangents. She had suddenly thought of Cyril. Wasn't it more usual for the only grandson to have the watch? And then dear Cyril was so appreciative and a good watch meant so much to a young man. Benny, it all probability, had quite got out of the habit of watches; men so seldom wore waistcoats in those hot climates. Whereas Cyril in London wore them from year's end to year's end. And it would be so nice for her and Constantia, when he came to tea, to know it was there. 'I see you've got on grandfather's watch, Cyril.' It would be somehow so satisfactory.

Dear boy! What a blow his sweet, sympathetic little note had been! Of course they quite understood; but it was most unfortunate.

'It would have been such a point, having him,' Josephine.

'And he would have enjoyed it so,' said Constantia, not thinking what she was saying.

However, as soon as he got back he was coming to tea with his aunties. Cyril to tea was one of their rare treats.

'Now, Cyril, You mustn't be frightened of our cakes. Your Auntie Con and I bought them at Buszard's this morning. We know what a man's appetite is. So don't be ashamed of making a good tea.'

Josephine cut recklessly into the rich dark cake that stood for her winter gloves or the soling and heeling of Constantia's only respectable shoes. But Cyril was most unmanlike in appetite.

'I say, Aunt Josephine, I simply can't. I've only just had lunch, you know.'

'Oh, Cyril, that can't be true! It's after four,' cried Josephine. Constantia sat with her knife poised over the chocolate-roll.

'It is, all the same,' said Cyril. 'I had to meet a man at Victoria, and he kept me hanging about till... there was only time to get lunch and to come on here. And he gave me – phew' – Cyril put his hand to his forehead – 'a terrific blow-out,' he said.

It was disappointing – today of all days. But still he couldn't be expected to know.

'But you'll have a meringue, won't you, Cyril?' said Aunt Josephine. 'These meringues were bought specially for you. Your dear father was so fond of them. We were sure you are, too.'

'I *am*, Aunt Josephine,' cried Cyril ardently. 'Do you mind if I take half to begin with?'

'Not at all, dear boy; but we mustn't let you off with that.'

'Is your dear father still so found of meringues?' asked Auntie Con gently. She winced faintly as she broke through the shell of hers.

'Well, I don't quite know, Auntie Con,' said Cyril breezily.

At that they both looked up.

'Don't know?' almost snapped Josephine. 'Don't know a thing like that about your own father, Cyril?'

'Surely,' said Auntie Con softly.

Cyril tried to laugh it off. 'Oh, well,' he said, 'it's such a long time since – ' He faltered. He stopped. Their faces were too much for him.

'Even *so*,' said Josephine.

And Auntie Con looked.

Cyril put down his teacup. 'Wait a bit,' he cried. 'Wait a bit, Aunt Josephine. What am I thinking of?'

He looked up. They were beginning to brighten. Cyril slapped his knee.

'Of course,' he said, 'it was meringues. How could I have forgotten? Yes, Aunt Josephine, you're perfectly right. Father's most frightfully keen on meringues.'

They didn't only beam. Aunt Josephine were scarlet with pleasure; Auntie Con gave a deep, deep sigh.

'And now, Cyril, you must come and see father,' said Josephine. 'he knows you were coming today.'

'Right,' said Cyril, very firmly and heartily. He got up from, his chair; suddenly he glanced at the clock.

'I say, Auntie Con, isn't your clock a bit slow? I've got to meet a man at – at Paddington just after five. I'm afraid I shan't be able to stay very long with grandfather.'

'Oh, he won't expect you to say *very* long!' said Aunt Josephine.

Constantia was still gazing at the clock. She couldn't make up her mind if it was fast or slow. It was one or the other, she felt almost certain of that. At any rate, it had been.

Cyril still lingered. 'Aren't you coming along, Auntie Con?'

'Of course,' said Josephine, 'we shall all go. Come on, Con.'

IX

They knocked at the door, and Cyril followed his aunts into grandfather's hot, sweetish room.

'Come on,' said Grandfather Pinner. 'Don't hang about. What is it? What've you been up to?'

He was sitting in front of a roaring fire, clasping his stick. He had a thick rug over his knees. On his lap there lay a beautiful pale-yellow silk handkerchief.

'It's Cyril, father,' said Josephine shyly. And she took Cyril's hand and led him forward.

'Good afternoon, grandfather,' said Cyril, trying to take his hand out of Aunt Josephine's. Grandfather Pinner shot his eyes at Cyril in the way he was famous for. Where was Auntie Con? She stood on the other side of Aunt Josephine; her long arms hung down in front of her; her hands were clasped. She never took her eyes off grandfather.

'Well', said Grandfather Pinner, beginning to thump, 'what have you got to tell me?'

What had he, what had he got to tell him? Cyril felt himself smiling like a perfect imbecile. The room was stifling, too.

But Aunt Josephine came to his rescue. She cried brightly, 'Cyril says his father is still very fond of meringues, father dear.'

'Eh?' said Grandfather Pinner, curving his hand like a purple meringue-shell over one ear.

Josephine repeated, 'Cyril says his father is still very fond of meringues.'

'Can't hear,' said old Colonel Pinner. And he waved Josephine away with his stick, then pointed with his stick to Cyril. 'Tell me what she's trying to say,' he said.

(My God!) 'Must I?' said Cyril, blushing and staring at Aunt Josephine.

'Do, dear,' she smiled. 'It will please him so much.'

'Come on, out with it!' cried Colonel Pinner testily, beginning to thump again.

And Cyril leaned forward and yelled, 'Father's still very fond of meringues.'

At that Grandfather Pinner jumped as though he had been shot.

'Don't shout!' he cried. 'What's the matter with the boy?' *Meringues*! What about 'em?'

Oh, Aunt Josephine, must we go on?' groaned Cyril desperately.

'It's quite all right, dear boy,' said Aunt Josephine, as though he and she were at the dentist's together. 'He'll understand in a minute.' And she whispered to Cyril, 'He's getting a bit deaf, you know.' Then she leaned forward and really bawled at Grandfather Pinner, 'Cyril only wanted to tell you, father dear, that *his* father is still very fond of meringues.'

Colonel Pinner heard that time, heard and brooded, looking Cyril up and down.

'What an esstrorordinary thing!' said old Grandfather Pinner. 'What an esstrorordinary thing to come all this way here to tell me!'

And Cyril felt it *was*.

'Yes, I shall send Cyril the watch,' said Josephine.

'That would be very nice,' said Constantia. 'I seem to remember last time he came there was some little trouble about the time.'

X

They were interrupted by Kate bursting through the door in her usual fashion, as though she had discovered some secret panel in the wall.

'Fried or boiled?' asked the bold voice.

Fried or boiled? Josephine and Constantia were quite bewildered for the moment. They could hardly take it in.

'Fried or boiled what, Kate?' asked Josephine, trying to begin to concentrate.

Kate gave a loud sniff. 'Fish.'

'Well, why didn't you say something immediately?' Josephine reproached her gently. 'How could you expect us to understand, Kate? There are a great many things in this world, you know, which are fried or boiled.' and after such a display of courage she said quite brightly to Constantia, 'Which do you prefer, Con?'

'I think it might be nice to have it fried,' said Constantia. 'On the other hand, of course, boiled fish is very nice. I think I prefer both equally well ... Unless you ... In that case –'

'I shall fry it,' said Kate, and she bounced back, leaving their door open and slamming the door of her kitchen.

Josephine gazed at Constantia; she raised her pale eyebrows until they rippled away into her pale hair. She got up. She said in a very lofty, imposing way, 'Do you mind following me into the drawing-room, Constantia? I've something of great importance to discuss with you.'

For it was always to the drawing-room they retired when they wanted to talk over Kate.

Josephine closed the door meaningly. 'Sit down, Constantia,' she said, very grand. She might have been receiving Constantia for the first time. And Con looked vaguely for a chair, as though she felt indeed quite a stranger.

'Now the question is,' said Josephine, bending forward, 'whether we shall keep her or not.'

'That is the question,' agreed Constantia.

'And this time,' said Josephine firmly, 'we must come to a definite decision.'

Constantia looked for a moment as though she might begin going over all the other times, but she pulled herself together and said, 'Yes, Jug.'

'You see, Con,' explained Josephine, 'everything is so changed now.' Constantia looked up quickly. 'I mean,' went on Josephine, 'we're not dependent on Kate as we were.' And she blushed faintly. 'There's not father to cook for.'

'That is perfectly true,' agreed Constantia. 'Father certainly doesn't want any cooking now whatever else –'

Josephine broke in sharply, 'You're not sleepy, are you, Con.'

'Sleepy, Jug?' Constantia was wide-eyed.

'Well, concentrate more,' said Josephine sharply, and she returned to the subject. 'What it comes to is, if we did' – and this she barely breathed, glancing at the door– 'give Kate notice' – she raised her voice again – 'we could manage our own food.'

'Why not?' cried Constantia. She couldn't help smiling. The idea was so exciting. She clasped her hands. 'What should we live on, Jug?'

'Oh, eggs in various forms!' said Jug, lofty again. 'And, besides, there are all the cooked foods.'

'But I've always heard,' said Constantia, 'they are considered so very expensive.'

'Not if one buys them in moderation,' said Josephine. But she tore herself away from this fascinating bypath and dragged Constantia after her.

'What we've got to decide now, however, is whether we really do trust Kate or not.'

Constantia leaned back. Her flat little laugh flew from her lips. 'Isn't it curious, Jug,' said she, 'that just on this one subject I've never been able to quite make up my mind?'

XI

She never had. The whole difficulty was to prove anything. How did one prove things, how could one? Suppose Kate had stood in front of her and deliberately made a face. Mightn't she very well have been in pain? Wasn't it impossible, at any rate, to ask Kate if she was making a face at her? If Kate answered 'No' – and, of course, she would say 'No' – what a position! How undignified! Then, again, Constantia suspected, she was almost certain that Kate went to her chest of drawers when she and Josephine were out, not to take things but to spy. Many times she had come back to find her amethyst cross in the most unlikely places, under her lace ties or on top her evening Bertha. More than once she had laid a trap for Kate. She had arranged things in a special order and then called Josephine to witness.

'You see, Jug?'

'Quite, Con.'

'Now we shall be able to tell.'

But, oh dear, when she did go to look, she was as far off from a proof as ever! If anything was displaced, it might so very well have happened as she closed the drawer; a jolt might have done it so easily.

'You come, Jug, and decide. I really can't. It's too difficult.' But after a pause and a long glare Josephine would sigh, 'Now you've put the doubt into my mind, Con, I'm sure I can't tell myself.'

'Well, we can't postpone it again,' said Josephine. 'If we postpone it this time –'

XII

But at that moment in the street below a barrel-organ struck up. Josephine and Constantia sprang to their feet together.

'Run, Con,' said Josephine. 'Run quickly. There's sixpence on the–'

Then they remembered. It didn't matter. They would never have to stop the organ-grinder again. Never again would she and Constantia be told to make that monkey take his noise somewhere else. Never would sound that loud, strange bellow when father thought they were not hurrying enough. The organ-grinder might ply there all day and the stick would not thump.

It never will thump again,
It never will thump again,

played the barrel-organ.

What was Constantia thinking? She had such a strange smile; she looked different. She couldn't be going to cry.

'Jug, Jug,' said Constantia softly, pressing her hands together. 'Do you know what day it is? It's Saturday. It's a week today, a whole week.'

A week since father died,
A week since father died,

cried the barrel-organ. And Josephine, too, forgot to be practical and sensible; she smiled faintly, strangely. On the Indian carpet there fell a square of sunlight, pale red; it came and went and came – and stayed, deepened – until it shone almost golden.

'The sun's out,' said Josephine, as though it really mattered.

A perfect fountain of bubbling notes shook from the barrel-organ, round, bright notes, carelessly scattered.

Constantia lifted her big, cold hands as if to catch them, and then her hands fell again. She walked over to the mantelpiece to her favourite Buddha. And the stone and gilt image, whose smile always gave her such a queer feeling, almost a pain and yet a pleasant pain, seemed today to be more than smiling. He knew something; he had a secret. 'I know something that you don't know,' said her Buddha. Oh, what was it, what could it be? And yet she had always felt there was ... something.

The sunlight pressed through the windows, thieved its way in, flashed its light over the furniture and the photographs. Josephine watched it. When it came to mother's photographs, the enlargement over the piano, it lingered as though puzzled to find so little remained of mother, except the ear-rings shaped like tiny pagodas and a black feather boa. Why did the photographs of dead people always fade so? wondered Josephine. As soon as a person was dead their photographs died too. But, of course, this one of mother was very old. It was thirty-five years old. Josephine remembered standing on a chair and pointing out that feather boa to Constantia and telling her that it was a snake that had killed their mother in Ceylon... Would everything have been different if mother hadn't died? She didn't see why. Aunt Florence had lived with them until they had left school, and they had moved three times and had their yearly holiday and ... and there'd been changes of servants, of course.

Some little sparrows, young sparrows they sounded, chirped on the window-ledge. *yeep – eyeep – yeep.* But Josephine felt they were not sparrows, not on the window ledge. It was inside her, that queer little crying noise. *Yeep – eyeep – yeep.* Ah, what was it crying, so weak and forlorn?

If mother had lived, might they have married? But there had been nobody for them to marry. There had been father's Anglo-Indian friends before he quarrelled with them. But after that she and Constantia never met a single man except clergymen. How did one meet men? Or even if they'd met them, how could they have got to know men well enough to be more than strangers? One read of people having adventures, being followed, and so on. But nobody had ever followed Constantia and her. Oh yes, there had been one year at Eastbourne a mysterious man at their boarding-house who had put a note on the jug of hot water outside their bedroom door! But by the time Connie had found it the steam had made the writing too faint to read; they couldn't even make out to which of them it was addressed. And he had left next day. And that was all. The rest had been looking after father and at the same time keeping out of father's way. But now? But now? The thieving sun touched Josephine gently. She lifted her face. She was drawn over to the window by gentle beams...

Until the barrel-organ stopped playing Constantia stayed before the Buddha, wondering, but not as usual, not vaguely. This time her wonder was like longing. She remembered the times she had come in here, crept out of bed in her night-gown when the moon was full, and lain on the floor with her arms outstretched, as though she was crucified. Why? The big, pale moon had made her do it. The horrible dancing figures on the carved screen had leered at her and she hadn't minded. She remembered too how, whenever they were at the seaside, she had gone off by herself and got as close to the sea as she could, and sung something, something she had made up, while she gazed all over that restless water. There had been this other life, running out, bringing things home in bags, getting things on approval, discussing them with Jug, and taking them back to get more things on approval, and arranging father's trays and trying not to annoy father. But it all seemed to have happened in a kind of tunnel. It wasn't real. It was only when she came out of the tunnel into the moonlight or by the sea or into a thunderstorm that she really felt herself. What did it mean? What was it she was always wanting? What did it all lead to? Now? Now?

She turned away from the Buddha with one of her vague gestures. She went over to where Josephine was standing. She wanted to say something to Josephine, something frightfully important, about – about the future and what...

'Don't you think perhaps-' she began.

But Josephine interrupted her. 'I was wondering if now-' she murmured. They stopped; they waited for each other.

'Go on, Con,' said Josephine.

'No, no, Jug; after you,' said Constantia.

'No, say what you were going to say. You began,' said Josephine.

'I ... I'd rather hear what you were going to say first,' said Constantia.

'Don't be absurd, Con.'

'Really, Jug.'

'Connie!'

'Oh, *Jug!*'

A pause. Then Constantia said faintly, 'I can't say what I was going to say, Jug, because I've forgotten what it was ... that I was going to say.'

Josephine was silent for a moment. She stared at a big cloud where the sun had been. The she replied shortly, 'I've forgotten too.'

Lalithambika Antarjanam
(1909-1987)

The word 'Antarjanam', means people who live indoors, or are secluded. It also indicates Lalithambika's caste affiliations. In Kerala, the Brahmin community of the Nambudiris practices a moral code which discriminates on the grounds of gender.

Lalithambika was born in a family which was deeply critical about this double code of morality and worked for social reform. They were enlightened people, people who were not afraid to discuss or debate contentious issues, but later her marriage into a conservative family exposed her to virtual seclusion. Educated at home in Malayalam and Sanskrit, she started writing by the time she was fourteen. In 1926, at age 17, she was married to Narayan Nambudiri and went on to have seven children.

It is not surprising that Lalithambika's stories repeatedly portray this world. The story, which is included in this anthology is about a real life happening which took place sometime between 1900-1910. Kuriyedath Tatri was a Nambudiri woman almost smothered by the confines of her existence. Her husband's neglect of her led to further frustration as did the depressing climate of her parental home which was a home full of dependent women. Rather than exchange one prison for another, Tatri entered into a life of liaisons with upper caste men and went on to keep proofs of their infidelity. Later, when brought before a trial jury, she shocked the public by the proofs she produced against many men otherwise considered respectable.

This episode of Kerala women's history has been fictionalised at least thrice. Besides Lalithambika's story originally titled *"Pratikara devata* (The Spirit of Revenge) there exist two others in the form of novels one by K.B. Sreedevi, titled *Yagnam* (Sacrifice) and *Brushte* (the polluted and hence the outcast) by Matampu Kunjukuttan.

Revenge Herself

Midnight. I sat alone in my study. Sleep beckoned me with compassion, caressing my work-weary body and soul. But if I should put away my writing materials, there would be no returning until the next day – to the same hour, the same weariness. Silence all around, broken only by the occasional chatter of the married mice in the attic, or the snoring of the sleeping children in the next room. From the solitary lamp on the table a pale light was cast, somehow terrifying against the dense darkness outside. Somewhere owls hooted in warning. I am a coward by nature, let me admit it. I was more so that night, in those eerie surroundings.

I shut the window and bolted it, adjusted the wicks of the oil lamp, checked on the children to see if they were awake, came back and sat in my usual place. I had to write. But what should I write about? Where to begin? The problem overwhelmed me. It is not easy to write a story, particularly for a woman in my position. I want to write out of my convictions, but I fear to hazard my name, my status. When my stories mirror the reality of society, I am open to the criticism of all kinds of people. When they abuse me, how should I retaliate? I dare not even approach the question of religious customs. And yet in spite of all these scruples, whom. will I displease this time? Which literary movement will I offend?

I threw my pen down in disgust, leaned back in the chair and shut my eyes. Many possible characters seemed to walk by: seen, unseen, alive, dead, women and men; suffering souls, voiceless, but with thunder and lightning in their hearts. Were they commanding me to record their lives? I was frightened, but exhilarated too.

Suddenly I heard the sound of approaching footsteps. What was this? I shivered and sat up. Had I forgotten to close the door and bolt it? I hadn't heard the sound of the door being opened. It was midnight, the time when spirits walk. And though I am not naturally superstitious, I was afraid. I felt faint, my eyes closed. The footsteps seemed to come nearer and nearer, yet I could not move.

Minutes ticked by. Five minutes? An hour? I don't know. After some time I heard a woman's voice nearby, speaking to me softly but firmly: 'Are you asleep? Or are you just scared?'

I did not stir. Or rather, I did not have the courage to stir. The voice continued in a slightly sarcastic tone: 'You claim to be a. writer, and yet you are afraid. I thought that experienced writers were accustomed to observing horror and tragedy without so much as batting an eyelid.'

My curiosity to see this person who knew this much about me, overcame my fear. I opened my eyes. Before me, as though from a dream, stood a woman, neither young nor old; ageless. Her expression seemed a mixture of sorrow, bitterness, hatred and despair. Her eyes seemed to burn with the intensity of revenge. I thought she was a figure from the pages of recent history – known but forgotten.

She continued authoritatively, yet with some kindness too. 'Mine is not a social visit. I thought you were in a dilemma, floundering without a theme for a story. I can offer you an excellent one: shelved and rotting, waiting to be written. With your permission – if you are not afraid . . .'

By this time I had pulled myself together somewhat.

'Yes', I said, 'I am scared. Of this night. Of all that is happening now. Who are you? How did you manage to come here? Weren't the doors closed?'

'Who am I?' She laughed aloud. 'So you would like to know who I am. You want to know whether I am human being or devil; ghost or evil spirit. You have courage.'

Her laughter had the sound of a wild river that had burst its dam. Wave upon wave of that unearthly laughter filled the room, echoing, reverberating. By this time I was prepared.

'I admit I am a coward. But tell me who you are. Without knowing that how can I proceed? As human beings we need to know – even about the remotest stars – their names and station.'

'As human beings? I would rather you didn't call me one', she cut in angrily. 'Once upon a time, I was proud to carry that name, and I struggled hard not to dishonour it. Now I no longer wish to be known as a human being, particularly a woman. One lesson I have learnt, and perhaps I have taught it too: the human condition is one of cruel betrayal and suffering.'

'Perhaps,' I agreed. 'But isn't suffering and pain the special gift granted to humankind – the golden chain that links human and divine?'

She dismissed the notion summarily.

'Suffering, a golden chain? What absolute nonsense! Just tell me one thing. As a means of bondage, is gold any different from iron? At least one knows where one is with iron. Gold hides behind its seductive facade. Iswara! That, after all, is the difference between devil and man too.'

By now, her face, charged with hatred, had taken on an inhuman aspect, though I could not quite understand how the change had come about. Sorrow, hatred, pride and revenge seemed to flit across it making it extraordinarily vivid, strangely attractive. I wondered what it was that she had endured in her past life.

'Are you waiting to hear my story?' she asked after a pause. 'Well, it is my intention to tell you. It is an old story, of true events that happened half a century ago. At that time it turned history on its head. You weren't even born then. Neither were these new-fangled social reformist organisations with their tall claims nor their leaders around then. Few characters from my story are alive now. But the echoes of those events have not quite died ... Did you ever hear of Tatri of – ?'

I shivered. So this was she. Whose name our mothers had prohibited us from speaking. A name which to us had become obscene. I was speechless.

She saw my hesitation. Sadly she said, 'O yes, which Nambudiri woman hasn't heard of Tatri, "fallen object", "tainted goods"? Though none of you will so much as admit to that knowledge. But child, can you now try and understand why that hated one gave up her life?

'To begin with, she was as innocent as any one of you. She too once made karuka garlands. She too prayed like you, raptly clasping her black string. She fasted on all auspicious days. She was innocent, she had neither looked upon a man nor spoken with him. Grandmothers used to uphold Tatri as a model of propriety to all the young girls who come of age.

'But you know that all those rituals are, after all, charades. You know that by the time we are seventeen or eighteen we are shrewd enough to control our most secret thoughts. On moonlit nights we sit in the inner verandah reciting prayers, our sighs suppressed. We sing "Parvati Swayamvaram" and "Mangala Atira" and dance, the catch in our voices unheard. And all the time we wait, with bated breath, for the men's voices in the outer verandah. We offer austere leaves of kuvalam in strict prayer, while our hearts are filled with the sensuous fragrance of mango blooms. And so we wait ... days, months, even years ... At last one day our mothers come with henna and silver ring. And our hands are given into the hands of a man old or young, invalid or lecher. That is our destiny. That is our entire life.

'Mine was a lucky fate, or so people said in those days. He was in his prime, it was his first marriage, he had sufficient means. So I began my marriage with no worries. I soon found he was a man with aggressive sexual needs. I learnt in time to meet those demands, to please him in his taste for sex with the same attention and care that I gave to his taste for food. After all, one's husband is considered the pratyaksha deivam, the "seen" God. And it was to please that God that I learnt the art of the prostitute. If it were not for that, dear sister, I too – like so many women of our community – would have remained a mere wife, a neglected and ignored wife. Perhaps, too, none of the wretched consequences would have followed. On the other hand, it might be, that in learning to serve him, I unleashed my own instinctual being. I don't know. But I swear to you that at that time he alone was at the centre of my life.

'So it was that when he started drifting away from me, I was desolate. Often he didn't come home at night. I used to think, at first, that he was at a festival or a private feast. Perhaps he was at the variyam or was needed at the palace. I would cry and sulk on the rare occasions when I saw him. There was no one else to share my grief.

'He laughed in response to my heartbroken complaints. A man, he said, is as free as a bird. His life should be one of enjoyment. Surely a man cannot be expected to waste away his entire youth married to one woman, and that a Nambudiri wife.

'Sometimes I was filled with anger and bitterness. Sometimes I even wished to put an end to my life. I often cursed my lot as a Nambudiri woman, thinking, if only I belonged to any other caste of Kerala, one which would have given me the right to reply, to match his male arrogance with my freedom.

'But no. Each month, upon the recurrence of his birthstar, I bathed and prayed that he should have a long life, making offerings of tumba flower garlands and neivillakku lit with ghee. When I came of age I had prayed to be granted a good husband; now I prayed that I should be granted my husband's love.

'The steward of our estate was a kind man who made sure I had plenty to eat. But what about one's inner hunger, that other greed? Once kindled it is not easily quenched. It flows like molten lava, like fire through the very life-blood. He, my husband, knew this too. But he was a man and I a woman. A woman: born in a cursed society.

I too would have suffered in silence like all those other Nambudiri women except for what happened unexpectedly. One night he came home with a new wife. They were to sleep that night in the very bedroom I had shared with him. I could even bring myself to serve food to this woman, but to be actually asked to prepare their nuptial bed! Yes, I had chanted the "Seelavati charitram" again and again ... But an Antarjanam is a human being too ... I cursed her aloud. In my grief and outrage, I called her a whore. On that instant I saw him turn into a devil. He flung my words back at me. "I know perfectly well she is a whore – I love her for what she is. If you could be like her, I might like you better."

'I could bear the physical violence, but those words were a far worse assault. I was numb with the horror of it. A pativrata, a woman of honour to be as much as told by her husband, "If you want me to love you, be a prostitute!" For a blinding moment, I was overcome by a furious thirst for revenge. Somehow I held myself together. But I knew I had had enough. I could not stay in that place a moment longer.

'I did not speak to him again. I withdrew into myself. Desolate and grief-stricken, yearning for consolation, I returned to my own home. There followed days without love; uneventful days. There were no rays of fight in the tunnel. All Nambudiri houses are dark prisons, after all. Is one any better than another? My father had died but his five wives were still alive. My brother was looking for a bride to replace his fourth wife who was now dead. My two widowed sisters were there too. The third one, driven insane because of the ill-treatment she had received from her husband, wandered about aimlessly. Two younger sisters, now grown up, were unmarried – a burden to the house and a grief to my mother. When I joined this lot, it was exactly like jumping from the frying pan into the fire. Living in such a bleak, claustrophobic world, who could be blamed for seeking some comfort? I was young, healthy, egoistic. I thought I was more beautiful than any of my husband's mistresses. In those days, when I combed my hair, freshened my face and glanced covertly through the windows, all I wanted was a glimpse of the outside world. I had an innocent desire to be seen and admired. There were some who caught those glances and smiled at me. I smiled in return. And that was all. Those aristocratic Nambudiris who were attracted to me knew well enough the consequences I would suffer for even this. As for themselves, they would have been ready for any kind of liaison provided it was discreet.

'Meaningful glances. Hushed whispers. Gossip and scandal The inmates of the inner rooms turned out to be fifth columnists. My mother never lost an opportunity to curse me. "You sinner, born to be the ruin of your family's reputation. I wish I had never carried you in my womb."

'And one day my sister-in-law was peremptory with her order: "Don't step into the kitchen."

I still cannot understand why I was punished so. I hadn't so much as touched a man other than my husband. I hadn't the boldness to nurture such a desire. There had been a few glances through the window. A few men had been attracted. Was that my fault? But the world was never concerned with reason or logic. The innuendos continued till they numbed my heart. Terror at the thought of dishonour threw me off balance; pushed me to the verge of the very abyss I dreaded. I was long past suffering. In all directions there was only darkness. It was as though through whirling coils of dark smoke my enemies waited, ready to strike, like snakes. To survive that final struggle I had to be a snake too. At last I gave way to those long quiescent storms of anger and revenge.

'If I should tell you what I decided to do, you would be appalled. But please remember, my sister, that it was done for you too, and for all Nambudiri women. As a matter of pride. As a show of strength. I enjoyed the humiliation of those men, for there never was any value attached to our own tears. Yet, after all, in the end I gained nothing, for even you women hated me, dreaded me more than the devil. Years have passed, but even to you of a modern time Tatri is no more than a fallen woman.'

As she spoke, her eyes filled with tears, and overcome with grief she laid her head upon the table. I watched her in silence, wondering what sort of future a woman such as she could have expected. If her life had been shattered and strewn around the wilderness like pieces of a broken bottle then was it her fault or that of society's? There could have been only two alternatives for her: madness or prostitution. Both tragic.

After a moment she sat up, her eyes dry once more and aflame with intensity. 'No, child,' she said, 'I shall not cry again. That was a momentary weakness.' She resumed her story. 'Nothing could shock me any more – neither the waves breaking the bounds of the sea, nor even the skies falling down. Life and death had all become the same. Yes, I made my decision. I thought that since I had chosen my destiny, it should also be an act of revenge on behalf of my mothers and sisters. If I should be victimised, it should not be on false grounds. If I should be made outcast, it should not be for being innocent. Women, too, I thought, can willingly choose the path of debasement. And if I should choose to fan, I would bring down, with me several cruel men who were the means of that fall. I would see to it that in the clear light of justice many more men than I should deserve excommunication.

'On a certain night a new courtesan appeared on the festival grounds and temple precincts. She was beautiful and witty. Her modesty attracted men even more than her beauty. Princes, courtiers and Nambudiris, all sought her company. At first she kept them all at arm's length, saying she was a married woman with a husband who was still alive. She withheld a crucial detail about herself, however, – the community to which she belonged. They brushed aside her pleas to be left alone. They argued that in Kerala, the land of Parasurama, a woman was allowed as many husbands as she chose. The only women who were outside this rule were the Nambudiris. The rest, they said, were free to enjoy their pleasure. O these men who seem so honourable, so saintly! Men who expect unquestioning faithfulness from their own wives, but who are quite willing to ruin another's!

'So many men were attracted to me. So different from the ostracism of the inner rooms. I melted, I was moved. I could not have enough of their adulation.

'The new courtesan grew famous. Those who came to her went away happy. From each of them, in return for their pleasure, she received – or took – gifts and mementos. And so, gradually and deliberately, she gained possession of the honour of many men who claimed to be pillars of our society.

'There was one man who was yet to come. There was one man for whom she waited and watched. She knew he would not fail to come, once he had heard of this true pleasure seeker. We had not seen each other for five years. But I recognised him the moment I met him at my usual rendezvous near the temple. He, however, did not know me. How could he see in this proud and famous woman his old Antarjanam?

'I shall not forget that night. For that night I had debased myself; for that night I had lived and waited. From the moment he had last spoken, this idea had rankled, then seeded and grown in my mind. If a woman should. go to the lengths of becoming a prostitute in order to please her husband, can she be called a pativrata? For if that were so, I too was one; a veritable "Seelavati". Through my corruption I could please him, and yes, he was pleased.

'Just before he left me, he said, "In all my life, I have never met a woman so beautiful and so clever. I wish I could live with you always."

'At the very moment that he slipped the ring – once again – on my finger, I asked him, "Are you. sure you have never before met one like me?"

'Holding his sacred thread with both hands, he said, "No, I swear by my Brahmasvam. No. I have never before met a woman of your wit and intelligence."

'I smiled with triumph. I raised my voice very slightly and said, "That's false. Think of your wife. Was she any worse than I?"

'In the hesitant light of that pale dawn he looked at me once again. A strangled cry escaped him. "O my God, my Lord Vadakkunatha, it is Tatri. Tatri." And he fled from my sight, disappearing immediately.

'That's all I need to tell you. You know very well all that happened afterwards. As an Antarjanam I was brought to trial for defilement, and under threat of losing caste. It was a trial that shook the whole of Kerala. As it got under way, they were all terrified – yes, princes and Nambudiris too – that their names would be spoken by the prostitute. Then some went into hiding. Others frantically made offerings to the gods. Each hoped desperately she had forgotten him.

'I had more than names, I had proofs; a golden ring with a name engraved upon it, a golden girdle, a gold bordered veshti. And so, sixty-five men, priests among, them, were brought to trial. I could have been the means of excommunicating sixty thousand men, not merely sixty-five. Any woman who was beautiful enough and clever enough could have done the same, such were the decadent landlords and Nambudiris of those days. I could have insisted on continuing the enquiry. But no. In the end, for all the submerged rage of all Nambudiri women, only sixty-five men were brought to trial. Those sixty-five were indicted. That was my revenge. Was it my revenge alone?

'And now, tell me sister. Which one do you think was worse, the man who led a woman into prostitution for his own satisfaction, or the woman who willed herself, into prostitution to counter him? Which one should you hate? Which one should you shun?'

I had not uttered a word throughout her strange account, and now I was dumbstruck. She misunderstood my silence and spoke in a voice full of disappointment and despair. Why did I come here? I made a mistake. Why did I try to speak to a slave of a woman who has no self-respect or honour? Oh no, you will never change.'

I was not offended by what she said. At last I began to speak. 'My poor wronged sister, I don't blame you. I do sympathise with you. I understand that you were speaking for many – for the weak against the strong, for women calling out for justice, for all human beings whose emotions and instincts have been stamped upon. What you did was not just an act of personal revenge, it was a protest born out of grief and despair.

'But then, think of this, too. Was it not impulsive and headstrong to take up such a responsibility on your own? Individual effort cannot yield lasting results; sometimes it, can be positively dangerous. Just think of that. That storm that you raised – what good did it possibly do to society as a whole? In the end, men used it as an excuse to victimise us even more: the memory of that event was a means of humiliating us, forcing us to hang our heads in shame. Remember too, that you hardly brought any consolation to the families and womenfolk of the excommunicated men.'

By this time, I too was stirred, my voice shook as I spoke. 'You must excuse me. But I have to say that for most of us, what you choose to describe as the sacrifice of Tatri was nothing more and nothing less than the trial of a prostitute. True, it created a storm, but it did not point to a clear direction for us. The end cannot justify the means, sister. Of course, I applaud your courage and your pride, but I have to denounce the path you took.

'But, all the same, we as Nambudiris can never forget Tatri. From your world of darkness and silence you hurled a random firecracker as a warning and a challenge. Nevertheless it ignited a torch for us in our generation, and there will be greater fires in times to come. Your revenge will be forgiven because of those radiant future fires.'

I held out my hands to her in love and compassion. But the face of the female form had paled, its eyes were lifeless, it vanished away into the morning fog, wailing. 'I must not let my shadow fall upon you. For you I am, and always will be, a sinner, a fallen woman, a devil.'

The cock crew. I woke up from that strange dream.

Mahasweta Devi

(b 1926)

Mahasweta Devi writes in Bengali but her work has been translated into several languages. Born in Dhaka in an artistic family, she inherited intellectual and literary talents from her parents. Her father was a novelist and a poet and her mother a social worker and writer. Mahasweta's writing is not only interlaced with social concerns but she is, in her own right, a social activist having taken up the burden of articulating tribal experience and exposing the oppressive tendencies of mainstream society.

It was only in 1956 that she began full-fledged writing choosing for her first book the biography of Laxmibai, Rani of Jhansi. Time and again she has written about revolutionary movements, whether it be the Naxalite movement, or the tribals' struggle for social space. The book which shot her to fame was *Aranyer Adhikar* (Rights Over the Forest), translated into Hindi as *Jungle Ke Davedar*.

Mahasweta's work reveals a deep concern for the subjugation of women who are easy targets of exploitation, as courtesans or prostitutes, as mothers and wives. It is remarkable that her women characters, instead of breaking down or withdrawing into insanity, respond with a sturdy boldness and raw courage. "Draupadi" is one such story which has been introduced into postcolonial constructs by Gayatri Spivak through her translation.

"Draupadi" turns the account of the Mahabharata episode of the *chirharan* (the public exposure attempted by the Kaurvas, wherein she was protected by the miraculous lengthening of the sari which covered her), on its head and uses nakedness as a symbol of indomitable courage where the body has ceased to matter and the fully clothed officers stand 'exposed' in every way. The use of legend, fable or myth lends itself to fresh myths in her work. She is a name to reckon with as activism and aesthetics continue to flow together in her work.

Draupadi

I

Name Dopdi Mejhen, age twenty-seven, husband Dulna Majhi (deceased), domicile Cherakhan, Bankrahjarh, scar on the shoulder (Dopdi was shot), information whether dead or alive and/or assistance in arrest, one hundred rupees ...

An exchange between two liveried *uniforms.*

First Livery: What's this, a tribal called Dopdi? The list of names I brought has nothing like it! How can anyone have an unlisted name?

Second: Draupadi Mejhen. Born the year her mother threshed rice at Surja Sahu (killed)'s at Bakuli. Surja Sahu's wife gave her the name.

First: These officers like nothing better than to write as much as they can in English. What's all this stuff about her?

Second: *Most notorious* female. *Long wanted in many ...*

Dossier: Dulna and Dopdi worked at harvests, *rotating between* Birbhum, Barddhaman, Murshidabad, and Bankura. In 1971, in the famous *Operation* Bakuli, when three villages were *cordoned off* and *machinegunned,* they too lay on the ground, faking dead. In fact, they were the *main criminals.* Murdering Surja Sahu and his son, occupying *upper-caste* wells and tubewells during the *drought,* not *surrendering* those three young men to the police. In all this they were the chief instigators. In the morning, at the time of the body count, the couple could not be found. The *blood-sugar* level of Captain Arjan Singh, the *architect* of *Operation* Bakuli, rose at once and proved yet again that diabetes can be a result of anxiety and depression. Diabetes has twelve husbands – among them *anxiety.*

Dulna and Dopdi went underground for a long time in a *Neanderthal* darkness. The Special Forces, attempting to pierce that dark by an armed search, compelled quite a few migrant Santals, male and female farmworkers, in the various districts of West Bengal to meet their Maker against their will. By the Indian Constitution, all human beings, regardless of caste or creed, are sacred. Still accidents like this do happen. Two sorts of reasons: (1) the underground couple's skill in self-concealment; (2) not merely the Santals but all tribals of the Austro-Asiatic Munda tribes appear the same to the Special Forces.

In fact, all around the ill-famed forest of Jhadkhani, which is under the jurisdiction of the police station at Bankrajharh (in this India of ours, even a worm is under a certain police station), even in the southeast and southwest corners, one comes across hair-raising details in the eyewitness records put together on the people who are suspected of attacking police stations, stealing guns (since the snatchers are not invariably well educated, they sometimes say 'give up your *chambers*' rather than give up your gun), killing grain brokers, landlords, moneylenders, law officers, bureaucrats and narks. A black-skinned couple ululated like police sirens before the episode. They sang jubilantly in a savage tongue, incomprehensible even to the Santals. Such as:

Samaray hijulenako mar goekope

and,

Hende rambra kechey kechey
Pundi rambra kechey kechey

This proves conclusively that they are the cause of Captain Arjan Singh's diabetes.

Government procedure being as incomprehensible as the Male Principle in Sankhya philosophy or Antonioni's early films to *hoi polloi*, it was Arjan Singh who was sent once again on *Operation Forest* Jhadkhani. Learning from Intelligence that the above-mentioned ululating and dancing couple were the escaped corpses, Arjan Singh fell for a bit into a *zombie* like state and finally acquired so irrational a dread of black-skinned people that whenever he saw a black person in a ballbag, he swooned, saying 'they're killing me', and drank and passed a lot of water. Neither uniform nor Scriptures could relieve that depression. At long last, under the shadow of a *premature* and *forced retirement,* it was possible to present him at the desk of Mr Senanayak, the elderly Bengali *specialist* in combat and extreme-Left politics.

Senanayak knows the activities and capacities of the opposition better than they themselves do. First, therefore, he presents an encomium on the military genius of the Sikhs. Then he explains further: Is it only the opposition that should find power at the end of the barrel of a gun? Arjan Singh's power also explodes out of the *male organ* of a gun. Without a gun even the 'five Ks' come to nothing in this day and age. These speeches he delivers to all and sundry. As a result, the fighting forces regain their confidence in the *Army Handbook.* It is not a book for everyone. It says that the most despicable and repulsive style of fighting is guerrilla warfare., with primitive weapons. Annihilation at sight of any and all practitioners of such warfare is the sacred duty of every soldier. Dopdi and Dulna belong to the category of such fighters, for they too kill by means of hatchet and scythe, bow and arrow, etc. In fact, their fighting power is greater than the gentlemen's. Not all gentlemen become experts in the explosion of 'chambers'; they think the power will come out on its own if the gun is held. But since Dulna and Dopdi are illiterate, their kind have practised the use of weapons generation after generation.

I should mention here that, although the other side make little of him, Senanayak is not to be trifled with. Whatever his practice, in theory he respects the opposition. Respects them because they could be neither understood nor demolished if they were treated with the attitude, 'It's nothing but a bit *of* impertinent game-playing with guns'. *In order to destroy the enemy, become one.* Thus he understood them by (theoretically) becoming one of them. He hopes to write on all this in the future. He has also decided that in his written work he will *demolish* the gentlemen and highlight the message *of* the migrant workers. These mental *processes* might seem complicated, but actually he is a simple man and is as pleased as his third great-uncle after a meal of turtle meat. In fact, he knows that, as in the old IPTA song, turn by turn the world will change. And in every world he must have the credentials to survive with honour. If necessary he will show the future to what extent he alone understands the matter in its proper *perspective.* He knows very well that what he is doing today the future will forget, but he also knows that if he can change colour from world to world, he can represent the particular world in question. Today he is getting rid of the young by means of *'apprehension and elimination',* but he knows people will soon forget the memory and lesson of blood. And at the same time, he, like Shakespeare, believes in delivering the world's *legacy* into youth's hands. He is Prospero as well.

At any rate, information is received that many young men and women, *batch by batch* and on jeeps, have attacked police station after police station, terrified and elated the region, and disappeared into the forest of Jhadkhani. Since after escaping from Bakuli, Dopdi and Dulna have worked at the house of virtually every landowner, they can efficiently inform the killers about their targets and announce proudly that they too are soldiers, *rank and file.* Finally the impenetrable forest of Jhadkhani is surrounded by real soldiers, the *army* enters and splits the battlefield, looking for fugitives. Cartographers make draughts of the forest. Soldiers in hiding guard the falls and springs that are the only source of drinking water; they are still guarding, still looking. On one such search, army informant Dukhiram Ghadari saw a young Santal man lying on his stomach on a flat stone, dipping his face to drink water. The soldiers shot him as he lay. As the .303 threw him off spread-eagled and brought a bloody foam to his mouth, he roared 'Ma—ho' and then went limp. They realized later that it was the redoubtable Dulna Majhi. What does 'Ma—ho' mean? Is this a violent slogan in the tribal language? Even after much thought, the Department of Defence could not be sure. Two tribal-specialist types are flown in from Calcutta, and they sweat over the dictionaries put together by worthies such as Hoffmann-Jeffer and Golden-Palmer. Finally the omniscient Senanayak summons Chamru, the Santal water-carrier of the *camp.* He giggles when he sees the two specialists, scratches his ear with his *bidi* and says, 'The Santals of Maldah did say that when they began fighting at the time of King Gandhi! It's a battle cry. Who said "Ma—ho" here? Did someone come from Maldah?'

The problem is thus solved. Then, leaving Dulna's body on the stone, the soldiers climb the trees in green *camouflage*. They embrace the leafy boughs like so many great god Pans and wait as the large red ants bite their private parts. To see if anyone comes to take away the body. This is the hunter's way, not the soldier's. But Senanayak knows that these brutes cannot be dispatched by the approved method. So he asks his men to draw the prey with a corpse as bait. All will come clear, he says, I have almost deciphered Dopdi's song.

The soldiers get going at his command. But no one comes to claim Dulna's corpse. At night the soldiers shoot at a scuffle and, descending, discover that they have killed two hedgehogs copulating on dry leaves. Improvidently enough, the soldiers' jungle scout Dukhiram gets a knife in the neck before he can claim the reward for Dulna's capture. Bearing Dulna's corpse, the soldiers suffer shooting pains as the ants, interrupted in their feast, begin to bite them. When Senanayak hears that no one has come to take the corpse, he slaps his *anti-Fascist paperback* copy of *The Deputy* and shouts, 'What?' Immediately one *of* the tribal specialists runs in with a joy as naked and transparent as Archimedes' and says, 'Get up, *sir! I* have discovered the meaning *of* that "hende rambra" stuff. It's Mundari *language.'*

Thus the search for Dopdi continues. In the forest *belt of* Jhadkhani, the *Operation* continues – will continue. It is a carbuncle on the government's backside. Not to be cured by the tested ointment, not to burst with the appropriate herb. In the first phase, the fugitives, ignorant *of* the forest's *topography,* are caught easily, and by the law *of* confrontation they are shot at the taxpayer's expense. By the law *of* confrontation their eyeballs, intestines, stomachs, hearts, genitals, and so on become the food *of* fox, vulture, hyena, wildcat, ant, and worm, and the untouchables go off happily to sell their bare skeletons.

They do not allow themselves to be captured in open combat in the next phase. Now it seems that they have found a trustworthy *courier.* Ten to one it's Dopdi. Dopdi loved Dulna more than her blood. No doubt it is she who is saving the fugitives now.

'They' is also a *hypothesis.*

Why?

How many went *originally?*

The answer is silence. About that there are many tales, many books in press. Best not to believe everything.

How many killed in six years' confrontation?

The answer is silence.

Why after confrontations are the skeletons discovered with arms broken or severed? Could armless men have fought? Why do the collarbones shake, why are legs and ribs crushed?

Two kinds of answer. Silence. Hurt rebuke in the eyes. Shame on you! Why bring this up? What will be will be ...

How many left in the forest? The answer is silence.

A *legion*? Is it *justifiable to* maintain a large battalion in that wild area at the taxpayer's expense?

Answer: *Objection.* 'Wild area' is incorrect. The battalion is provided with supervised nutrition, arrangements to worship according to religion, opportunity to listen to 'Vividh-Bharati' and to see Sanjeev Kumar and the Lord Krishna face-to-face in the movie *This is Life.* No. The area is not 'wild'.

How many are left?

The answer is silence.

How many are left? Is there anyone *at all?*

The answer is long.

Item: *Well, action* still goes on. Moneylenders, landlords, grain brokers, anonymous brothel keepers, ex-narks are still terrified. The hungry and naked are still defiant and irrepressible. In some *pockets* the migrant workers are getting a *better wage.* Villages sympathetic to the fugitives are still silent and hostile. These events cause one to think ...

Where in this picture does Dopdi Mejhen fit?

She must have connections with the fugitives. The case for fear is elsewhere. The ones who remain have lived a long time in the primitive world of the forest. They keep company with the poor migrant workers and the tribals. They must have forgotten book learning. Perhaps they are *orienting* their book learning to the soil they live on and learning new combat and survival techniques. One can shoot and get rid of the ones whose only recourse is extrinsic book learning and sincere intrinsic enthusiasm. Those who are working practically will not be exterminated so easily.

Therefore *Operation* Jhadkhani *Forest* cannot stop. Reason: the words of warning in the *Army Handbook.*

II

Catch Dopdi Mejhen. She will lead us to the others.

Dopdi was proceeding slowly, with some rice knotted into her belt. Mushai Tudu's wife had cooked her some. She does so occasionally. When the rice is cold, Dopdi knots it into her waistcloth and walks slowly. As she walked, she picked out and killed the lice in her hair. If she had some *kerosene,* she'd rub it into her scalp and get rid of the lice. Then she could wash her hair with baking soda. But the bastards put traps at every bend of the falls. If they smell *kerosene* in the water, they will follow the scent.

Dopdi!

She doesn't respond. She never responds when she hears her own name. She has seen in the Panchayat office just today the notice for the reward in her name. Mushai Tudu's wife had said, 'What are you looking at? Who is Dopdi Mejhen. Money if you give her up!'

'How much?'

'Two-hundred!'

'Oh God!'

Mushai's wife said outside the office: 'A lot of preparation this time. All new policemen.'

'Hm.'

'Don't come again.'

'Why?'

Mushai's wife looked down. 'Tudu says that Sahib has come again. If they catch you, the village, our huts ...

'They'll burn again.'

'Yes. And about Dukhiram

'The Sahib knows?'

'Shomai and Budhna betrayed us.'

'Where are they?'

'Ran away by train.'

Dopdi thought of something. Then said, 'Go home. I don't know what will happen, if they catch me don't know me.'

'Can't you run away?'

'No. Tell me, how many times can I run away? What will they do if they catch me? They will *kounter* me. Let them.'

Mushai's wife said, 'We have nowhere else to go.'

Dopdi said softly, 'I won't tell anyone's name.'

Dopdi knows, has learned by hearing so often and so long, how one can come to terms with torture. If mind and body give way under torture, Dopdi will bite off her tongue. That boy did it. They *kountered* him. When they *kounter* you, your hands are tied behind you. All your bones are crushed, your sex is a terrible wound. *Killed by police in an encounter ... unknown male ... age twenty-two...*

As she walked thinking these thoughts, Dopdi heard someone calling, Dopdi!

She didn't respond. She doesn't respond if called by her own name. Here her name is Upi Mejhen. But who calls?

Spines of suspicion are always furled in her mind. Hearing 'Dopdi' they stiffen like a hedgehog's. Walking, she *unrolls the film* of known faces in her mind. Who? Not Shomra, Shomra is on the run. Shomai and Budhna are also on the run, for other reasons. Not Golok, he is in Bakuli. Is it someone from Bakuli? After Bakuli, her and Dulna's names were Upi Mejhen, Matang Majhi. Here no one but Mushai and his wife knows their real names. Among the young gentlemen, not all of the previous *batches* knew.

That was a troubled time. Dopdi is confused when she thinks about it. *Operation* Bakuli in Bakuli, Surja Sahu arranged with Biddi-babu to dig two tubewells and three wells within the compound of his two houses. No water anywhere, drought in Birbhum. Unlimited water at Surja Sahu's house, as clear as a crow's eye.

Get your water with canal tax, everything is burning.

What's my profit in increasing cultivation with tax money?

Everything's on fire.

Get out of here. I don't accept your Panchayat nonsense. Increase cultivation with water. You want half the paddy for sharecropping. Everyone is happy with free paddy. Then give me paddy at home, give me money. I've learned my lesson trying to do you good.

What good did you do?

Have I not given water to the village?

You've given it to your kin Bhagunal.

Don't you get water?

No. The untouchables don't get water.

The quarrel began there. In the drought, human patience catches fire easily. Satish and Jugal from the village and that young gentleman, was Rana his name?, said a landowning moneylender won't give a thing, put him down.

Surja Sahu's house was surrounded at night. Surja Sahu had brought out his gun. Surja was tied up with cow rope. His whitish eyeballs turned and turned, he was incontinent again and again. Dulna had said, I'll have the first blow, brothers. My great-grandfather took a bit of paddy from him, and I still give him free labour to repay that debt.

Dopdi had said, His mouth watered when he looked at me. I'll pull out his eyes.

Surja Sahu. Then a telegraphic message from Siuri. *Special train. Army.* The jeep didn't come up to Bakuli. *March-march-march.* The *crunch-crunch-crunch* of gravel under hobnailed boots. *Cordon up. Commands* on the *mike.* Jugal Mandal, Satish Mandal, Rana *alias* Prabir *alias* Dipak, Dulna Majhi-Dopdi Mejhen, *surrender surrender surrender. No surrender surrender. Mow-mow-mow* down the village. Putt—putt putt-putt *cordite* in the air—putt-putt – *round the clock*—putt-putt. Flame thrower. Bakuli is burning. *More men and women, children... fire-fire. Close canal approach. Over-over-over by nightfall.* Dopdi and Dulna had crawled on their stomachs to safety.

They could not have reached Paltakudi after Bakuli. Bhupati and Tapa took them. Then it was decided that Dopdi and Dulna would work around the Jhadkhani belt. Dulna had explained to Dopdi. Dear, this is best! We won't get family and children this way. But who knows? Landowner and moneylender and policemen might one day be wiped out!

Who called her from the back today?

Dopdi kept walking. Villages and fields, bush and rock – *Public Works Department* markers – sound of running steps at her back. Only one person running. Jharkhani Forest still about two miles away. Now she thinks of nothing but entering the forest. She must let them know that the police have set up notices for her again. Must tell them that that bastard Sahib has appeared again. Must change *hideouts*. Also, the plan to do to Lakkhi Bera and Naran Bera what they did to Surja Sahu on account of the trouble over paying the field hands in Sandara must be cancelled. Shomai and Budhna knew everything. There was the *urgency* of great danger under Dopdi's ribs. Now she thought there was no shame as a Santal in Shomai and Budhna's treachery. Dopdi's blood was the pure unadulterated black blood of Champadhumi. From Champa to Bakuli the rise and set of a million moons. Their blood could have been contaminated; Dopdi felt proud of her forefathers. They stood guard over their women's blood with the poison of the black *armor*. Shomai and Budhna are half-breeds. The fruits of the war. Contributions to Radhbhumi by the American soldiers stationed at Shiandanga. Otherwise, crow would eat crow's flesh before Santal would betray Santal.

Footsteps at her back. The steps keep a distance. Rice in her belt, tobacco leaves tucked at her waist. Arijit, Malini, Shamu, Mantu – none of them smokes or even drinks tea. Tobacco leaves and limestone powder. Best medicine for scorpion bite. Nothing must be given away.

Dopdi turned left. This way is the *camp*. Two miles. This is not the way to the forest. But Dopdi will not enter the forest with a nark at her back.

I swear by my life. By my life Dulna, by my life. Nothing must be told.

The footsteps turn left. Dopdi touches her waist. In her palm the comfort of a half-moon. A baby scythe. The smiths at Jhadkhani are fine artisans. Such an edge we'll put on it, Upi, a hundred Dukhirams – Thank God, Dopdi is not a gentleman. Actually, perhaps they have understood scythe, hatchet, and knife best. They do their work in silence. The lights of the *camp* at a distance. Why is Dopdi going this way? Stop a bit, it turns again. Huh! I can tell where I am if I wander all night with my eyes shut. I won't go in the forest, I won't lose him that way. I won't outrun him. You fucking jackal of a nark, deadly afraid of death, you can't run around in the forest. I'd run you out of breath, throw you in a ditch, and finish you off.

Not a word must be said. Dopdi has seen the new *camp,* she has sat in the bus station, passed the time of day, smoked a bidi and found out how many police convoys had arrived, how many radio vans. Squash four, onions seven, peppers fifty, a straightforward account. This information cannot now be passed on. They will understand Dopdi Mejhen. has been *kountered.* Then they'll run. Arijit's voice. If anyone is caught, the others must catch the *timing* and *change* their *hideout.* If Comrade Dopdi arrives late, we will not remain. There will be a sign of where we've gone. No comrade will let the others be *destroyed* for her own sake.

Arijit's voice. The gurgle of water. The direction of the next *hideout* will be indicated by the tip of the wooden arrowhead under the stone.

Dopdi likes and understands this. Dulna died, but, let me tell you, he didn't lose anyone else's life. Because this was not in our heads to begin with, one was *kountered* for the other's trouble. Now a much harsher rule, easy and clear. Dopdi returns – good; doesn't return – bad. *Change hideout.* The clue will be such that the *opposition* won't see it, won't understand even if they do.

Footsteps at her back. Dopdi turns again. These $3\frac{1}{2}$ miles of land and rocky ground are the best way to enter the forest. Dopdi has left that way behind. A little level ground ahead. Then rocks again. The army could not have struck camp on such rocky terrain. This area is quiet enough. It's like a maze, every hump looks like every other. That's fine. Dopdi will lead the nark to the burning ghat. Patitpaban of Saranda had been sacrificed in the name of Kali of the Burning Ghats.

Apprehend!

A lump of rock stands up. Another. Yet another. The elderly Senanayak was at once triumphant and despondent. *If you want to destroy the enemy, become one.* He had done so. As long as six years ago he could *anticipate their every move.* He still can. Therefore he is elated. Since he has kept up with literature, he has read *First Blood* and seen approval of his thought and work.

Dopdi couldn't trick him, he is unhappy about that. Two sorts of reasons. Six years ago he published an article on the basis of statistics stored in his brain cells. He demonstrated in that piece that he supported this struggle from the point of view of the migrant workers. Dopdi is a migrant worker. *Veteran fighter. Search and destroy.* Dopdi Mejhen. is about to be *apprehended*. Will be *destroyed*. Regret.

Halt!

Dopdi stops short. The steps behind come around to the front. Under Dopdi's ribs the canal dam breaks. No hope. Surja Sahu's brother Rotoni Sahu. The two lumps of rock come forward. Shomai and Budhna. They had not escaped by train.

Arijit's voice. Just as you must know when you've won, you must also acknowledge defeat and start the activities of the next stage.

Now Dopdi spreads her arms, raises her face to the sky, turns towards the forest, and ululates with the force of her entire being. Once, twice, three times. At the third burst the birds in the trees at the outskirts of the Jhadkhani forest awake and flap their wings. The echo of the call travels far.

III

Draupadi Mejhen was apprehended at 6.57 p.m. It took an hour to get her to *camp*. Questioning took another hour exactly. No one touched her, and she was allowed to sit on a canvas camp stool. At 8.57 Senanayak's dinner hour approached, and saying, 'Make her. *Do the needful,*' he disappeared.

Then a billion moons pass. A billion lunar years. Opening her eyes after a million light years, Draupadi, strangely enough, sees sky and moon. Slowly the bloodied nailheads shift from her brain. Trying to move, she feels her arms and legs still tied to four posts. Something sticky under her arse and waist. Her own blood. Only the gag has been removed. Incredible thirst. In case she says 'water', she catches her lower lip in her teeth. She senses that her vagina is bleeding. How many came to make her?

Shaming her, a tear trickles out of the corner of her eye. In the muddy moonlight she lowers her lightless eye, sees her breasts and understands that, indeed, she's been made up right. It would please Senanayak now. Her breasts are bitten raw, the nipples torn. How many? Four – five – six – seven – then Draupadi had passed out.

She turns her eyes and sees something white. Her own cloth. Nothing else. Suddenly she hopes against hope. Perhaps they have abandoned her. For the foxes to devour. But she hears the scrape of feet. She turns her head, the guard leans on his bayonet and leers at her. Draupadi closes her eyes. She doesn't have to wait long. Again the process of making her begins. Goes on. The moon vomits a bit of light and goes to sleep. Only the dark remains. A compelled spread-eagled still body. Active *pistons* of flesh rise and fall, rise and fall over it.

Then morning comes.

Then Draupadi Mejhen is brought to the tent and thrown on the straw. Her piece of cloth is thrown over her body.

Then, after *breakfast,* after reading the newspaper and sending the *radio message* 'Draupadi Mejhen. *apprehended',* etc., Senanayak orders Draupadi Mejhen to be brought in.

Suddenly there is trouble.

Draupadi sits up as soon as she hears 'Move!' and asks, Where do you want me to go?

To the Burra Sahib's tent.

Where is the tent?

Over there.

Draupadi fixes her red eyes on the tent. Says, Come, I'll go.

The guard pushes the water pot forward.

Draupadi stands up. She pours the water down on the ground. Tears her piece of cloth with her teeth. Seeing such strange behaviour, the guard says, She's gone crazy, and runs for orders. He can lead the prisoner out but doesn't know what to do if the prisoner behaves incomprehensibly. So he goes to ask his superior.

The commotion is as if the alarm had sounded in a prison. Senanayak walks out surprised and sees Draupadi, naked, walking towards him in the bright sunlight with her head high. The nervous guards trail behind.

What is this? He is about to cry, but stops.

Draupadi stands before him, naked. Thigh and pubic hair matted with dry blood. Two breasts, two wounds.

What is this? He is about to bark.

Draupadi comes closer. Stands with her hand on her hip, laughs and says, The object of your search, Dopdi Mejhen. You asked them to make me up, don't you want to see how they made me?

Where are her clothes?

Won't put them on, sir. Tearing them.

Draupadi's black body comes even closer. Draupadi shakes with an indomitable laughter that Senanayak simply cannot understand. Her ravaged lips bleed as she begins laughing. Draupadi wipes the blood on her palm and says in a voice that is as terrifying, sky splitting and sharp as her ululation, What's the use of clothes? You can strip me, but how can you clothe me again? Are you a man?

She looks around and chooses the front of Senanayak's white bush shirt to spit a bloody gob at and says, There isn't a man here that I should be ashamed. I will not let you put my cloth on me. What more can you do? Come on, *kounter* me—come on, *kounter* – me?

Draupadi pushed Senanayak with her two mangled breasts, and for the first time Senanayak is afraid to stand before an unarmed *target*, terribly afraid.

Translated by Gayatri Chakravorty Spivak

Alice Munro
(b 1931)

Alice Munro was born in 1931 in Wingham, and grew up in the aftermath of the Great Depression of 1929. Her father was a breeder of silver foxes and her mother sold the furs to help the family survive. These tales of courage and determination are at the back of most of her writing which is largely based on women's experiences.

The form of the short story is Munro's favourite genre as she locates her stories in familiar landscapes and carries forth her characters from one narrative to another. In an interview given to Alan Twigg she has talked of her early experiences as those of exclusion:

'We lived outside the whole social structure because we didn't live in the town and we didn't live in the country. We lived in this kind of little ghetto where all the bootleggers and prostitutes and hangers on lived. Those were the people I knew. It was a community of outcasts. I had that feeling about myself.'

She began writing at the early age of twelve and her juvenilia was imitative and adventurous. Amongst her collections of short stories *Lives of Girls and Women, Who Do you Think You Are?* and *The Dance of the Happy Shades* are the ones which have come into prominence. "The Peace of Utrecht" was written in the summer of 1959. "It was the first story I absolutely had to write and wasn't writing to see If I could write that kind of story" (in an interview given to J.R. Struther). Based upon personal experience, her own mother's illness and the conflictual emotions it aroused, it is a postmortem of the relationship and a combating with the feelings of guilt which were aroused as she became aware of her own need for freedom. The experience, despite being so specific, is one which is shared by many women as they are torn between a sense of compassion and duty and the need to hold on to the reality of their own physical and emotional needs.

The Peace of Utrecht

I have been at home now for three weeks and it has not been a success. Maddy and I, though we speak cheerfully of our enjoyment of so long and intimate a visit, will be relieved when it is over. Silences disturb us. We laugh immoderately. I am afraid – very likely we are both afraid – that when the moment comes to say goodbye, unless we are very quick to kiss, and fervently mockingly squeeze each other's shoulders, we will have to look straight into the desert that is between us and acknowledge that we are not merely indifferent; at heart we reject each other, and as for that past we make so much of sharing we do not really share it at all, each of us keeping it jealously to herself, thinking privately that the other has turned alien, and forfeited her claim.

At night we often sit out on the steps of the verandah and drink gin and smoke diligently to defeat the mosquitoes and postpone until very late the moment of going to bed. It is hot; the evening takes a long time to burn out. The high brick house, which stays fairly cool until midafternoon, holds the heat of the day trapped until long after dark. It was always like this, and Maddy and I recall how we used to drag our mattress downstairs onto the verandah, where we lay counting falling stars and trying to stay awake till dawn. We never did, falling asleep each night about the time a chill drift of air came up off the river, carrying a smell of reeds and the black ooze of the riverbed. At half-past ten a bus goes through the town, not slowing much; we see it go by at the end of our street. It is the same bus I used to take when I came home from college, and I remember coming into Jubilee on some warm night, seeing the earth bare around the massive roots of the trees, the drinking fountain surrounded by little puddles of water on the main street, the soft scrawls of blue and red and orange light that said BILLIARDS and CAFÉ; feeling as I recognized these signs a queer kind of oppression and release, as I exchanged the whole holiday world of school, of friends and, later on, of love, for the dim world of continuing disaster, of home. Maddy making the same journey four years earlier must have felt the same thing. I want to ask her: is it possible that children growing up as we did lose the ability to believe in – to be at home in – any ordinary and peaceful reality? But I don't ask her; we never talk about any of that. No exorcising here, says Maddy in her thin, bright voice with the slangy quality I had forgotten, we're not going to depress each other. So we haven't.

One night Maddy took me to a party at the Lake, which is about thirty miles west of here. The party was held in a cottage a couple of women from Jubilee had rented for the week. Most of the women there seemed to be widowed, single. separated or divorced; the men were mostly young and unmarried – those from Jubilee so young that I remember them only as little boys in the lower grades. There were two or three older men, not with their wives. But the women – they reminded me surprisingly of certain women familiar to me in my childhood, though of course I never saw their party-going personalities, only their activities in the stores and offices, and not infrequently in the Sunday schools, of Jubilee. They differed from the married women in being more aware of themselves in the world, a little brisker, sharper and coarser (though I can think of only one or two whose respectability was ever in question). They wore resolutely stylish though matronly clothes, which tended to swish and rustle over their hard rubber corsets, and they put perfume, quite a lot of it, on their artificial flowers. Maddy's friends were considerably modernized; they had copper rinses on their hair, and blue eyelids, and a robust capacity for drink.

Maddy I thought did not look one of them, with her slight figure and her still carelessly worn dark hair; her face has grown thin and strained without losing entirely its girlish look of impertinence and pride. But she speaks with the harsh twang of the local accent, which we used to make fun of, and her expression as she romped and drank was determinedly undismayed. It seemed to me that she was making every effort to belong with these people and that shortly she would succeed. It seemed to me too that she wanted me to see her succeeding, to see her repudiating that secret, exhilarating, really monstrous snobbery which we cultivated when we were children together, and promised ourselves, of course, much bigger things than Jubilee.

During the game in which all the women put an article of clothing – it begins decorously with a shoe – in a basket, and then all the men come in and have a race trying to fit things on to their proper owners, I went out and sat in the car, where I felt lonely for my husband and my friends and listened to the hilarity of the party and the waves failing on the beach and presently went to sleep. Maddy came much later and said, "For heaven's sake !" Then she laughed and said airily like a lady in an English movie, "You find these goings-on distasteful?" We both laughed; I felt apologetic, and rather sick from drinking and not getting drunk. "They may not be much on intellectual conversation but their hearts are in the right place, as the saying goes." I did not dispute this and we drove at eighty miles an hour from Inverhuron to Jubilee. Since then we have not been to any more parties.

But we are not always alone when we sit out on the steps. Often we are joined by a man named Fred Powell. He was at the party, peaceably in the background remembering whose liquor was whose and amiably holding someone's head over the rickety porch railing. He grew up in Jubilee as we did but I do not remember him, I suppose because he went through school some years ahead of us and then went away to the war. Maddy surprised me by bringing him home to supper the first night I was here and then we spent the evening, as we have spent many since, making this strange man a present of our childhood, or of that version of our childhood which is safely preserved in anecdote, as in a kind of mental cellophane. And what fantasies we build around the frail figures of our childselves, so that they emerge beyond recognition incorrigible and gay. We tell stories together well. "You girls have got good memories," Fred Powell says, and sits watching us with an air of admiration and something else – reserve, embarrassment, deprecation – which appears on the faces of these mild deliberate people as they watch the keyed-up antics of their entertainers.

Now thinking of Fred Powell I admit that my reaction to this – this *situation* as I call it – is far more conventional than I would have expected; it is even absurd. And I do not know what situation it really is. I know that he is married. Maddy told me so, on the first evening, in a merely informative voice. His wife is an invalid. He has her at the Lake for the summer, Maddy says, he's very good to her. I do not know if he is Maddy's lover and she will never tell me. Why should it matter to me? Maddy is well over thirty. But I keep thinking of the way he sits on our steps with his hands set flat on his spread knees, his mild full face turned almost indulgently toward Maddy as she talks; he has an affable masculine look of being diverted but unimpressed. And Maddy teases him, tells him he is too fat, will not smoke his cigarettes, involves him in private, nervous tender arguments which have no meaning and no end. He allows it. (And this is what frightens me, I know it now: he allows it; *she needs it.)* When she is a little drunk she says in tones of half-pleading mockery that he is her only real friend. He speaks the same language, she says. Nobody else does. I have no answer to that.

Then again I begin to wonder: is he only her friend? I had forgotten certain restrictions of life in Jubilee – and this holds good whatever the pocket novels are saying about small towns – and also what strong, respectable, never overtly sexual friendships can flourish within these restrictions and be fed by them, so that in the end such relationships may consume half a life. This thought depresses me (unconsummated relationships depress outsiders perhaps more than anybody else) so much that I find myself wishing for them to be honest lovers.

The rhythm of life in Jubilee is primitively seasonal. Deaths occur in the winter; marriages are celebrated in the summer. There is good reason for this; the winters are long and full of hardship and the old and weak cannot always get through them. Last winter was a catastrophe, such as may be expected every ten or twelve years; you can see how the pavement in the streets is broken up, as if the town had survived a minor bombardment. A death is dealt with then in the middle of great difficulties; there comes time now in the summer to think about it, and talk. I find that people stop me in the street to talk about my mother. I have heard from them about her funeral, what flowers she had and what the weather was like on that day. And now that she is dead I no longer feel that when they say the words "your mother" they deal a knowing, cunning blow at my pride. I used to feel that; at those words I felt my whole identity, that pretentious adolescent construction, come crumbling down.

Now I listen to them speak of her, so gently and ceremoniously, and I realize that she became one of the town's possessions and oddities, its brief legends. This she achieved in spite of us, for we tried, both crudely and artfully, to keep her at home, away from that sad notoriety; not for her sake, but for ours, who suffered such unnecessary humiliation at the sight of her eyes rolling back in her head in a temporary paralysis of the eye muscles, at the sound of her thickened voice, whose embarrassing pronouncements it was our job to interpret to outsiders. So bizarre was the disease she had in its effects that it made us feel like crying out in apology (though we stayed stiff and white) as if we were accompanying a particularly tasteless sideshow. All wasted, our pride; our purging its rage in wild caricatures we did for each other (no, not caricatures, for she was one herself; imitations). We should have let the town have her; it would have treated her better.

About Maddy and her ten-years vigil they say very little, perhaps they want to spare my feelings, remembering that I was the one who went away and here are my two children to show for it, while Maddy is alone and has nothing but that discouraging house. But I don't think so; in Jubilee the feelings are not spared this way. And they ask me point-blank why I did not come home for the funeral; I am glad I have the excuse of the blizzard that halted air travel that week, or I do not know if I would have come anyway, after Maddy had written so vehemently urging me to stay away. I felt strongly that she had a right to be left alone with it, if she wanted to be, after all this time.

After all this time. Maddy was the one who stayed. First, she went away to college, then I went. You give me four years, I'll give you four years, she said. But I got married. She was not surprised; she was exasperated at me for my wretched useless feelings of guilt. She said that she had always meant to stay. She said that Mother no longer "bothered" her. "Our Gothic Mother," she said, "I play it out now, I let her be. I don't keep trying to make her *human* any more. You know." It would simplify things so much to say that Maddy was religious, that she felt the joys of self-sacrifice, the strong, mystical appeal of total rejection. But about Maddy who could say that? When we were in our teens, and our old aunts, Aunt Annie and Auntie Lou, spoke to us of some dutiful son or daughter who had given up everything for an ailing parent, Maddy would quote impiously the opinions of modern psychiatry. Yet she stayed. All I can think about that, all I have ever been able to think, to comfort me, is that she may have been able and may even have chosen to live without time and in perfect imaginary freedom as children do, the future untampered with, all choices always possible,

To change the subject, people ask me what it is like to be back in Jubilee. But I don't know, I am still waiting for something to tell me, to make me understand that I am back. The day I drove up from Toronto with my children in the back seat of the car I was very tired, on the last lap of a twenty-five-hundred-mile trip. I had to follow a complicated system of highways and sideroads, for there is no easy way to get to Jubilee from anywhere on earth. Then about two o'clock, in the afternoon I saw ahead of me, so familiar and unexpected, the gaudy, peeling cupola of the town hall, which is no relation to any of the rest of the town's squarely built, dingy grey-and-red-brick architecture. (Underneath it hangs a great bell, to be rung in the event of some mythical disaster.) I drove up the main street – a new service station, new stucco front on the Queen's Hotel – and turned into the quiet, decaying side streets where old maids live, and have birdbaths and blue delphiniums in their gardens. The big brick houses that I knew, with their wooden verandahs and gaping, dark-screened windows, seemed to me plausible but unreal. (Anyone to whom I have mentioned the dreaming, sunken feeling of these streets wants to take me out to the north side of town where there is a new soft-drink bottling plant, some new ranch-style houses and a Tastee-Freez.) Then I parked my car in a little splash of shade in front of the house where I used to live. My little girl, whose name is Margaret, said neutrally yet with some disbelief, "Mother, is that your house?"

And I felt that my daughter's voice expressed a complex disappointment – to which, characteristically, she seemed resigned, or even resigned *in advance;* it contained the whole flatness and strangeness of the moment in which is revealed the source of legends, the unsatisfactory, apologetic and persistent reality. The red brick of which the house is built looked harsh and hot in the sun and was marked in two or three places by long grimacing cracks; the verandah, which always had the air of an insubstantial decoration, was visibly falling away. There was – there is – a little blind window of coloured glass beside the front door. I sat staring at it with a puzzled lack of emotional recognition. I sat and looked at the house and the window shades did not move, the door did not fly open, no one came out on the verandah; there was no one at home. This was as I had expected, since Maddy works now in the office of the town clerk, yet I was surprised to see the house take on such a closed, bare, impoverished look, merely by being left empty. And it was brought home to me, as I walked across the front yard to the steps, that after all these summers on the Coast I had forgotten the immense inland heat, which makes you feel as if you have to carry the whole burning sky on your head.

A sign pinned to the front door announced, in Maddy's rather sloppy and flamboyant hand: VISITORS WELCOME, CHILDREN FREE, RATES TO BE ARRANGED LATER (YOU'LL. BE SORRY) WALK IN. On the hall table was a bouquet of pink phlox whose velvety scent filled the hot air of a closed house on a summer afternoon. "Upstairs!" I said to the children, and I took the hand of the little girl and her smaller brother, who had slept in the car and who rubbed against me, whimpering, as he walked. Then I paused, one foot on the bottom step, and turned to greet, matter-of-factly, the reflection of a thin, tanned, habitually watchful woman, recognizably a Young Mother, whose hair, pulled into a knot on top of her head, exposed a jawline no longer softly fleshed, a brown neck rising with a look of tension from the little sharp knobs of the collarbone this in the hall mirror that had shown me, last time I looked, a commonplace pretty girl, with a face as smooth and insensitive as an apple, no matter what panic and disorder lay behind it.

But this was not what I had turned for; I realized that I must have been waiting for my mother to call, from her couch in the dining-room, where she lay with the blinds down in the summer heat, drinking cups of tea which she never finished, eating – she had dispensed altogether with mealtimes, like a sickly child – little bowls of preserved fruit and crumblings of cake. It seemed to me that I could not close the door behind me without hearing my mother's ruined voice call out to me, and feeling myself go heavy all over as I prepared to answer it. Calling, *Who's there?*

I led my children to the big bedroom at the back of the house, where Maddy and I used to sleep. It has thin, almost worn-out white curtains at the windows and a square of linoleum on the floor; there is a double bed, a washstand which Maddy and I used as a desk when we were in high school, and a cardboard wardrobe with little mirrors on the inside of the doors. As I talked to my children I was thinking-but carefully, not in a rush of my mother's state of mind when she called out *Who's there?* I was allowing myself to hear – as if I had not dared before – the cry for help – undisguised, oh, shamefully undisguised and raw and supplicating – that sounded in her voice. A cry repeated so often, and, things being as they were, so uselessly, that Maddy and I recognized it only as one of those household sounds which must be dealt with, so that worse may not follow. *You go and deal with Mother,* we would say to each other, or *I'll be out in a minute, I have to deal with Mother.*

It might be that we had to perform some of the trivial and unpleasant services endlessly required, or that we had to supply five minutes' expediently cheerful conversation, so remorselessly of the real state of affairs, never a glint of pity to open the way for one of her long debilitating sieges of tears. But the pity denied, the tears might come anyway; so that we were defeated, we were forced – to stop that noise – into parodies of love. But we grew cunning, unfailing in cold solicitude; we took all emotion away from our dealings with her, as you might take away meat from a prisoner to weaken him; till he died.

We would tell her to read, to listen to music and enjoy the changes of season and be grateful that she did not have cancer. We added that she did not suffer any pain, and that is true if imprisonment is not pain. While she demanded our love in every way she knew, without shame or sense, as a child will. And how could we have loved her, I say desperately to myself, the resources of love we had were not enough, the demand on us was too great. Nor would it have changed anything.

"Everything has been taken away from me," she would say. To strangers, to friends of ours whom we tried always unsuccessfully to keep separate from her, to old friends of hers who came guiltily infrequently to see her, she would speak like this, in the very slow and mournful voice that was not intelligible or quite human; we would have to interpret. Such theatricality humiliated us almost to death; yet now I think that without that egotism feeding, stubbornly even on disaster she might have sunk rapidly into some dim vegetable life. She kept herself as much in the world as she could, not troubling about her welcome; restlessly she wandered through the house and into the streets of Jubilee. Oh, she was not resigned; she must have wept and struggled in that house of stone (as I can, but will not, imagine) until the very end.

But I find the picture is still not complete. Our Gothic Mother, with the cold appalling mask of the Shaking Palsy laid across her features, shuffling, weeping, devouring attention wherever she can get it, eyes dead and burning, fixed inward on herself; this is not all. For the disease is erratic and leisurely in its progress; some mornings (gradually growing fewer and fewer and farther apart) she wakes up better; she goes out to the yard and straightens up a plant in such a simple housewifely way; she says something calm and lucid to us; she listens attentively to the news. She has wakened out of a bad dream; she tries to make up for lost time, tidying the house, forcing her stiff trembling hands to work a little while at the sewing machine. She makes us one of her specialties, a banana cake or a lemon meringue pie. Occasionally since she died I have dreams of her (I never dreamt of her when she was alive) in which she is doing something like this, and I think, why did I exaggerate so to myself, see, she is all right, only that her hands are trembling –

At the end of these periods of calm a kind of ravaging energy would come over her; she would make conversation insistently and with less and less coherence; she would demand that we rouge her cheeks and fix her hair; sometimes she might even hire a dressmaker to come in and make clothes for her, working in the dining room where she could watch – spending her time again more and more on the couch. This was extravagant, unnecessary from any practical point of view (for why did she need these clothes, where did she wear them?) and nerve-racking, because the dressmaker did not understand what she wanted and sometimes neither did we. I remember after I went away receiving from Maddy several amusing, distracted, quietly overwrought letters describing these sessions with the dressmaker. I read them with sympathy but without being able to enter into the once-familiar atmosphere of frenzy and frustration which my mother's demands could produce. In the ordinary world it was not possible to re-create her. The picture of her face which I carried in my mind seemed too terrible, unreal. Similarly the complex strain of living with her, the feelings of hysteria which Maddy and I once dissipated in a great deal of brutal laughter, now began to seem partly imaginary; I felt the beginnings of a secret, guilty estrangement.

I stayed in the room with my children for a little while because it was a strange place, for them it was only another strange place to go to sleep. Looking at them in this room I felt that they were particularly fortunate and that their life was safe and easy, which may be what most parents think at one time or another. I looked in the wardrobe but there was nothing there, only a hat trimmed with flowers from the five-and-ten, which one of us must have made for some flossy Easter. When I opened the drawer of the washstand I saw that it was crammed full of pages from a loose-leaf notebook. I read: "The Peace of Utrecht, 1713, brought an end to the War of the Spanish Succession." It struck me that the handwriting was my own. Strange to think of it lying here for ten years more; it looked as if I might have written it that day.

For some reason reading these words had a strong effect on me; I felt as if my old life was lying around me, waiting to be picked up again. Only then for a few moments in our old room did

I have this feeling. The brown halls of the old High School (a building since torn down) were, re-opened for me, and I remembered the Saturday nights in spring, after the snow had melted and all the country people crowded into town. I thought of us walking up and down the main street, arm in arm with two or three other girls, until it got dark, then going in to Al's to dance, under a string of little coloured lights. The windows in the dance hall were open; they let in the raw spring air with its smell of earth and the river; the hands of farm boys crumpled and stained our white blouses when we danced, And now an experience which seemed not at all memorable at the time (in fact Al's was a dismal place and the ritual of walking up and down the street to show ourselves off we thought crude and ridiculous, though we could not resist it) had been transformed into something curiously meaningful for me, and complete; it took in more than the girls dancing and the single street, it spread over the whole town, its rudimentary pattern of streets and its bare trees and muddy yards just free of the snow, over the dirt roads where the lights of cars appeared, jolting towards the town, under an immense pale wash of sky.

Also: we wore ballerina shoes, and full black taffeta skirts and short coats of such colours as robin's egg blue, cerise red, lime green. Maddy wore a great funereal bow at the neck of her blouse and a wreath of artificial daisies in her hair. These were the fashions, or so we believed, of one of the years after the war. Maddy; her bright skeptical look; my sister.

I ask Maddy, "Do you ever remember what she was like before?"

"No," says Maddy!. "No, I can't."

"I sometimes think I can," I say hesitantly. "Not very often."

Cowardly tender nostalgia, trying to get back to a gentler truth.

"I think you would have to have been away," Maddy says, "You would have to have been away these last quite a few – years to get those kind of memories."

It was then she said: No exorcising.

And the only other thing she said was, "She spent a lot of time sorting things. All kinds of things. Greeting cards. Buttons and yarn. Sorting and putting them into little piles. It would keep her quiet by the hour."

II

I have been to visit Aunt Annie and Auntie Lou. This is the third time I have been there since I came home and each time they have been spending the afternoon making rugs out of dyed rags. They are very old now. They sit in a hot little porch that is shaded by bamboo blinds; the rags and the half-finished rugs make an encouraging, domestic sort of disorder around them. They do not go out any more, but they get up early in the mornings, wash and powder themselves and put on their shapeless print dresses trimmed with rickrack and white braid. They make coffee and porridge and then they clean the house, Aunt Annie working upstairs and Auntie Lou down. Their house is very clean, dark and varnished, and it smells of vinegar and apples. In the afternoon they lie down for an hour and then put on their afternoon dresses, with brooches at the neck, and sit down to do hand work.

They are the sort of women whose flesh melts or mysteriously falls away as they get older. Auntie Lou's hair is still black, but it looks stiff and dry in its net as the dead end of hair on a ripe ear of corn. She sits straight and moves her bone-thin arms in very fine, slow movements; she looks like an Egyptian, with her long neck and small sharp face and greatly wrinkled, greatly darkened skin. Aunt Annie, perhaps because of her gentler, even coquettish manner, seems more humanly fragile and worn. Her hair is nearly all gone, and she keeps on her head one of those pretty caps designed for young wives who wear curlers to bed. She calls my attention to this and asks if I do not think it is becoming. They are both adept at these ironies and take a mild delight in pointing out whatever is grotesque about themselves. Their company manners are exceedingly lighthearted and their conversation with each other falls into an accomplished pattern of teasing and protest. I have a fascinated glimpse of Maddy and myself, grown old, caught back in the web of sisterhood after everything else has disappeared, making tea for some young, loved, and essentially unimportant relative-and exhibiting just such a polished relationship; what will anyone ever know of us? As I watch my entertaining old aunts I wonder if old people plan, such stylized and simplified roles with us because they are afraid that anything more honest might try our patience; or if they do it out of delicacy to fill the social time – when in reality they feel so far away from us that there is no possibility of communicating with us at all.

At any rate I felt held at a distance by them, at least until this third afternoon when they showed in front of me some signs of disagreement with each other. I believe this is the first time that has happened. Certainly I never saw them argue in all the years when Maddy and I used to visit them, and we used to visit them often – not only out of duty but because we found the atmosphere of sense and bustle reassuring after the comparative anarchy, the threatened melodrama, of our house at home.

Aunt Annie wanted to take me upstairs to show me something. Auntie Lou objected, looking remote and offended, as if the whole subject embarrassed her. And such is the feeling for discretion, the tradition of circumlocution in that house, that it was unthinkable for me to ask them what they were talking about.

"Oh, let her have her tea," Auntie Lou said, and Aunt Annie said, "Well. When she's *had* her tea."
"Do as you like then. That upstairs is hot."
"Will you come up, Lou?"
"Then who's going to watch the children?"
"Oh, the children. I forgot."

So Aunt Annie and I withdrew into the darker parts of the house. It occurred to me, absurdly, that she was going to give me a five-dollar bill. I remembered that sometimes she used to draw me into the front hall in this mysterious way and open her purse. I do not think that Auntie Lou was included in that secret either. But we went on upstairs, and into Aunt Annie's own bedroom, which looked so neat and virginal, papered with timid flowery wallpaper, the dressers spread with white scarves. It was really very hot, as Auntie Lou had said.

"Now," Aunt Annie said, a little breathless. "Get me down that box on the top shelf of the closet."

I did, and she opened it and said with her wistful conspirator's gaiety, "Now I guess you wondered what became of all your mother's clothes?"

I had not thought of it. I sat down on the bed, forgetting that in this house the beds were not to be sat on; the bedrooms had one straight chair apiece, for that. Aunt Annie did not check me. She began to lift things out, saying, "Maddy never mentioned them, did she?"

"I never asked her," I said.

"No. Nor I wouldn't. I wouldn't say a word about it to Maddy. But I thought I might as well show you. Why not? Look," she said. We washed and ironed what we could and what we couldn't we sent to the cleaners. I paid the cleaning myself. Then we mended anything needed mending. It's all in good condition, see?"

I watched helplessly while she held up for my inspection the underwear which was on top. She showed me where things had been expertly darned and mended and where the elastic had been renewed. She showed me a slip which had been worn, she said, only once. She took out nightgowns, a dressing gown, knitted bed-jackets. "This was what she had on the last time I saw her," she said. "I think it was. Yes." I recognized with alarm the peach-coloured bed-jacket I had sent for Christmas.

"You can see it's hardly used. Why, it's hardly used at all."

"No," I said.

"Underneath is her dresses." Her hands rummaged down through those brocades and flowered silks, growing yearly more exotic, in which my mother had wished to costume herself. Thinking of her in these peacock colours, even Aunt Annie seemed to hesitate. She drew up a blouse. "I washed this by hand, it looks like new. There's a coat hanging up in the closet. Perfectly good. She never wore a coat. She wore it when she went into the hospital, that was all. Wouldn't it fit you?"

"No," I *said. "No."* For Aunt Annie was already moving towards the closet. "I just got a new coat. I have several coats. Aunt Annie!"

"But why should you go and buy," Aunt Annie went on in her mild stubborn way, "when there are things here as good as new."

"I would rather buy," I said, and was immediately sorry for the coldness in my voice. Nevertheless I continued, "When I need something, I do go and buy it." This suggestion that I was not poor any more brought a look of reproach and aloofness into my aunt's face. She said nothing. I went and looked at a picture of Aunt Annie and Auntie Lou and their older brothers and their mother and father which hung over the bureau. They stared back at me with grave accusing Protestant faces, for I had run up against the simple unprepossessing materialism which was the rock of their lives. Things must be used; everything must be used up, saved and mended and made into something else and used again; clothes were to be worn. I felt that I had hurt Aunt Annie's feelings and that furthermore I had probably borne out a prediction of Auntie Lou's, for she was sensitive to certain attitudes in the world that were too sophisticated for Aunt Annie to bother about, and she had very likely said that I would not want my mother's clothes.

"She was gone sooner than anybody would have expected," Aunt Annie said. I turned around surprised and she said, "Your mother." Then I wondered if the clothes had been the main thing after all; perhaps they were only to serve as the introduction to a conversation about my mother's death, which Aunt Annie might feel to be a necessary part of our visit. Auntie Lou would feel differently; she had an almost superstitious dislike of certain rituals of emotionalism; such a conversation could never take place with her about.

"Two months after she went into the hospital," Aunt Annie said. "She was gone in two months." I saw that she was crying distractedly, as old people do, with miserable scanty tears. She pulled a handkerchief out of her dress and rubbed at her face.

"Maddy told her it was nothing but a check-up," she said. "Maddy told her it would be about three weeks. Your mother went in there and she thought she was coming out in three weeks." She was whispering as if she was afraid of us being overheard. "Do you think she wanted to stay in there where nobody could make out what she was saying and they wouldn't let her out of her bed? She wanted to come home!"

"But she was too sick," I said.

"No, she wasn't, she was just the way she'd always been, just getting a little worse and a little worse as time went on. But after she went in there she felt she would die, everything kind of closed in around her, and she went down so fast."

"Maybe it would have happened anyway," I said. "Maybe it was just the time."

Aunt Annie paid no attention to me. "I went up to see her," she said. "She was so glad to see me because I could tell what she was saying. She said Aunt Annie, they won't keep me in here for good, will they? And I said to her, No. I said, No.

"And she said, Aunt Annie ask Maddy to take me home again or I'm going to die. She didn't want to die. Don't you ever think a person wants to die, just because it seems to everybody else they have got no reason to go on living. So I told Maddy. But she didn't say anything. She went to the hospital every day and saw your mother and she wouldn't take her home. Your mother told me Maddy said to her, I won't take you home."

"Mother didn't always tell the truth," I said. "Aunt Annie, you know that."

"Did you know your mother got out of the hospital?"

"No," I said. But strangely I felt no surprise, only a vague physical sense of terror, a longing not to be told-and beyond this a feeling that what I would be told I already knew, I had always known.

"Maddy, didn't she tell you?"

"No."

"Well she got out the side door where the ambulance comes in, it's the only door that isn't locked. It was at night when they haven't so many nurses to watch them. She got her dressing gown and her slippers on, the first time she ever got anything on herself in years, and she went out and there it was January, snowing, but she didn't go back in. She was away down the street when they caught her. After that they put the board across her bed."

The snow, the dressing gown and slippers, the board across the bed. It was a picture I was much inclined to resist. Yet I had no doubt that this was true, all this was true and exactly as it happened. It was what she would do; all her life as long as I had known her led up to that flight.

"Where was she going?" I said, but I knew there was no answer.

"I don't know. Maybe I shouldn't have told you. Oh, Helen, when they came after her she tried to run. She tried to *run.*"

The flight that concerns everybody. Even behind my aunt's soft familiar face there is another, more primitive old woman, capable of panic in some place her faith has never touched.

She began folding the clothes up and putting them back in the box. "They nailed a board across her bed. I saw it. You can't blame the nurses. They can't watch everybody. They haven't the time."

"I said to Maddy after the funeral, Maddy may it never happen like that to you. I couldn't help it, that's what I said." She sat down on the bed herself now, folding things and putting them back in the box, making an effort to bring her voice back to normal and pretty soon succeeding, for having lived this long who would not be an old hand at grief and self-control?

"We thought it was hard," she said finally. "Lou and I thought it was hard."

Is this the last function of old women, beyond making rag rugs and giving us five-dollar bills – making sure the haunts we have contracted for are with us, not one gone without?

She was afraid of Maddy – through fear, had cast her out for good. I thought of what Maddy had said: nobody speaks the same language.

When I got home Maddy was out in the back kitchen making a salad. Rectangles of sunlight lay on the rough linoleum. She had taken off her high-heeled shoes and was standing there in her bare feet. The back kitchen is a large untidy pleasant room with a view, behind the stove and the drying dishtowels, of the sloping back yard, the CPR station and the golden, marshy river that almost encircles the town of Jubilee. My children who had felt a little repressed in the other house immediately began to play under the table.

"Where have you been?" Maddy said.

"Nowhere. Just to see the Aunts."

"Oh, how are they?"

"There fine. They're indestructible."

"Are they? Yes I guess they are. I haven't been to see them for a while. I don't actually see that much of them any more."

"Don't you?" I said, and she knew then what they had told me.

"They were beginning to get on my nerves a bit, after the funeral. And Fred got me this job and everything and I've been so busy." She looked at me, waiting for what I would say, smiling a little derisively, patiently.

"Don't be guilty, Maddy," I said softly. All this time the children were running in and out and shrieking at each other between our legs.

"I'm not guilty," she said. "Where did you get that? I'm not guilty." She went to turn on the radio, talking to me over her shoulder. "Fred's going to eat with us again since he's alone. I got some raspberries for dessert. Raspberries are almost over for this year. Do they look all right to you?"

"They look all right," I said. "Do you want me to finish this?"

"Fine," she said. "I'll go and get a bowl."

She went into the dining room and came back carrying a pink cut-glass bowl, for the raspberries.

"I couldn't go on," she said. "I wanted my life."

She was standing on the little step between the kitchen and the dining room and suddenly she lost her grip on the bowl, either because her hands had begun to shake or because she had not picked it up properly in the first place; it was quite a heavy and elaborate old bowl. It slipped out of her hands and she tried to catch it and it smashed on the floor.

Maddy began to laugh. "Oh, hell," she said. "Oh, hell, oh Hel-en," she said, using one of our old foolish ritual phrases of despair. "Look what I've done now. In my bare feet yet. Get me a broom."

"Take your life, Maddy. Take it."

"Yes I will," Maddy said. "Yes I will."

"Go away, don't stay here."

"Yes I will."

Then she bent down and began picking up the pieces of broken pink glass. My children stood back looking at her with awe and she was laughing and saying, "It's no loss to me. I've got a whole shelf full of glass bowls. I've got enough glass bowls to do me the rest of my life. Oh, don't stand there looking at me, go and get me a broom!" I went around the kitchen looking for a broom because I seemed to have forgotten where it was kept and she said, "But why can't I, Helen? *Why can't I?"*

Bessie Head
(1937-1986)

Born of a mixed parentage – a white mother and a black father – Bessie Head's work reveals an ongoing concern with oppression of all kinds. It is not merely or only racism which results in oppression, there are a whole lot of other practices, rituals, orthodoxies and familial pressures which become oppressive. In this larger context, it is again women who emerge as the most oppressed.

In her life of forty-nine years, she had to combat both poverty and exclusion. For the greater part Bessie Head lived in Botswana where she took up permanent exile and her writing reflects her experiences there. She published three novels, *When Rain Clouds Gather, Maru* and *A Question of Power*, and several short stories which have been brought together in *The Collector of Treasures*. In 1981 she also brought out a volume of social history *The Serowe Village of the Rain-wind*, about the Botswanian community. The autobiographical piece *A Woman Alone,* and *Tenderness and Power* were published posthumously.

One can trace a strong critiquing of colonialism in her work as well as a sharp criticism of tribal conventions, practices which are often brutal and insensitive. "Property" is a very dense story which brings out details of tribal practices, like the bride price, the material aspects of marriage, the mother's control, the bargaining which underlies relationships, and the social discouragement of any change in masculine norms. The one-word title is applicable to both the human beings and to the property they have.

The strength of the story lies in the juxtaposition and the conflict between 'masculine' and 'feminine' values, between individual needs and social norms, and between the desired and the possible.

Property

He had paid for his wife with twelve head of cattle and the marriage had been arranged by an uncle, one of the elder brothers of his mother. She should therefore have been his property, an impersonal something acquired to assist his mother in tilling the fields, fetching water from the river collecting firewood from the bush and cooking the meals. But there was something wrong somehow and after the first few weeks of marriage the young wife sensed it and it unnerved her.

True enough she was well-trained in the duties of a wife and of an apparently docile subservient temperament as women of her background are supposed to be; but in reality she was as lovely as the tall cool grasses that swayed in the summer wind. At least, the man saw her that way with his own magic eyes. People were all kinds of things to him: nothing like the dull pretentious clothes of custom which they all wore; but in flashes, and at moments of crisis they revealed their real selves: some were giant icy mountains, some were wide wind-swept plains in breadth of thought and depth of suffering; some were stark bare twigs perpetually bent before the storms and winters of life and some, like his mother were the evening sunsets. And because his wife was young she had no way of concealing that she was the grass that swayed in the summer wind. This caused him to look at her with a strange delight in his eyes and a quiet half-smile about his mouth. She always dropped her eyes in embarrassment because she could not understand it.

'Perhaps I have married a mad man', she thought with fear in her heart, longing for the thoughtless, chattering companionship of her sisters.

And she became more and more sure of this as the days passed. One evening they were alone in their hut, the man enquired gently:

'Are you tired?'

She looked at him in a quick suspicious way and bent her head with an equally quick movement for that smile about his mouth and that awful look was in his eyes as though he was silently pleading for more than the contract allowed. No slave owner asked a purchased slave if the slave was tired. In fact, if something was your property you expected it to keep the place spick and span and occasionally you roughed it up with a good beating to keep it in its place; to assert your male dominance. But these beatings were profitable to the purchased slave's family. The slave ran home and the condition of return was that its family be made richer by one beast. The young wife wondered how she would ever be able to provoke the necessary quarrel with this soft, unmanly man. Yet there was nothing unmanly about his love-making at night and this one direct, though inarticulate, expression of his love she confused, to her regret, with the mistaken feeling that he was the slave of her body.

A change took place. It was the young wife who began to dominate the household because she despised her husband and hated her mother-in-law whom she privately blamed for the womanliness of her husband and it seemed to her as though there was a conspiracy of secret understanding between them. They looked so alike. They smiled alike and had a way of communicating with each other by a mere glance. And really, contrary to custom the man had grown up almost entirely under the influence of his mother. The men of the family clan, who should have accepted responsibility for him after his father had died when he was barely one year old, turned out to be a restless lot with their hearts drawn to the big cities of South Africa. But they were always sending money home for the purchase of cattle and then always in one way or an other getting killed in the cities. Thus, the man eventually found himself almost the sole inheritor of huge herds of cattle. On the other hand, the young wife's family had clung to the old tribal way of life. They were a large clan with few beasts and their joy and greed and relief were great at the marriage of one of their own to the richest man in the area.

A little of this clan greed made the young wife careless of her behaviour. A flounce developed in her walk and a contemptuous smile often played around her mouth. The mother was quick to notice these things and though she often looked at her son anxiously, she said nothing. The son, meanwhile, was still wrapped in his own vision of a woman who walked like grass that swayed in the summer wind.

But very soon a certain incident brought him out of the clouds. One evening he noticed that his wife had a deep cut on her arm and in his odd gentle fashion enquired the cause, whereupon she burst into laughter. He could not mistake the contempt in her eyes and without a word, he stood up and left the room, not to appear again that night, nor three nights after that. On the fourth day the young wife was goaded through frustration into remarking that the man sought comfort from his mother; whereupon the man picked up a thick stick and beat her severely; whereupon the young wife ran home. The family were overjoyed. The bruises and bumps were immense. They would demand three head of cattle as compensation.

Days passed and no word arrived demanding the return of the young wife. The family's joy turned to anxiety and an elder of the clan was sent to enquire the cause.

'Tell them that I no longer require her as my wife', the man said.

Anxiety turned to alarm but the man seemed stone deaf and blind to any appeal. Cunning persuasion was turned on the mother. The young wife was expecting a child. Who knows, it might be a boy to carry on the family name. And so, in turn, the mother persuaded the son to accept his wife back. In relief, the young wife's family forgot to press for the compensation of the three beasts.

Back in her routine, the young wife found that things had indeed changed. That magic look and half-smile had disappeared from her husband's face and you could not tell him apart from all the other men of the area. Theirs was a normal marriage at last.

But it was barely a month later that the man left the reserve for the city and barely a month passed before the two women received the news that he had been killed in the city.

The two women did not grieve long, however, for six months later a son was born in the exact image of his father. They called him Mbuya, which means, he-has-come-back. And this event drew the two women close together. The child was their whole life and he grew up in an excess of womanly smothering and petting. As he was to inherit such huge herds of cattle, neither woman gave a thought to his education. The boy Mbuya remedied this omission in an unexpected way on the day he turned fourteen years old.

His birthday was also kept as a family feast day for his dead father and early that morning his mother asked him to take a goat to her old home where the feast was held. On delivering the goat, his maternal grandmother ordered two of his cousins to prepare him some tea. These cousins had been to the city for an education and were in the process of training to be teachers. They were snobbish about it and as soon as the grandmother was out of earshot one of the cousins passed a remark that so wounded the boy that he almost fainted on the spot.

'Hmm', she said. 'I really don't know why the old hag orders us to make tea for such an uneducated person. He ought to be our servant. I suppose we must honour him for his wealth.'

He cried silently: 'Stop, you are hurting me.'

But they chattered on in their artificial manner.

'Really', said the other. 'We must get back to civilisation as soon as possible.'

And they both turned and gave the boy a nasty look to emphasise what they thought about making tea for uneducated people.

At the first opportunity, the boy mentioned his new plans to his mother.

'I am going to school', he said.

She opened her eyes in surprise.

'Why?' she asked. 'One day you will be the richest man in the district and where have you ever heard of a rich man who needs an education? Education is for those who have to work.'

'Is that so?' he said. 'Well then, I shall slaughter all the cattle.'

His mother had had some frightening experiences with the stubborn, wilful spirit in him. In distress she fled to the paternal grandmother. The paternal grandmother bent her eyes to hide their gleam of joy: 'The spirit of my son is indeed in the boy', she thought.

Aloud she said: 'You must take the boy to the city for his education.'

Her family clan objected strenuously. They thought of the boy and the cattle as their possession and they feared what an education might do to him. He above all had to stay in the old way of life, till some natural gravitational law this huge wealth fell into their hands, oh, maybe when the paternal grandmother died. And all the while the boy secretly threatened the mother with the slaughter of the cattle. She knew he would do it. There was something in him which was capable of anything.

The day they left for the city he made a silent vow : 'I shall never return.'

He started at the bottom and by the time he was twenty six he had completed matriculation. What next? And while he stopped to think, certain happenings in the city attracted his attention. One of these is politics and since he concentrated on politics as much as he had on his studies, he was soon jailed for two years. On release from jail he was considered an African who was unfit to live in the city and given a restriction order to remain permanently in his tribal reserve.

The day of his arrival back home, the young man Mbuya, noticed a vast crowd of maternal aunts, uncles and so on assembling in the yard of his paternal grandmother's home. Soon his mother said:

'Pay attention, my son.'

Then one of the elders of the clan spoke:

'I wish to enquire, on behalf of the family, if there is anything wrong with you, my son.'

The young man looked them over warily. He was not sure what they wanted and he had a need to escape in a few days.

'There is nothing wrong with me, uncle', he said.

'We are very pleased to hear that, my son', the elder said.

'Now, since you are in good health, we further wish to enquire as to why you have not married.'

'I have not had the time', he said, surprised, yet on guard.

'That is what we thought too, my son', continued the elder. 'Accordingly, we have arranged for a suitable marriage partner for you. The general agreement was that if you do not marry we shall lose you."

The young man kept silent a while. Then he said.

'I hope someone will agree to abide with this poor girl because I cannot.'

'Please explain', said the elder.

'I have a different view of my future wife', he said. 'For one thing, I shall choose her for myself. For another, my wife shall never be property. She will never be purchased to be the slave in my mother's home. She will never carry a pot of water on her head and she will never collect firewood in the bush. As for the cattle which belong to me, you may do with them as you wish.'

There was a brief, stunned silence. The women started a terrible wail. His eyes passed casually over the gathering. He did not care. He really did not care and he felt so detached as though no one had ever belonged to him. What startled him, however, was the expression on the face of his paternal grandmother. Even when addressed by the elder, she could not suppress the fact that she had been smiling:

'Tell us, Elder Sister, about the mentality of this child', said the elder.

'He has this tendency to know his own mind', she said. 'Younger sister and I have often been amazed to note that he is one person whose word and deed agree. Due to this we avoided any interference in the child's life. I am most anxious that you therefore do nothing rash about this proposed marriage as we shall indeed create a problem for the maiden.'

And the young man was not aware of his rudeness. He had an escape plan to work out. The discussion seemed un-ending. He stood up abruptly and looked at the gathering; absent-mindedly, distantly. He even smiled, perhaps in his mind's eye a magic life they would never know. Only his mother recognised it, that magic look and half-smile that had so terrified her when she was a woman who walked like the grass swaying in the summer wind.

Yasmine Gooneratne

(b 1935)

Yasmine Gooneratne, poet, novelist and critic was born in 1935 in Colombo, Sri Lanka, from where she graduated in 1959 and went on to work for her doctoral degree at Cambridge University in England. In 1972 she moved to Australia where she teaches at Macquarie University and has the chair in Postcolonial Studies. She has been honoured with several academic and literary awards.

Amongst her writings are poems, short stories, and novels. The first novel *A Change of Skies* appeared in 1991 and is concerned with diasporic dislocations while the second *The Pleasure of Conquest* (1995) is about East-West relationships. Deeply attached to her Sri Lankan heritage, she extends her understanding to South Asian cultures and concerns. Gooneratne has also written a memoir, *Relative Merits,* which is a personal narrative based on the interviews with her family, the Bandaranaikes.

The story "Masterpiece" is a very finely crafted narrative which interconnects some of Gooneratne's main concerns – east-west relationships, past as it finds itself reflected in the present, the social construction of the human ego, and the gender inequality through the ages. There is also a strong sense of irony underlying the narrative. There are multiple frameworks and parallelisms: the visiting scholar versus the native scholar, the journey to the village versus the journey into the past, the native scholar's recounting of the past and the invited storyteller's narration as it is embedded in the main narrative. There are two narrators and two audiences working simultaneously but not necessarily running parallel. Parallelisms are violated. Within the embedded narrative are recurring references to the subordinated role of the wife – one who is passive, complaisant and 'homely' (the Indianism expressing 'homey'), and the clash between cultural constructs of meaning. There is a commentary on the writer and his relationship (a) with his work and (b) with his wife. The creation of the 'masterpiece' is not the work of a single hand. In the process of writing identities shift, merge and disguise themselves and creativity is a layered and a collaborative work.

Masterpiece

Our small village, said my Indian colleague, as the train on which we were travelling from Delhi to Hyderabad paused briefly to admit more passengers, has recently been discovered by the West. For many centuries it had gone its own way, content and quiet, celebrating harvest festivals and weddings, and mourning funerals. But now there is a Literature and Language Research Center in the middle of our village, with beautiful gardens all around it, and to this Center from every part of the world come scholars with an interest in India's classical literature. The master of the local school, at which I studied as a boy, is proud that our village has been picked for a project of such international importance.

And so am I: but I am not surprised. You see, it was in this very village, nine centuries ago, that a literary masterpiece came to be created. This masterpiece was the *Gita Govinda* or (as they call it in the West) "The Song of the Shepherd" a poem composed in Sanskrit in the twelfth century, about the love of the God Krishna for Radha the herd-girl. To have such a phenomenon emerge from our locality was a most unusual thing, since ours is a village of farmers who do not go in for literary masterpieces. True, our farmers often sing as they work, or hum under their breath, but what emerges from them at such times cannot be called literature, since it has not been written down on parchment or paper.

Quite recently, my friend continued, I was honored with an invitation to attend a seminar at our Literature and Language Research Center. Many eminent persons had come from abroad to attend this meeting, as well as visiting professors, staff and graduate students from our own universities in Delhi, Hyderabad, Mysore and Kerala. The subject chosen for discussion was the *Gita Govinda* itself, its status in relation to India's classical heritage and to world literature, its literary qualities, and the process of its composition. On this latter aspect of the poem, a well-known storyteller of our district had been asked to speak. I was so struck by the discussion we had that day that I would like to tell you about it.

The author of this great poem, the storyteller told us, had not been a man of our area, but an established city poet. He had been born and brought up in another district, far to the south, but he had settled among us because he wished, he said, to walk in the forest glades in which Lord Krishna had walked and played his flute. He had heard the old tales which link our village with that dark and handsome god, and it seems that he believed them. Poets of every age, though educated, are of course somewhat eccentric, and their little weaknesses should be overlooked in view of their genius.

Being in his late middle age at this time, the poet Sri Jayadeva was a man of settled habits. Very early every day, before the sun was up, he would rise, perform his morning ablutions, worship at his household shrine, and eat the breakfast his wife had prepared for him. Then he would work without a break for three or four hours before walking down to the river to bathe. When he returned, his wife would have his noon meal ready for him, and she would fan him with her palm leaf fan while he ate. After which he would retire for an afternoon nap, and rise again in order to write for two hours more, until the fading light prevented further labors.

He would probably have worked through the night, if he had lived in our own day, with electricity to light up his page and power his word processor. As it was, by keeping these regular hours with the help of his delightful and nonargumentative wife, Sri Jayadeva made rapid progress. Stanza by stanza, the poem grew under the poet's stylus. It was rumored that the poem, once completed, would be recited at a festival before an audience consisting of the principal poets of our land and the king, who himself was as everyone knew, a poet of distinction.

Our ancestors were not learned people. But they were proud to know that their village would be associated with such eminent persons through this wonderful poem. They knew that the flowering groves in which the divine lovers would walk in the poem were *their* banana groves, the flowing stream by which they would sit (and which Lord Krishna in the poem would compare to his sweetheart's long hair) was the very stream in which *they* fished. Lord Krishna, with his beautiful body and strong shoulders, is every villager's son. Radha of the long, lustrous eyes and shy smile is every village woman's daughter. Our village ancestors longed to see the poem completed, they longed to hear it recited, for the image of their village had never been reflected in art before that time, and who knew when, or if, it would ever be so reflected again?

For all these reasons, Sri Jayadeva became a focus of deep interest among our village people. This is not to say that they queued up to ask him for his opinion on world affairs, or hounded him for his autograph, as happens in many countries today when a person of the locality becomes a celebrity. Not at all: they kept themselves at a discreet distance from the genius and from his household, and if our men accidentally encountered the poet some evening at the temple, or our women met his wife by chance at the village fair, they would greet them with respect, smile and pass on.

But one day disaster struck both poet and poem. Sri Jayadeva sat down to his writing table one fine spring morning, he spread the palm-leaf parchment before him, intoned his usual prayer to Saraswati, Goddess of Wisdom, picked up his stylus – and found that he could not write. Try as he might, the couplet he wanted, the couplet that he knew was already in his mind – he only had to shine his light in the right direction and discover it – would not reveal itself to him. Sri Jayadeva sat back, composed his mind, and started again, performing each of his little writerly rituals one by one, spreading his parchment, repeating his prayer, picking up his stylus. It was no use. The words would not come.

"Writer's Block," said a voice in the auditorium.

"I beg your pardon, sir," the storyteller said. "I did not catch that. Would you kindly repeat it?"

"Writer's Block. Happens to us all."

The storyteller was not pleased by the implied comparison. "Excuse me, sir, Sri Jayadeva was a genius. Unlike you or me. There can be no comparison. A genius does not suffer writer's or any other block, especially when he works with the blessings of the gods. You are not doubting that he had such blessings in plenty?"

"Oh, not for a moment," said the voice. "I wish I had half his luck. Wonderful scenery, regular hours, a staff of servants, a complaisant wife.... No wonder he got his writing done. Having an attack of Writer's Block just shows he was human."

"Let me finish, sir, if you please," the storyteller said. "You will learn something, I think, about the god-given nature of inspiration."

"Good-oh," said the voice. "Carry on."

The poet rose from his seat, placed over his shoulder the pure white towel his wife had provided for him, and prepared to leave the house.

"You are taking your bath early, husband," his wife said. "Is the poem finished, then?"

"No, the poem is not finished," the poet replied. "I will continue to work on it when I return."

His wife watched him go down the hill, and she saw how his body seemed bowed in despair. The sight struck her with sorrow because, young as she was, she greatly respected her elderly husband, and considered that her duty in life was to support his literary work. She returned to the kitchen, knowing she must have the midday meal prepared earlier than usual, but she could not get her husband's sad mood out of her mind.

After a while, glancing out of the window as she ground coriander and cardamom on her kitchen stone, she saw her husband returning up the hill. Even from a distance she could see that his mood had changed. He held his head high, there was a youthful spring in his step. She heard him come in at the door, and waited joyfully to hear his voice. But he did not call for his noon meal as usual. Instead he went straight to his writing desk and sat down before it.

"Do not tell the master his food is ready. Let him alone, to write," said the wife to her servant. "We must not interrupt the flow of his ideas."

"Tell me, sir, do all women in this country resemble the poet's wife?" asked the irrepressible questioner in the audience.

"All, all," said the storyteller irritably. "She was a typical Indian wife, dutiful, obedient and homely."

"Homely?" said the questioner "I had got the impression that she was an attractive young woman."

"By homely I mean that she was skilled in household matters. Whether she was attractive or not is unimportant in the context of literature. It is the poet, not the poet's wife, whom we are discussing here. Please do not keep interrupting the story."

"Sorry," the questioner said. "But I need to know. I am an Australian, on a visiting appointment in Delhi, and I have just got married, to a graduate student of mine as it happens. Your answer may make a big difference to my life."

"Okay," said the storyteller "She was a typical Indian wife. Any more questions? No? Then let us continue."

The poet's wife took up her sewing, and waited patiently until her husband was ready for his meal. When he appeared in the doorway, she looked up expectantly.

"Is the poem finished, husband?" she asked.

"It has been completed," he answered. "But not by me."

Sri Jayadeva told his wife that on his return from the river bank he had gone straight to his desk. There, in the blank space he had left on the palm leaf when inspiration had failed him, he found that some unknown hand had inscribed the very couplet he had been seeking.

"Who has been visiting this house in my absence?" he asked his wife. "Who has been sitting at my desk and writing with my stylus?"

"No man has come into this house but yourself, husband," replied she. "Why, have you forgotten? You returned early from the river, and you did not pause to eat but went straight to your desk to write your poem."

Husband and wife looked at each other in amazement.

"Someone has been here," said Sri Jayadeva. "And it was not I."

What should have been a day of rejoicing for them both now turned into a day of suspicion for the poet, and sorrow for his wife. Sri Jayadeva could not get the idea out of his mind that his wife had been secretly entertaining another man, a lover – and a poet, too! he thought unhappily. He tried not to show his feelings, but his wife knew very well what he was thinking. That evening she asked him to go with her to the temple.

"Let us give thanks to Lord Krishna, husband," said she, "since your poem is now complete."

When they entered the building, Sri Jayadeva told the priest he had completed his masterpiece.

"Why, then, this look of sorrow and despair, brother?" said the priest. "You should be celebrating this auspicious event."

On hearing this, the poet's wife began to cry. She told the priest how her husband's poem had been mysteriously completed. She told him how her husband had been in mental turmoil ever since. The priest listened to her sympathetically, but it was obvious that he had problems of his own. The statue of Lord Krishna in the temple shrine-room, he said, had suffered a curious change in the course of that day. On the little finger of the god's right hand, fully in view as it curved around the stem of his famous flute, a black stain had mysteriously appeared that no one could explain.

The news had spread, and people from the countryside round about had begun making their way to the temple to see this phenomenon for themselves,

"It is a sign of prosperity for our district," said some.

"It is a prophecy of evil to come," remarked the doomsayers. "It is a sign of war or famine."

The priest feared for the reputation of his temple, and he feared even more for his own reputation as guardian of the statue. Sri Jayadeva entered the shrine-room and examined the stain.

"That's ink," he said. "I should know. I use it every day."

"An ink stain on the finger of Lord Krishna!" exclaimed the temple priest. "And your poem completed by an unknown hand!"

He lifted his palms in thanksgiving.

"It is a miracle!" he said.

Well, from that day forward a new legend was added to the tales of Lord Krishna which flourish in our village. A new legend in which the god himself descended in glory from his lotus throne in the temple, and climbed the hill to a poet's house in order to complete a classic poem.

The tale ended amidst tumultuous applause. To his surprise, the storyteller heard himself questioned yet again.

"Yes, yes? What is it?" he said.

"I have a theory," said the foreign professor in the audience. "And it is this. In my opinion, the poet's wife completed the poem."

For a moment, it seemed that the storyteller had been deprived of the power of speech.

"The Gita Govinda? A woman complete the Gita Govinda?"

"Why not?"

"Sir, if I may say so, you appear to have women on the brain," the storyteller said. "What you are suggesting is sacrilegious. Besides, it is impossible."

"Why is it impossible?"

"Because, as a respectable young woman of twelfth century India, palm leaf and stylus would have been carefully kept out of her reach. What man in his senses would marry a girl who could read and write?"

"Perhaps her husband might have taught her?" the questioner said. "Or she might have taught herself?"

"Nonsense. Such a young lady could not have been a writer. She would have knowledge of music, yes, and perhaps of dancing. Essentially, sir, she would have been a kitchen-knowing songstress. How could she have learned to write?"

"I don't know, sir. You're the expert. Perhaps she learned to write by scratching her letters on a smoke blackened kitchen wall."

"You are speaking insultingly of oriental culture, sir. In any case, if the poet's wife did complete the poem – and I do not agree for one moment that she did – why did she not say so, and claim the credit for it?"

"Perhaps it would have cost her more than her life was worth to say so," said the questioner. "So she let Lord Krishna take the credit."

"If you wish your married life to bring you happiness," the storyteller said, after a slight pause, "let me advise you, sir, to keep your theories to yourself, and study instead the art of interruption. It is not that we do not welcome interruption. We do. But it must be constructive interruption. A person may say 'Yes?' Or he may say, 'And so, what happened next?' Such interruptions allow the story to move smoothly onwards, to a proper conclusion."

"And I have got the art of constructive interruption wrong?"

"With all due respect, sir, you have got it wrong. Please consult your wife, she will set you right on this matter. You have done what must never be done, sir. You have proposed an alternative story."

Shashi Deshpande

(b 1938)

One of India's leading novelists, Shashi Deshpande commenced her literary journey a little late in life, graduating to it through journalism. Born in a Brahmin family, Deshpande grew up in Dharwar, later lived in Mumbai (Bombay) and now lives in Bangalore with her husband who is a pathologist. She inherited a literary legacy from her father, Adya Rangachar, better known as Sriranga, a well-known playwright and a much-respected writer in Kannada. He was instrumental in encouraging her to seek publication.

Deshpande simultaneously inhabits several worlds of languages and cultures. She was exposed to both Marathi (her mother's language) and Kannada (her father's language) right from early childhood, and grew up to write in English. Her concerns send her to urban as well as to small town areas, her compassion compels her to move across class and caste. In fact, she is one of those rare writers whose marginal characters like domestic servants and slum dwellers cross the margins and acquire a personhood. She also moves comfortably between classics like the *Mahabharata* and the *Upanishdas* and the world of Hindi films focusing on the impact of the media on the imagination of the young.

To date Deshpande has published nine novels, several collections of short stories and a book of non-fiction. Her concerns are social, but she chooses to work from within the psyche of a woman, articulate female silences and work on relationships. Another major strand which works from novel to novel is the strand of mortality and the subsequent bereavement. How do the living manage without those who are now dead?

The story in this collection has been taken from *The Stone Women and Other Stories* published in 2000. The collection reworks the stories from the *Mahabharata* from a feminist perspective. "Hear Me, Sanjaya" is a long monologue by Kunti as she traverses over the past, her decisions and actions, Draupadi's life, the manner in which women work against other women in false allegiance to their conventional roles dictated by tradition, and through this review upsets the traditional interpretations.

Hear Me, Sanjaya

Shall we sit down here, Sanjaya? Just for a while? I know you are anxious about your King, I. know you want go get back to him soon; but I need to rest. Not for long, just for a while. And shall I say something to you, Sanjaya? There is no need for you to be so anxious about the King any more. Have you not seen how different he seems ever since Gandhari uncovered her eyes? He seems at peace with himself, as if an ancient wrong has been righted. She should have done it long back, yes, she should have done this long ago. What use was it blinding herself? Oh, these futile vows! I sometimes think they're just a cover for the wilfulness of self-willed people. Look at Bhishma! Do you remember those two queens, our mothers-in-law, Gandhari's and mine? No, no, what am I saying how can you remember them? You never saw them, I sometimes forget how young you are. You seem to have been always with us. Why, even I can scarcely remember how they looked. They rarely spoke, except to each other – and that only in whispers – and moved about so little and so silently it was hard to remember they were there. But later, when I went back to the palace – you know, after we returned from the forest – they began to haunt me. As if the walls had absorbed their whispers, I could feel their words in the air about me. And it was then that I learned their story – and of the third sister no one ever spoke of and how and why she died.

But why am I talking of those poor, long-dead women? *Oh,* Yes, vows, that's right, I was speaking of vows. You know, Sanjaya sometimes I think – if only Bhishma had given up his vow, if he had had children of his own, then perhaps those sisters would have lived normal, happy lives. Who knows? What do you think?

Let it go. I know I shouldn't say such things about someone we revered so much. I shouldn't even think like this. But what can you do to the mind, Sanjaya? It goes its own way and... All right, I won't say anything more. I can see it makes you uncomfortable to hear me speak this way. Or, are you just impatient? Don't be in a hurry, Sanjaya, let us leave the king and my sister to themselves for a while. You don't seem pleased? Are you sorry, does it hurt you to let her become his eyes after you have played that role for so long? I know how you feel. I felt the same way when my sons let go my hand and began to walk, when they began to run. But never mind, Sanjaya, he will still need your eyes. The world you gave him is the world he is familiar with. I wonder, yes, I really wonder if he will be as comfortable with Gandhari's world? She will show him a different world, of course she will. No, I don't mean you didn't do your job well. It's just that – she is a woman and much older and what she sees will be – yes, different. But yes, I think it's your world he will feel more at home in. And you know Sanjaya, we don't like change, not at our age. You are smiling. I know what you are thinking. We have changed our lives so much by coming here, by getting away from the palace – that's what you are thinking of, aren't you? But this is not change, my son. We are on the same road, still walking on the same path we have been walking on all these years. We have gone on ahead, much further ahead, that's all.

You know, Sanjaya, I don't think I want to sit here, after all; let us go somewhere else. I don't like to be so close to the river. The sound of the river makes me uneasy, it fills me with strange thoughts. Shall we walk on? Does it tire you to listen to my talk? I don't know why I am speaking so much today. But, maybe, this is restful for you, just listening instead of talking. Do you know, I used to listen to you sometimes when you described the war to the king. My ears thirsted for news then, oh, how my heart hungered for good news. But I wanted the truth, Sanjaya – that was why it was *your* account I always wanted to listen to. Sanjaya will speak the truth, I used to think, he will not exaggerate, he will not hide things. But you did bend the truth – yes, a little – sometimes, didn't you? Your face told me when you did that. The king could not see your face and so he never guessed. But I knew. No, no, Sanjaya, don't feel ashamed, I am not blaming you or censuring you. We all do it, moving away from the truth, just a little bit, maybe, but away nevertheless. Yes, we all did it, specially during the war...

Why am I speaking of the war? Have you noticed we never speak of it? Not a word, no, neither about the living, nor the dead. It's as if it never happened. But sometimes, at night, I hear the king moaning, I hear him muttering the names of his sons. Gandhari hears him too, I know she is awake though she never stirs. And in the morning when we wake up, we wipe the knowledge out of our minds. Wholly. Nothing happened. Nothing. Here we are, three old people and one young man – that's all there is. Why are you smiling? Because I called you young? But to me you are young. I always think of you as that splendid young man I saw in charge of the king's chariot. You seemed then like Surya's charioteer. Shining and radiant. Yes, yes, I mean it, that was how you looked. Truly.

But all that is over. Tell me, Sanjaya, do you have regrets about having left these things behind? Tell me, honestly, are you happy here? No, no, I'm being stupid, I shouldn't ask you this question. I know the answer myself. Mother, Yudhishtira said to me, I can't bear to think of the three of you living here like this. Like what? I asked him. We lack nothing here, I told him. But he thinks we are suffering. I tried to tell him we are not. We are free. You feel it too, don't you? There's something here that wipes away everything that is not true, everything that is not real. Now Gandhari knows what I meant when I told her – oh, all those years ago when I came back with my five young sons to Hastinapura – I told her that my children needed no pity because they had lived in the forests until then. She thought me proud. Proud! Perhaps I am a proud woman; but it is true that I never felt sorry for the children when we lived in the forest. Sorry for them when they lived away from walls, from servants, from spies and scheming sycophants? We knew this freedom, the children and I, in those days. There was danger, sometimes there was fear, but they were young – and yes, so was I – and they laughed and played and enjoyed everything new that they saw. For me it was not new, I had lived in such surroundings even before they were born. With my husband and Madri ... But that was different, very different...

Why do I suddenly remember them? I have not thought of them for a long time, a very long time. For years, for ages. They seem like people I knew in some past life, not part of this one at all. And yet there was a time when I used to brood over them every minute of the day. Do you know how unfair life is to a woman who does not have beauty, Sanjaya? The day they brought Madri home I knew I was not beautiful. Until then I had not known it, perhaps I had not thought about it. But after I saw her, every day, each moment of each day ...

No, I won't think of it. It was so long ago and what profit is there in reviving old bitterness? And how little it means now I can still remember how threatened I felt by her two sons. Now it sounds so strange doesn't it? Those two her sons? Why, they are much more my sons than even my own. Take my sons, she said. You have to look after them. And I was angry. She's escaping, I thought. She's taking away all the glory, dying with her husband, leaving the struggle, the drudgery for me. But she was right to go. He needed her more, even in that other world he would have pined for her. I remember sometimes I used to listen to them talking; he had so many pet names for her, so many endearments. For me, there was only one name. You look away, Sanjaya. Are you embarrassed? Do you feel awkward listening to me speaking of such things? All right, I won't go on. Why should I bring back all that anger and grief now? Sometimes I think that when they died, I died too and a new woman was born. I had to become – yes, a charioteer. I know how you feel, how you felt when you were driving the chariot, I know the impatience, the pride, the confidence, the joy of being in control, the fear of losing it ...

I tried to say all these things to Draupadi when she entered our home. I thought she could – I thought she would take over my burdens. But she was never one to listen. She was impatient and oh, so impetuous! I sometimes think they do girls a great wrong when they pamper them and make much of them as children. They make them think that they matter, they make them imagine they will always matter. Draupadi was too much petted, too much indulged by her father and brother. Oh, I don't blame them; she must have been such a lively and sparkling child. How could they not have pampered her? But it does not help, no, it never helps girls to be brought up that way. Only her mother – and it was Draupadi who told me this herself – only her mother kept warning her – *'don't think you can always get what you want'*. Draupadi must have had a 'why?' I even for that, I'm sure. Poor girl.

Girl! What am I thinking of? She is a woman, a hard-faced woman who has no more questions now, not since she knew her sons were dead. No tears after that one bout of crying, either She was tearless, dry-eyed when she bid me farewell. I remember that. But – how strange, it comes back to me only now – her cheeks were wet after she took leave of Gandhari. Gandhari, the mother of her worst enemy. But they clung to each other and Gandhari's eyes were flowing as well. I can remember that, yes, very clearly. I know now why their tears mingled – they were both mothers who had lost their children. Looking at me, Draupadi must have thought – and Gandhari too: *what does she know of sorrow, she who has lost no child?* They forget, they all forget...

Perhaps, the real truth is that Draupadi has not yet forgiven me. Why do you look so amazed? Don't you know I have wronged her? Yes, I have, I know that. Each time I looked at her I remembered that, I thought of it. She entered our hut that day with joy, such joy, Sanjaya! I can never forget her face as she looked up at Arjuna. But I saw something else; I saw the faces of my other four sons. And for their sakes I took away the joy from hers. I saw Yudhishtira's face light up, as it so rarely did, when I told him what they should do, I saw Bhima's unbelieving joy. I did not look at her then, but later, when I did, it was as if the light had been dimmed. I know people think I did it out of cunning, that I knew it was the only way to keep my sons together, to get the kingdom back. Yes, that too, maybe; I never denied it, I was always silent when I heard this said. Let people think this way; in a way, it's a better reason than the real one. But what difference does it make to Draupadi? I wronged her, whatever my, reason I did her a great wrong – she should have been the wife of the one man she loved – Arjuna. She would have looked up to Yudhishtira like a father and Nakul and Sahadev – they would have been her friends. Why, they were her friends more than anything else! All three of them were uncomfortable being anything else; I could see that whenever I saw them together.

But what about Bhima then? He – his face when he looked at Draupadi – his eyes ... No, I did what I had to do. I had no choice, I have tried to tell myself often that I had no choice; but that is not true. There is always a choice. And yet I must have been a very hard woman to have made the choice I did that day. But I am a hard woman, Sanjaya. If I had not been hard would I have survived?

You know, Sanjaya, I think it was a good thing that I was brought up the way I was. I was never pampered and indulged. But who would have pampered me anyway? My father gave me away – how easily he gave me away. As if I was a bit of property. Don't you think it queer, Sanjaya? And I can't even remember if it made me angry? Did I just accept it as normal? But I remember I was frightened. I thought my father had given me away to his friend because he was displeased with me, because I had done something wrong. And I thought – what if I displease this man too? Will he give me away to someone else? And so I did everything I could to please him, I tried hard, oh so hard, never to displease him.

But I hated my new name. Kunti! I never realised it was I they wanted when someone called out that name. Now, if someone called me Pritha, I would not know who it was they wanted. But there was someone who called me Pritha – yes, even after I became Kunti, there was someone who called me by my childhood name. Who was it? This it one of the burdens of being old. Some things come back easily and others ... Who was it who called me by the name? You are smiling, you are wondering why it matters so much. I don't know, but it seems terrible to misplace a memory. Memories are all we have at our age, Sanjaya, they are precious to us. Who was it now? *Pritha, Pritha* – I can hear someone saying that and crying. It was by a river, I remember that ...

Yes, now it comes back to me. Nothing is too long ago, is it, Sanjaya? The consequences of an act go on and on. It was my nurse who called me, Pritha. But that day, by the river, I told her – *I am Kunti now, call me by no other name. I* sent her away, I remember that. I wanted to be alone. But even when she left me and went away, there was no silence. I could still hear the cries of the child, cries that drowned the sounds of the river. I kept hearing them; however far I went from the river, wherever I went, I could still hear the crying. It was only that day, when I went to meet him – and yes, again by the river – a grown man now, and he turned and faced me, his face cold and distant – it was only after that that I stopped hearing the cries. As if the child had died at last. There were so many things I could have said *to* him that day: *I was too young. I was only a child, I did not understand what I was doing,* I only *did what they told me to do. I* could have said all these things, but what was the use? He would not have heard me. We had put a bit of armour by him when we put him in the river – it was my nurse who had done that. Let them know he is a Kshatriya, she had said. When I met him after all those years, it was as if he was wearing that armour. Nothing I said would have penetrated. *My son,* I called him, but he never called me 'Mother'. Not once. Perhaps he was more honest. But he thought too much of his birth, I always felt that. That bit of armour – no, it did him no good, no good at all.

I have no sons, my husband used to cry out in despair. He was frightened, like his father had been, of going into the darkness. It was I who had the courage to light that darkness; Madri dared only when she saw my sons. Yes, we gave him sons, Madri and I. Five splendid sons. The sons of Pandu, that's what they called them. Pandu's sons! And I could never claim my own son. It makes me want to laugh sometimes. I never laughed much when I was young. I used to wonder when I heard Madri laughing, beautiful, easy laughter. Perhaps it's easy to laugh when you are loved. Is that why Krishna could laugh so much, so easily? He could make others laugh too, couldn't he, Sanjaya? I remember how angry Draupadi was when she knew about Subhadra. Krishna soothed her and comforted her, though it was he who had brought Arjun and Subhadra together. And he made Draupadi laugh, finally, yes, he did, the rogue. Why, Sanjaya, you are frowning, you seem displeased. Is it because I called Krishna a rogue? I know how you revere him, but don't forget, I love him. I love him like my own. He is my brother's son, I know him so well. Do I? Do I really know him? I don't know. But I remember he made Draupadi laugh. She was still angry with Subhadra, though, for long she nursed her anger. Yet, when Abhimanyu died, she was inconsolable.

Dead ... is he really dead, Sanjaya? Did it all really happen and are they all dead, all our sons? Are they really dead? Or is it one of those terrible dreams we are happy to wake out of? No, it's true, it happened. Like Gandhari, we have opened our eyes a little too late. What mistakes we make, Sanjaya, what terrible mistakes! Is that why we don't speak of the war? Because we are afraid we will ask ourselves – why? What was it all for? Why didn't we speak? Why didn't we stop it? I remember the few feeble shouts that greeted my sons when it was all over. Victors, they called them. They the victors? No, it's the dead who are the victors. They know it too now. Yudhishtira moves about like a puppet, Arjuna's eyes are empty and even Bhima ...

You know, Sanjaya, seeing the animals here, I have begun thinking that we are wrong, we are foolish in clinging to our roles for so long. Does a grown deer seek its mother? At some time the bond should snap, it should be over. That is natural, that is wiser. No? You don't agree? But then one shouldn't live long enough to see the sight I did. These tired old men my sons, I thought? It frightened me ...

That is enough. I am a fool to have spoken of these things. We are wiser not to speak of them. And what need is there? It is all over now. We are at peace, Gandhari, the king and I. We want nothing any more, not for ourselves, not for our children. That is real freedom, isn't it? You know, it too, don't you? Is that why ...?

But we must go back now, Sanjaya. We have been away too long. Come, Sanjaya, we must go. The king and my sister must be wondering what has happened to us, the king must be getting impatient for you. Where is Sanjaya, he must be asking the queen. Why did you let him go? Come, let us go back to them. Look, the sun is setting. How bright the light is. It is like ... The sun setting? So soon? It can't be, there is still time for that, night is far away. But what is that then? There – look there. What is it, Sanjaya, what is it, why are you hurrying? You know I am too old, I can't walk fast. Look, it is spreading, the brightness ...

Oh, now I know. Is it not the sunset. I know why the birds are suddenly silent. Yes, Sanjaya, let's hurry. I have to be with them, with my sister and the king, we need to be together. But not you, Sanjaya, not you. You must leave us. You are stubborn, but you will have to obey the king, I know you will. Yes, there they are, waiting for us. How still they are standing! Look at the king, his head held high, his nose sniffing the smoke – he knows, yes, they both know what is happening. And they are smiling. Let me go to them, Sanjaya, let me hurry. No, not you, you have to go away from here. But I must go to them, yes, I must ...

Lakshmi Kannan

(b 1947)

Lakshmi Kannan was born in Mysore where she spent her childhood with her mother's parents, and went on to the universities at Delhi and Jadavpur. A much travelled person, Kannan has abandoned an academic career for her literary pursuits.

A bilingual writer, Kannan writes both in Tamil and English. Poet, shortstory writer, novelist, she is also a translator and critic. She writes in Tamil under the pseudonym of Kaaveri, a name she has chosen because of her childhood fascination for the river which flowed past her house. Art runs in the family. Her mother is a painter and has been interested in music – these audio-visual talents are reflected in her sense of rhythm and language, in the visual images she draws with words. Kannan has three collections of poems, a few novellas and several collections of short stories.

Her Tamil novel *Athukku Poganum* has been translated by the author herself as *Going Home*. In the Preface to the novel she says: "I wrote to break a long, oppressive silence, a mute, dull, numbing pain with which I witnessed women, many of them from families that could be defined as 'upper caste/class', formally educated, wealthy and apparently socially 'respectable'. But they continued to perpetuate an unchanging, set pattern of deprivation on their women." The novel discusses these deprivations, and the control of patriarchy not only over life and property but also over space and freedom. Even as she focuses attention on feminist concerns she stresses the need for the reader/critic to recognise the multivalence of women's writing.

"Muniyakka" is the story of a woman who is outside this notion of respectability, a widow, no longer young and the mother of sons. Despite all this, she is lonely and abandoned and caught between the inner compulsion of adhering to the 'dead' rituals for the dead husband and her equally compelling need to live for herself.

Muniyakka

Muniyakka had mastered the art of soliloquy. She would keep muttering to herself as she walked, mutter to herself fluently, without any hesitation. The most meaningful conversations she had were the ones she had with herself. Everyone was used to the way this old woman freely held forth with herself.

Carrying herself on thin, spindly legs that looked more like a pair of drumsticks, Muniyakka was surprisingly mobile as she went about her work, shivering in the cold winter of Bangalore. Sweeping, mopping, washing vessels and clothes, cleaning the courtyard in front of the houses, sweeping the front yards and decorating them with *kolam* patterned skilfully with finely powdered rice. As she went about doing all the work, she would tirelessly and continuously talk to herself, 'argue' with her relations and her enemies, supplying herself with suitable replies from them. Children playing on the sides of the street would laugh at her and cry out: "There goes Muniyakka, the walkie-talkie!" Adults who chanced upon her, noticed her in passing, mildly amused. Muniyakka meanwhile went about nonchalant, perpetuating a habit that seemed to sustain her even as she worked.

Washing vessels in Anjaneyulu's house brought her twenty rupees. She received another thirty-five for sweeping, mopping the floor and washing the clothes at Vasudev Chetty's. Having worked for a long period at Rama Rao's, she now received a kind of gratuity from them and they had allowed her to build a small hut in a corner of their garden for herself. It was convenient. There was a tap near the hut and a raised stone platform over a cemented surface on which she washed her own clothes as well as those of the Rao household. She put out her rags to dry on a short washing line tied to a *neem* tree and a coconut tree.

On finishing her work, Muniyakka would return to the Rao bungalow. Mrs Ratna Rao had a genial temperament and she treated Muniyakka as an old member of the family. No festivities would take place in the house without the participation of Muniyakka. Ratna Rao shared some of her free moments with the old woman, chatting about various things in a semi-serious vein. Only Ratna could truly relate to Muniyakka's strange ways and she found the old woman's queer humour truly enjoyable. Every day, Muniyakka concluded her day's work with her duties in the temple close by. This fetched her fifteen rupees apart from a sense of fulfilment. At the end of the day she cleaned and washed the floor of the temple, after which she gratefully took refuge in her hut. Then she would heave a sigh of relief and call it a day. Lighting an earthen oil lamp and guided by the dim glow, she got a log-fire crackling in a rather functional oven, got a pot to boil her broth. After preparing the broth, she cooked the flour of ragi, cooked it real soft and tender and made some curry to go with it. Then she sat down to eat.

Alone in the hut she ate, helping herself to large handfuls of the food. Sweeping up food with her palm she swallowed lump after lump, freely scolding her dead husband and her absent sons. Eventually shaking off the feeling that she was alone in the hut, her appetite whetted by her own anger, she ate her food ravenously.

She was pleasantly suffused with a satisfaction of eating the food earned through her own hard labour.

After finishing her meal, she cleaned up the hut, and with a piece of jaggery in hand, emerged from the hut to sit outside for sometime. She nibbled lingeringly on the jaggery. After swallowing the last little morsel, she sat back and chewed lazily on an *areca nut* her eyes fixed on some distant point in the darkness. In that still moment, she felt evacuated – her mind swept clean like the interior of the hut, purged of all disturbing thoughts and stilled to a mute point. Not a fibre of her being moved. And yet, this sense of peace never lasted for long....

With the failing vision of her old eyes, she peered into the inky darkness around her. The Rao bungalow was surrounded by a large garden. Segregated on one side was a group of coconut trees. Beyond the coconut grove, sprawled a large jack-fruit tree. Nestling under its shade was Muniyakka's hut. The gardens and groves in Bangalore invariably howled in the strong breeze at night. To Muniyakka's eyes, the coconut trees seemed to sway around with their "hair" loosely flying in the breeze, dancing the dance of the devil in the darkness of the night. Kokkina Halli, Muniyakka's village was a few miles away from Bangalore. The people of that village always described ghosts and devils this way, essentially in their female forms. The devil was personified as a wild, mad woman – her incisors in her row of teeth curving over her lips revealed a hideous smile, as her voice cackled and echoed resoundingly in the cloud capped night sky. Hair swaying in the breeze and over the face, the devil danced in a trance to a mad rhythm.

Outside the house and above the wall that enclosed the garden, a big *peepul* tree stood under the dim glow of the moon. The oily gloss of the *peepul* leaves, shimmered in the night light. It was a garden pampered by the care and attention of the Raos. It had a dense variety of plants and many flower and fruit bearing trees. It looked a picture of health bursting with flowers, fruits and vegetables, exuding a great sense of luxurious well-being so characteristic of any well-maintained garden in Bangalore. Looking at it, one might forget for a moment that things like abject poverty, squalor or disease existed elsewhere. Collectively, the trees and plants looked like children who had been brought up with care and affection. Muniyakka was very fond of the garden and lavished her affection on it. In the afternoons, she would try to compete with the gardener and pour buckets of water, covering the entire garden, even if the exercise threatened to break her back. For a few moments, the flowers and fruits would take on a golden hue under the Midas touch of the setting sun. Taking in the sight, Muniyakka would feel infinitely enriched, as if she had somehow inherited a vast, great wealth. And yet, when the sky darkened....

She was back in her retreat again, squatting outside her hut in the darkness and looking at the same swaying plants and trees in the menacing form of the devil's dance. Her heart quickened as it learned to keep pace with the devil's beat outside. In the turbulence of the breeze, the branches hissed like so many snakes and, in the fury of the hissing, Muniyakka could completely identify herself. Her mind danced, pulsating with the rhythm of the *dhvamsha* of Kali.

The sounds of windows being slammed and bolted – the servants of the Rao household and his eldest daughter were securing the windows against the cold and stormy wind outside. Through the glass windows, the light of the house spread a quiet glow in the middle of the dark garden. There was peace inside. But storm outside, with Bangalore being lashed by cold gusts of wind like whiplashes. The night, pitch dark. Each of the leaves of the trees, fanning out like the enlarged hood of a snake, sighing "Hoos" "Hoos" as they collectively surrounded the solitary Muniyakka like a thousand snakes.

Snakes, snakes, and more snakes... everywhere a snake, hissing. If it slithers in green or brown colours in front of us, or if we find it curling down from the caves of the ceiling, then we take a sturdy bamboo pole and bring it down hard on the snake, beat it instantly! Beat it till it quivers in agony and is smashed into a pulp. But if the same genus of serpent comes crowned with the title of "cobra" and we see the proud tilt of its hood and feel the heat of its hissing breath, then we reach for some milk instantly. Offer the milk most humbly to the cobra, kneel down and do your obeisance. If the same cobra does not slide or slither but is frozen as a stone in a corner of a temple, or under a black-berry tree, then there is no limit to our worship. We apply *kumkum* on the stone snake, dash our foreheads on the curved stone as we entreat favours and dreams that need to be fulfilled. Offer flowers to the stone snake, break coconuts and let the tender coconut-water bathe the stone as we repeat our prayers, shivering and damp from our holy ablutions, our stomachs caved in from a devout fast. These women, muttering their prayers, going round and round the stone snakes and the black-berry tree, round and round dizzily, like fervent dervishes. Ripe berries dropping from the tree on the stone snakes below, smashing their rich pulp against the stone, dyeing it in vivid spots of blue and purple. The dumb mouths of the snakes, carrying the sweets smeared by the women. Armies of large, black ants filing in orderly rows towards the sweets. Stones scarred with crazy lines of *kumkum, haldi,* sandalwood paste, and the smudgy sprinkling of withered flowers.

It was Muniyakka's responsibility to wash the stones clean of all the stains. She doused the stones with buckets of water, and with a rough coir brush in her hand, fiercely scrubbed the stains away. With the broomstick held firmly in her hand, she swept away the stones of the half-eaten berries dropped by the squirrels. She cursed the women who came to worship and made such a mess at the temple. 'Foolish women... banging their brows on stone begging for favours – Give me a son, Lord of Snakes, great Nagaraj! Please give me a son... Idiots! I was like you when I was a young woman, bruising my brow on this stone and praying for sons. The result? Today I have three useless sons in whom I once had a deep, implicit faith. I visited their homes so eagerly, but not one of them would even give me a single, tepid bowl of broth. Each worthless son, lusting after his own wife. They don't need a mother any more. Shameless bastards. Naturally! For they were after all fathered by an equally worthless man, Bairappa. That husband of mine, dying after leading a life of waste smoking, drinking, gambling-squandering my hard-earned money... Bairappa be damned!'

"So, what news *Ajji?* Finished your work for the day?" asked Thimmayya the temple gardener, emerging from the bushes.

"Yes Thimmayya, I've finished my work. But I will have to get up early tomorrow. It is the death anniversary of that worthless man I had married. I will do my duty and have a small *sraddha* in my hut. Come tomorrow and have a special lunch. Will you come?"

"Of course *Ajji, I'll* certainly come," said Thimmayya, with a big grin. Then he asked: "Ajji, have you bought all the necessary things for the *sraddha* or has anything been left out? You always take care not to leave any gaps in Bairappa's banana leaf – it must be complete with his favourite brand of *bidi,* sweet buns made with jaggery, then spiced rice... even the toddy... Hum..." Thimmayya licked his lips in candid anticipation of an appetising meal.

Muniyakka laughed aloud. "Alright then, come tomorrow. You can have everything from the wretch Bairappa's leaf," she smiled. Picking up her bucket and the broomstick, she went out of the temple.

Bairappa's *sraddha.* It was done just the way it had been all these years in the past. Muniyakka performed the rites that should rightfully have been performed by her sons. Her sons ignored the day. She kept all her husband's favourite dishes on a clean banana leaf. This was meant to appease his departed soul. The gleaming leaf carried fish curry, tenderly cooked cabbage, sweet buns made with jaggery, spiced rice, a small bottle of toddy and a packet of his favourite brand of *bidis.* On this day, Muniyakka had a youthful glow on her face. This day she felt emboldened to have a large, round *kumkum* on her forehead. Flowers on her hair. A clean cotton saree wrapped around her old, withered body. She briskly attended to all the rites and rituals of the *sraddha,* all the while freely cursing her husband. Ratna Rao saw the items on the banana leaf and had a good laugh. She teased Muniyakka pleasantly in Kannada, her voice ringing lightly like silver bells. Muniyakka blushed at the teasing but joined Mrs Rao in her light-hearted laughter. When she had got through with all the work, Muniyakka began to sweep and clean the hut and her face registered a subtle transformation: "Husband! Son! What a humbug all these relationships are... Hmm!" She came out of the hut as usual and squatted outside, her back resting on the wall, eyes peering into the darkness. The tree began to dance in the darkness. Muniyakka enjoyed the devil's dance once more, with a vicarious pleasure. In that lonely hour, she experienced her own sense of isolation with a private thrill. Felt the damp air caressing her hollow cheeks. The pleasant smell. of earth dampened by the prelude of a drizzle. Even the language of Kannada seemed to have mingled with the damp earth and now it reached her nostrils delicately. Muniyakka smelt everything around her and heard the distant thunder. I don't have to water the garden tomorrow, she thought. There will be a heavy downpour. Thunder will crack the sky and rain will pour down on all the trees. On the plants. And on this hut, here. The temple. The stone snakes—everything will be washed clean.

In the strong breeze, the branches waved wildly. Muniyakka sat in the darkness, a small speck, peering, watching, thinking. 'Who's a devil and who's not a devil? Who am I? And you? Who the devil are you? Where are we going? How far?... and for what?'

Githa Hariharan

(b 1954)

Githa Hariharan lives in Delhi and has written short stories as well as novels. Her first novel won her instant fame as it was awarded the Commonwealth Writers Prize for the first novel. This novel, *The Thousand Faces of Night* (1992), explores the power of myth to create and to destroy, to confine and to liberate as the heroine works through her relationship with her husband on the cross-junction of the same myths narrated differently first by her grandmother and then by her father-in-law.

Her next novel *Ghosts of Vasu Master* (1994) uses a male protagonist but once again through narrating fables subverts the traditional pattern of education. She followed it by *When Dreams Travel* (1999) which reverses the Arabian Nights' narratives and is framed by fantasy and magic realism. Her most recent publication is *In Times of Siege*.

Hariharan has also published a collection of short stories, *The Art of Dying and Other Stories*. The story "The Remains of the Feast" is from that volume. The particular strength of this story lies in its ironical reversal, and in the close tie between the great grandmother and the great granddaughter, the old woman's total disassociation from social conventions and emotional relationships, the concentrated focus on the sensual aspects of life and concern with the repressed desires of her youth. The old woman wants a final fling at life and in the process wants to bid goodbye to the memories of deprivation of widowhood and loss. The narrative is invested with a certain sense of comedy as is some of Hariharan's other work. This subtle sense of humour, of ironic reversal is something she shares with Nayantara Sahgal and it serves as a fine contrast to the themes of oppression and claustrophobia which she discusses. "The Remains of the Feast" has its own inbuilt sense of loss but the juxtaposition of the medical student's detached study of anatomy, the description of the cancerous tumour, and the sensuousness of touch, smell and taste ending up finally in the smell of decay, holds the opposing elements of sorrow and pleasure together in a precarious balance.

The Remains of the Feast

The room still smells of her. Not as she did when she was dying, an overripe smell that clung to everything that had touched her, sheets, saris, hands. She had been in the nursing home for only ten days but a bedsore grew like an angry red welt on her back. Her neck was a big hump, and she lay in bed like a moody camel that would snap or bite at unpredictable intervals. The goitred lump, the familiar swelling I had seen on her neck all my life, that I had stroked and teasingly pinched as a child, was now a cancer that spread like a fire down the old body, licking clean everything in its way.

The room now smells like a pressed, faded rose. A dry, elusive smell. Burnt, a candle put out.

We were not exactly room-mates, but we shared two rooms, one corners of the old ancestral house, all my twenty-year-old life.

She was Rukmini, my great-grandmother. She was ninety when she died last month, outliving by ten years her only son and daughter-in-law. I don't know how she felt when they died, but later she seemed to find something hilarious about it all. That she an ignorant village-bred woman, who signed the papers my father brought her with a thumb-print, should survive; while they, city-bred, ambitious, should collapse of weak hearts and arthritic knees at the first sign of old age.

Her sense of humour was always quaint. It could also be embarrassing. She would sit in her corner, her round, plump face reddening, giggling like a little girl. I knew better than ask her why, I was a teenager by then. But some uninitiated friend would be unable to resist, and would go up to my great-grandmother and ask her why she was laughing. This, I knew, would send her into uncontrollable peals. The tears would flow down her cheeks, and finally, catching her breath, still weak with laughter, she would confess. She could fart exactly like a train whistling its way out of the station, and this achievement gave her as much joy as a child might get when she saw or heard a train.

So perhaps it is not all that surprising that she could be so flippant about her only child's death, especially since ten years had passed.

'Yes, Ratna, you study hard and become a big doctor-madam,' she should chuckle, when I kept the lights on all night and paced up and down the room, reading to myself.

'The last time I saw a doctor, I was thirty years old.'

'Your grandfather was in the hospital for three months. He would faint every time he saw his own blood.'

And as if that summed up the progress made between two generations, she would pull her blanket over her head and begin snoring almost immediately.

I have two rooms, the entire downstairs to myself now, since my great-grandmother died. I begin my course at medical college next month, and I am afraid to be here alone at night.

I have to live up to the gold medal I won last year. I keep late hours, reading my anatomy textbook before the course begins. The body is a solid, reliable thing. It is a wonderful, resilient machine. I hold on to the thick, hard-bound book and flip through the new-smelling pages greedily. I stop every time I find an illustration, and look at it closely. It reduces us to pink, blue and white, colour-coded, labelled parts. Muscles, veins, tendons. Everything has a name. Everything is linked, one with the other, all parts of a functioning whole.

It is poor consolation for the nights I have spent in her warm bed, surrounded by that safe, familiar, musty smell.

She was cheerful and never sick. But she was also undeniably old, and so it was no great surprise to us when she took to lying in bed all day a few weeks before her ninetieth birthday.

She had been lying in bed for close to two months, ignoring concern, advice, scolding, and then she suddenly gave up. She agreed to see a doctor.

The young doctor came out of her room, his face puzzled and angry. My father begged him to sit down and drink a tumbler of hot coffee.

'She will need all kinds of tests,' the doctor said. 'How long has she had that lump on her neck? Have you had it checked?'

My father shifted uneasily in his cane chair. He is a cadaverous looking man, prone to nervousness and sweating. He keeps a big jar of antacids on his office desk. He has a nine to five accountant's job in a government-owned company, the kind that never fires its employees.

My father pulled out the small towel he uses in place of a handkerchief. Wiping his forehead, he mumbled, 'You know how these old women are. Impossible to argue with them.'

'The neck,' the doctor said more gently. I could see he pitied my father.

'I think it was examined once, long ago. My father was alive then. There was supposed to have been an operation, I think. But you know what they thought in those days. An operation meant an unnatural death. All the relatives came over to scare her, advise her with horror stories. So she said no. You know how it is. And she was already a widow then, my father was the head of the household. How could he, a fourteen-year-old, take the responsibility?'

'Hm,' said the doctor. He shrugged his shoulders. 'Let me know when you want to admit her in my nursing home. But I suppose it's best to let her die at home.'

When the doctor left, we looked at each other, the three of us, like shifty accomplices. My mother, practical as always, broke the silence and said, 'Let's not tell her anything. Why worry her? And then we'll have all kinds of difficult old aunts and cousins visiting, it will be such a nuisance. How will Ratna study in the middle of all that chaos?'

But when I went to our room that night, my great-grandmother had a sly look on her face. 'Come here, Ratna,' She said. 'Come here, my darling little gem.'

I went, my heart quaking at the thought of telling her. She held my hand and kissed each finger, her half-closed eyes almost flirtatious.

'Tell me something, Ratna,' she began in a wheedling voice.

'I don't know, I don't know anything about it,' I said quickly.

'Of course you do!' She was surprised, a little annoyed. 'Those small cakes you got from the Christian shop that day. Do they have eggs in them?'

I was speechless with relief.

'Do they?' she persisted. 'Will you,' and her eyes narrowed with cunning, 'will you get one for me?'

So we began a strange partnership, my great-grandmother and I. I smuggled cakes and ice cream, biscuits and samosas, made by non-Brahmin hands, into a vegetarian invalid's room. To the deathbed of a Brahmin widow who had never eaten anything but pure, home-cooked food for almost a century.

She would grab it from my hand, late at night after my parents had gone to sleep. She would hold the pastry in her fingers, turn it round and round, as if on the verge of an earthshaking discovery.

'And does it really have egg in it?' she would ask again, as if she needed the password for her to bite into it with her gums.

'Yes, yes,' I would say, a little tired of midnight feasts by then. The pastries were a cheap yellow colour, topped by white frosting with hard, gray pearls.

'Lots and lots of eggs,' I would say, wanting her to hurry up and put it in her mouth. 'And the bakery is owned by a Christian. I think he hires Muslim cooks too.'

'Ooooh,' she would sign. Her little pink tongue darted out and licked the frosting. Her toothless mouth worked its way steadily, munching, making happy sucking noises.

Our secret was safe for about a week. Then she became bold. She was bored with the cakes, she said. They gave her heartburn.

She became a little more adventurous every day. Her cravings were varied and unpredictable. Laughable and always urgent.

'I'm thirsty,' she moaned, when my mother asked her if she wanted anything. 'No, no, I don't want water, I don't want, juice.' She stopped the moaning and looked at my mother's patient exasperated face. 'I'll tell you what I want', she whined. 'Get me a glass of that brown drink Ratna bought in the bottle. The kind that bubbles and makes a popping sound when you open the bottle. The one with the fizzy noise when you pour it out.'

'A Coca-Cola?' said my mother, shocked. 'Don't be silly, it will make you sick.'

'I don't care what it is called,' my great-grandmother said and started moaning again. 'I want it.'

So she got it and my mother poured out a small glassful, tight-lipped, and gave it to her without a word. She was always a dutiful grand-daughter-in-law.

'Ah,' sighed my great-grandmother, propped up against her pillows, the steel tumbler lifted high over her lips. The lump on her neck moved in little gurgles as she drank. Then she burped a loud, contented burp, and asked, as if she had just thought of it, 'Do you think there is something in it? You know, alcohol?'

A month later, we had got used to her unexpected, inappropriate demands. She had tasted, by now, lemon tarts, garlic, three types of aerated drinks, fruitcake laced with brandy, bhel-puri from the fly-infested bazaar nearby.

'There's going to be trouble,' my mother kept muttering under her breath. 'She's losing her mind, she is going to be a lot of trouble.'

And she was right, of course. My great-grandmother could no longer swallow very well. She would pour the coke into her mouth and half of it would trickle out of her nostrils, thick, brown, nauseating.

'It burns, it burns,' she would yell then, but she pursed lips tightly together when my mother spooned a thin gruel into her mouth, 'No, no,' she screamed deliriously. 'Get me something from the bazaar. Raw onions. Fried bread. Chickens and goats.'

Then we knew she was lost to us. She was dying.

She was in the nursing home for ten whole days. My mother and I took turns sitting by her, sleeping on the floor by the hospital cot.

She lay there quietly, the pendulous neck almost as big as her face. But she would not let the nurses near her bed. She would squirm and wriggle like a big fish that refused to be caught. The sheets smelled, and the young doctor shook his head. 'Not much to be done now,' he said. 'The cancer has left nothing intact.'

The day she died, she kept searching the room with her eye. Her arms were held down by the tubes and needle, criss-cross, in, out. The glucose dripped into her veins but her nose still ran, the clear, thin liquid trickling down like dribble on to her chin. Her hands clenched and unclenched with the effort and she whispered, like a miracle, 'Ratna.'

My mother and I rushed to her bedside. Tears streaming down her face, my mother bent her head before her and pleased, 'Give me your blessings, Paati. Bless me before you go.'

My great-grandmother looked at her for a minute, her lips working furiously, noiselessly. For the first time in my life I saw a fine veil of perspiration on her face. The muscles on her face twitched in mad, frenzied jerks. Then she pulled one arm free of the tubes, in a sudden, crazy spurt of strength, and the I.V. pole crashed to the floor.

'Bring me a red sari,' she screamed. 'A red one with a big wide border of gold. And,' her voice cracked, 'bring me peanuts with chilli powder from the corner shop. Onion and green chilli bondas deep-fried in oil.'

Then the voice gurgled and gurgled, her face and neck swayed, rocked like a boat lost in a stormy sea. She retched, and as the vomit flew out of her mouth and her nose, thick like the milkshakes she had drunk, brown like the alcoholic coke, her head slumped forward, her rounded chin buried in the cancerous neck.

When we brought the body home – I am not yet a doctor and already I can call her that – I helped my mother to wipe her clean with a wet, soft cloth. We wiped away the smells, the smell of the hospital bed, the smell of an old woman's juices drying. Her skin was dry and papery. The stubble on her head – she had refused to shave her head once she got sick – had grown, like the soft, white bristles of a hairbrush.

She had had only one child though she had lived so long. But the skin on her stomach was like crumpled, frayed velvet, the creases running to and fro in fine, silvery rivulets.

'Bring her sari,' my mother whispered, as if my great-grandmother could still hear her.

I looked at the stiff, cold body that I was seeing naked for the first time. She was asleep at last, quiet at last. I had learnt, in the last month or two, to expect the unexpected from her. I waited, in case she changed her mind and sat up, remembering one more taboo to be tasted.

'Bring me your eyebrow tweezers,' I heard her say. 'Bring me that hair-removing cream. I have a moustache and I don't want to be an ugly old woman.'

But she lay still, the wads of cotton in her nostrils and ears shutting us out. Shutting out her belated ardour.

I ran to my cupboard and brought her the brightest, reddest sari I could find: last year's Diwali sari, my first silk.

I unfolded it, ignoring my mother's eyes, which were turning aghast. I covered her naked body lovingly. The red silk glittered like her childish laughter.

'Have you gone mad,' my mother whispered furiously. 'She was a sick old woman, she didn't know what she was saying.'

She rolled up the sari and flung it aside, as if it had been polluted. She wiped the body again to free it from foolish, trivial desires.

They burnt her in a pale-brown sari, her widow's weeds. The prayer beads I had never seen her touch encircled the bulging, obscene neck.

I am still a novice at anatomy. I hover just over the body, I am just beneath the skin. I have yet to look at the insides, the entrails of memories she told me nothing about, the pain congealing into a cancer.

She has left me behind with nothing but a smell, a legacy that grows fainter every day. For a while I haunt the dirtiest bakeries and tea-stalls I can find. I search for her, my sweet great-grandmother, in plate after plate of stale confections, in needle-sharp green chillies, deep-fried in rancid oil. I plot her revenge for her, I give myself diarrhoea for a week.

Then I open all the windows and her cupboard and air the rooms. I tear her dirty, grey saris to shreds. I line the shelves of her empty cupboard with my thick, newly-bought, glossy-jacketed texts, one next to the other. They stand straight and solid, row after row of armed soldiers. They fill up the small cupboard quickly.

Theoretical Formulations: Questionings and Contestations

Mary Wollstonecraft
(1759-97)

Mary Wollstonecraft was one of the first intellectual women to win both fame and notoriety in her short life. Of Anglo-Irish origins, Mary was one of six children. Her father was a difficult man to live with and Mary's mother died when Mary was barely eleven. Coming from such an unsettled background, Mary went out to earn her livelihood when she was barely nineteen.

Of her works *A Vindication of the Rights of Woman* (1792) is the best known. But there are several others equally valuable works which deserve to be recognised and the 70s wave of feminist thought has drawn attention to it. Her early work *Thoughts on the Education of Daughters: With Reflections on Female Conduct, in the More Important Duties of Life* (1787) was the result of her own experience of having established a school in collaboration with her sister. Women's education was of great significance as the role of women was being transformed by the industrial society.

In 1790, Wollstonecraft also wrote *Vindication of the Rights of Man* in response to Edmund Burke's *Reflections on the Revolution in France.* Her novel *Mary* had already been published in 1788. Later when she went to Paris in 1792, she wrote another work on the French Revolution expressing her own views. A radical thinker she refused to be confined by social conventions. Nevertheless, after her relationship with Imlay collapsed, she married William Godwin in the interest of their (Godwin's and Mary's) unborn child. She died in 1797 of postnatal fever, after giving birth to Mary, the future Mary Shelley and the writer of *Frankenstein*.

William Godwin went on to publish her memoir which drew a lot of criticism and threw Wollstonecraft into disrepute.

The Rights of Woman: The Prevailing Opinion of a Sexual Character Discussed

To account for, and excuse the tyranny of man, many ingenious arguments have been brought forward to prove, that the two sexes, in the acquirement of virtue, ought to aim at attaining a very different character; or, to speak explicitly, women are not allowed to have sufficient strength of mind to acquire what really deserves the name of virtue. Yet it should seem, allowing them to have souls, that there is but one way appointed by providence to lead *mankind* to either virtue or happiness.

If then women are not a swarm of ephemeron triflers, why should they be kept in ignorance under the specious name of innocence? Men complain, and with reason, of the follies and caprices of our sex, when they do not keenly satirise our headstrong passions and grovelling vices. Behold, I should answer, the natural effect of ignorance! The mind will ever be unstable that has only prejudices to rest on, and the current will run with destructive fury when there are no barriers to break its force. Women are told from their infancy, and taught by the example of their mothers, that a little knowledge of human weakness, justly termed cunning, softness of temper, *outward* obedience, and a *scrupulous* attention to a puerile kind of propriety, will obtain for them the protection of man; and should they be beautiful, everything else is needless, for at least twenty years of their lives.

Thus, Milton describes our first frail mother; though when he tells us that women are formed for softness and sweet attractive grace, I cannot comprehend his meaning, unless, in the true

Mahometan strain, he meant to deprive us of souls, and insinuate that we were beings only designed by sweet attractive grace, and docile blind obedience, to gratify the senses of man when he can no longer soar on the wing of contemplation.

How grossly do they insult us who thus advise us only to render ourselves gentle, domestic brutes! For instance, the winning softness so warmly and frequently recommended, that governs by obeying. What childish expressions, and how insignificant is the being – can it be an immortal one? – who will condescend to govern by such sinister methods? "Certainly," says Lord Bacon, "man is of kin to the beasts by his body; and if he be not of kin to God by his spirit, he is a base and ignoble creature!" Men, indeed, appear to me to act in a very unphilosophical manner, when they try to secure the good conduct of women by attempting to keep them always in a state of childhood. Rousseau was more consistent when he wished to stop the progress of reason in both sexes, for if men eat of the tree of knowledge, women will come in for a taste; but, from the imperfect cultivation which their understandings now receive, they only attain a knowledge of evil.

Children, I grant, should be innocent; but when the epithet is applied to men, or women, it is but a civil term for weakness. For if it be allowed that women were destined by Providence to acquire human virtues, and, by the exercise of their understandings, that stability of character which is the firmest ground to rest our future hopes upon, they must be permitted to turn to the fountain of light, and not forced to shape their course by the twinkling of a mere satellite. Milton, I grant, was of a very different opinion; for he only bends to the indefeasible right of beauty, though it would be difficult to render two passages which I now mean to contrast, consistent. But into similar inconsistencies are great men often led by their senses:

> To whom thus Eve with *perfect beauty* adorn'd
> My author and disposer, what thou bid'st
> Unargued I obey; so God ordains:
> God is *thy law, thou mine:* to know no more
> Is woman's happiest knowledge and her *praise*.

These are exactly the arguments that I have used to children; but I have added, your reason is now gaining strength, and till it arrives at some degree of maturity, you must look up to me for advice, – then you ought to *think*, and only rely on God.

Yet in the following lines Milton seems to coincide with me, when he makes Adam thus expostulate with his Maker:

> Hast Thou not made me here Thy substitute,
> And these inferior far beneath me set?
> Among *unequals* what society
> Can sort, what harmony or true delight?
> Which must be mutual, in proportion due
> Given and received; but in *disparity*
> The one intense, the other still remiss
> Cannot well suit with either, but soon prove
> Tedious alike: of *fellowship* I speak
> Such as I seek, fit to participate
> All rational delight–

In treating therefore of the manners of women, let us, disregarding sensual arguments, trace what we should endeavour to make them in order to co-operate, if the expression be not too bold, with the Supreme Being.

By individual education, I mean, for the sense of the word is not precisely defined, such an attention to a child as will slowly sharpen the senses, form the temper, regulate the passions as they begin to ferment, and set the understanding to work before the body arrives at maturity; so that the man may only have to proceed, not to begin, the important task of learning to think and reason.

To prevent any misconstruction, I must add, that I do not believe that a private education can work the wonders which some sanguine writers have attributed to it. Men and women must be educated, in a great degree, by the opinions and manners of the society they live in. In every age there has been a stream of popular opinion that has carried all before it, and given a family character, as it were, to the century. It may then fairly be inferred, that, till society be differently constituted, much cannot be expected from education. It is, however, sufficient for my present purpose to assert that, whatever effect circumstances have on the abilities, every being may become virtuous by the exercise of its own reason; for if but one being was created with vicious inclinations, that is positively bad, what can save us from atheism? or if we worship a god, is not that God a devil?

Consequently, the most perfect education, in my opinion, is such an exercise of the understanding as is best calculated to strengthen the body and form the heart. Or, in other words, to enable the individual to attain such habits of virtue as will render it independent. In fact, it is a farce to call any being virtuous whose virtues do not result from the exercise of its own reason. This was Rousseau's opinion respecting men; I extend it to women, and confidently assert that they have been drawn out of their sphere by false refinement, and not by an endeavour to acquire masculine qualities. Still the regal homage which they receive is so intoxicating, that until the manners of the times are changed, and formed on more reasonable principles, it may be impossible to convince them that the illegitimate power which they obtain by degrading themselves is a curse, and that they must return to nature and equality if they wish to secure the placid satisfaction that unsophisticated affections impart. But for this epoch we must wait – wait perhaps till kings and nobles, enlightened by reason, and, preferring the real dignity of man to childish state, throw off their gaudy hereditary trappings; and if then women do not resign the arbitrary power of beauty – they will prove that they have *less* mind than man.

I may be accused of arrogance; still I must declare what I firmly believe, that all the writers who have written on the subject of female education and manners, from Rousseau to Dr. Gregory, have contributed to render women more artificial, weak characters, more useless members of society. I might have expressed this conviction in a lower key, but I am afraid it would have been the whine of affectation, and not the faithful expression of my feelings, of the clear results which experience and reflection have led me to draw. When I come to that division of the subject, I shall advert to the passages that I more particularly disapprove of, in the works of the authors I have just alluded to; but it is first necessary to observe that my objection extends to the whole purport of those books, which tend, in my opinion, to degrade one-half of the human species, and render women pleasing at the expense of every solid virtue.

Though, to reason on Rousseau's ground, if man did attain a degree of perfection of mind when his body arrived at maturity, it might be proper, in order to make a man and his wife *one,* that she should rely entirely on his understanding; and the graceful ivy, clasping the oak that supported it, would form a whole in which strength and beauty would be equally conspicuous. But, alas! husbands, as well as their helpmates, are often only overgrown children, – nay, thanks to early debauchery, scarcely men in their outward form, – and if the blind lead the blind, one need not come from heaven to tell us the consequence.

Many are the causes that, in the present corrupt state of society, contribute to enslave women by cramping their understandings and sharpening their senses. One, perhaps, that silently does more mischief than all the rest, is their disregard of order.

To do everything in all orderly manner is a most important precept, which women, who, generally speaking, receive only a disorderly kind of education, seldom attend to with that degree of exactness that men, who from their infancy are broken into method, observe. This negligent kind of guesswork – for what other epithet can be used to point out the random exertions of a sort of instinctive common sense never brought to the test of reason? – prevents their generalising matters of fact; so they do today what they did yesterday, merely because they did it yesterday.

This contempt of the understanding in early life has more baneful consequences than is commonly supposed; for the little knowledge which women of strong minds attain is, from various circumstances, of a more desultory kind than the knowledge of men, and it is acquired more by sheer observations on real life than from comparing what has been individually observed with the results of experience generalised by speculation. Led by their dependent situation and domestic employment more into society, what they learn is rather by snatches; and as learning is with them in general only a secondary thing, they do not pursue any one branch with that persevering ardour necessary to give vigour to the faculties and clearness to the judgement. In the present state of society a little learning is required to support the character of a gentleman, and boys are obliged to submit to a few years of discipline. But in the education of women, the cultivation of the understanding is always subordinate to the acquirement of some corporeal accomplishment. Even when enervated by confinement and false notions of modesty, the body is prevented from attaining that grace and beauty which relaxed half-formed limbs never exhibit. Besides, in youth their faculties are not brought forward by emulation; and having no serious scientific study, if they have natural sagacity, it is turned too soon on life and manners. They dwell on effects and modifications, without tracing them back to causes; and complicated rules to adjust behaviour are a weak substitute for simple principles.

Riches and hereditary honours have made cyphers of women to give consequence to the numerical figure; and idleness has produced a mixture of gallantry and despotism into society, which leads the very men who are the slaves of their mistresses to tyrannise over their sisters, wives , and daughters. This is only keeping them in rank and file, it is true. Strengthen the female mind by enlarging it, and there will be an end to blind obedience; but as blind obedience is ever sought for by power, tyrants and sensualists are in the right when they endeavour to keep woman in the dark, because the former only want slaves, and the latter a plaything. The sensualist, indeed, has been the most dangerous of tyrants, and women have been duped by their lovers, as princes by their ministers, whilst dreaming that they reigned over them.

I now principally allude to Rousseau, for his character of Sophia is undoubtedly a captivating one, though it appears to me grossly unnatural. However, it is not the superstructure, but the foundation of her character, the principles on which her education was built, that I mean to attack; nay, warmly as I admire the genius of that able writer, whose opinions I shall often have occasion to cite, indignation always takes place of admiration, and the rigid frown of insulted virtue effaces the smile of complacency which his eloquent periods are wont to raise when I read his voluptuous reveries. Is this the man who, in his ardour for virtue, would banish all the soft arts of peace, and almost carry us back to

Spartan discipline? Is this the man who delights to paint the useful struggles of passion, the triumphs of good dispositions, and the heroic flights which carry the glowing soul out of itself? How are these mighty sentiments lowered when he describes the pretty foot and enticing airs of his little favourite ! But for the present I waive the subject, and instead of severely reprehending the transient effusions of overweening sensibility, I shall only observe that whoever has cast a benevolent eye on society must often have been gratified by the sight of humble mutual love not dignified by sentiment, or strengthened by a union in intellectual pursuits. The domestic trifles of the day have afforded matters for cheerful converse, and innocent caresses have softened toils which did not require great exercise of mind or stretch of thought; yet has not the sight of this moderate felicity excited more tenderness than respect? – an emotion similar to what we feel when children are playing or animals sporting; whilst the contemplation of the noble struggle of suffering merit has raised admiration, and carried our thoughts to that world where sensation will give place to reason.

Women are therefore to be considered either as moral beings, or so weak that they must be entirely subjected to the superior faculties of men.

Let us examine this questions. Rousseau declares that a woman should never for a moment feel herself independent, that she should be governed by fear to exercise her *natural* cunning, and made a coquettish slave in order to render her a more alluring object of desire, a *sweeter* companion to man, whenever he chooses to relax himself. He carries the arguments, which he pretends to draw from the indications of nature, still further, and insinuates that truth and fortitude the corner-stones of all human virtue, should be cultivated with certain restrictions, because, with respect to the female character, obedience is the grand lesson which ought to be impressed with unrelenting rigour.

What nonsense! When will a great man arise with sufficient strength of mind to puff away the fumes which pride and sensuality have thus spread over the subject? If women are by nature inferior to men, their virtues must be the same in quality, if not in degree, or virtue is a relative idea; consequently their conduct should be founded on the same principles, and have the same aim.

Connected with man as daughters, wives, and mothers, their moral character may be estimated by their manner of fulfilling those simple duties; but the end, the grand end, of their exertions should be to unfold their own faculties, and acquire the dignity of conscious virtue. They may try to render their road pleasant; but ought never to forget, in common with man, that life yields not the felicity which can satisfy an immortal soul. I do not mean to insinuate that either sex should be so lost in abstract reflections or distant views as to forget the affections and duties that lie before them, and are, in truth, the means appointed to produce the fruit of life; on the contrary, I would warmly recommend them, even while I assert, that they afford most satisfaction when they are considered in their true sober light.

Probably the prevailing opinion that woman was created for man, may have taken its rise from Moses' poetical story; yet as very few, it is presumed, who have bestowed any serious thought on the subject ever supposed that Eve was, literally speaking, one of Adam's ribs, the deduction must be allowed to fall to the ground, or only be so far admitted as it proves that man, from the remotest antiquity, found it convenient to exert his strength to subjugate his companion, and his invention to show that the ought to have her neck bent under the yoke, because the whole creation was only created for his convenience or pleasure.

* * *

It is not necessary to inform the sagacious reader, now I enter on my concluding reflections, that the discussion of this subject merely consists in opening a few simple principles, and clearing away the rubbish which obscured them. But, as all readers are not sagacious, I must be allowed to add some explanatory remarks to bring the subject home to reason – to that sluggish reason, which supinely takes opinions on trust, and obstinately supports them to spare itself the labour of thinking.

Moralists have unanimously agreed, that unless virtue be nursed by liberty, it will never attain due strength – and what they say of man, I extend to mankind, insisting that in all cases morals must be fixed on immutable principles; and, that the being cannot be termed rational or virtuous, who obeys any authority, but that of reason.

To render women truly useful members of society, I argue that they should be led, by having their understanding cultivated on a large scale, to acquire a rational affection for their country, founded on knowledge, because it is obvious that we are little interested about what we do not understand. And to render this general knowledge of due importance, I have endeavoured to show that private duties are never properly fulfilled unless the understanding enlarges the heart; and that public virtue is only an aggregate of private. But, the distinctions established in society undermine both, by beating out the solid gold of virtue, till it becomes only the tinsel-covering of vice; for whilst wealth renders a man more respectable than virtue, wealth will be sought before virtue; and, whilst women's persons are caressed, when a childish simper shows an absence of mind – the mind will lie fallow. Yet, true voluptuousness must proceed from the mind – for what can equal the sensations produced by mutual affection, supported by mutual respect? What are the cold, or feverish caresses of appetite, but sin embracing death, compared with the modest overflowings of a pure heart and exalted imagination? Yes, let me tell the libertine of fancy when he despises understanding in woman – that the mind, which he disregards, gives life to the enthusiastic affection from which rapture, short-lived as it is, alone can flow! And, that, without virtue, a sexual attachment must expire, like a tallow candle in the socket, creating intolerable disgust. To prove this, I need only observe, that men who have wasted great part of their lives with women, and with whom they have sought for pleasure with eager thirst, entertain the meanest opinion of the sex. Virtue, true refiner of joy! – if foolish men were to fright thee from earth, in order to give loose to all their appetites without a check – some sensual weight of taste would scale the heavens to invite thee back, to give a zest to pleasure!

That women at present are by ignorance rendered foolish or vicious, is, I think, not to be disputed; and, that the most salutary effects tending to improve mankind might be expected from a REVOLUTION in female manners, appears, at least, with a face of probability, to rise out of the observation. For as marriage has been termed the parent of those endearing charities which draw man from the brutal herd, the corrupting intercourse that wealth, idleness, and folly, produce between the sexes, is more universally injurious to morality than all the other vices of mankind collectively considered. To adulterous lust the most sacred duties are sacrificed, because before marriage, men, by a promiscuous intimacy with women, learned to consider love as a selfish gratification – learned to separate it not only from esteem, but from the affection merely built on habit, which mixes a little humanity with it. Justice and friendship are also set at defiance, and that purity of taste is vitiated which would naturally lead a man to relish an artless display of affection rather than affected airs. But that noble simplicity of affection, which dares to appear unadorned, has few attractions for the libertine, though it be the charm, which by cementing the matrimonial tie, secures to the pledges of a warmer passion the necessary parental attention; for children will never be properly educated till friendship subsists between parents. Virtue flies from a house divided against itself – and a whole legion of devils take up their residence there.

The affection of husbands and wives cannot be pure when they have so few sentiments in common, and when so little confidence is established at home, as must be the case when their pursuits are so different. That intimacy from which tenderness should flow, will not, cannot subsist between the vicious.

Contending, therefore, that the sexual distinction which men have so warmly insisted upon, is arbitrary, I have dwelt on an observation, that several sensible men, with whom I have conversed on the subject, allowed to be well founded; and it is simply this, that the little chastity to be found amongst men, and consequent disregard of modesty, tend to degrade both sexes; and further, that the modesty of women, characterized as such, will often be only the artful veil of wantonness instead of being the natural reflection of purity, till modesty be universally respected.

From the tyranny of man, I firmly believe, the greater number of female follies proceed; and the cunning, which I allow makes at present a part of their character, I likewise have repeatedly endeavoured to prove, is produced by oppression.

Were not dissenters, for instance, a class of people, with strict truth, characterised as cunning? And may I not lay some stress on this fact to prove, that when any power but reason curbs the free spirit of man, dissimulation is practised, and the various shifts of art are naturally called forth? Great attention to decorum, which was carried to a degree of scrupulosity, and all that puerile bustle about trifles and consequential solemnity, which Butler's caricature of a dissenter brings before the imagination, shaped their persons as well as their minds in the mould of prim littleness. I speak collectively, for I know how many ornaments in human nature have been enrolled amongst sectaries; yet, I assert, that the same narrow prejudice for their sect, which women have for their families, prevailed in the dissenting part of the community, however worthy in other respects; and also that the same timid prudence, or headstrong efforts, often disgraced the exertions of both. Oppression thus formed many of the features of their character perfectly to coincidence with that of the oppressed half of mankind; for is it not notorious that dissenters were, like women, fond of deliberating together, and asking advice of each other, till by a complication of little contrivances, some little end was brought about? A similar attention to preserve their reputation was conspicuous in the dissenting and female world, and was produced by a similar cause.

Asserting the rights which women in common with men ought to contend for, I have not attempted to extenuate their faults; but to prove them to be the natural consequence of their education and station in society. If so, it is reasonable to suppose that they will change their character, and correct their vices and follies, when they are allowed to be free in a physical, moral, and civil sense.

Let woman share the rights, and she will emulate the virtues of man; for she must grow more perfect when emancipated, or justify the authority that chains such a weak being to her duty. If the latter, it will be expedient to opened a fresh trade with Russia for whips: a present which a father should always make to his son-in-law on his wedding day, that a husband may keep his whole family in order by the same means; and without any violation of justice reign, wielding this sceptre, sole master of his house, because he is the only thing in it who has reason; – the divine, indefeasible earthly sovereignty breathed into man by the Master of the universe. Allowing this position, women have not any inherent rights to claim; and, by the same rule, their duties vanish, for rights and duties are inseparable.

Be just then, O ye men of understanding; and mark not more severely what women do amiss than the vicious tricks of the horse or the ass for whom ye provide provender – and allow her the privileges of ignorance, to whom ye deny the rights of reason, or ye will be worse than Egyptian task-master, expecting virtue where Nature has not given understanding.

Margaret Fuller
(1810-1850)

Margaret Fuller was a talented woman who died young. Though her reputation as a feminist rests on her 1845 book *Women in the Nineteenth Century,* her contribution to political and social ideas was much more than this.

Fuller grew up under the tutelage of a possessive father who educated her to a point which wrecked her childhood. But she survived this to become a brilliant conversationalist and seminarist. Her seminars were very popular and well attended and these attracted housewives, social reformers and a host of other people. She was a transcendalist and an associate of Emerson, in collaboration with whom she founded the journal *The Dial* in 1840. *The Dial* had a short life of 4 years after which she shifted to New York to work as a literary and cultural critic for the *New York Tribune.* This experience exposed her to urban poverty and she became even more seriously focused an social reform including prison reform and worked for educational and political equality for minorities. Then followed a trip to Europe where she decided to live in Rome and became involved in the Italian movement for unification. Margaret Fuller fell in love with one of the leaders, Ossoli, married him and bore him a son. But on their journey to America in 1850 the couple and their young son were drowned as the ship sank.

Women in the Nineteenth Century takes note of the common prejudices against women, prejudices which work to subtract from their strength and character. Much of the writing of this period had to be defensive and had to concentrate on building up women's character values and justifying their rational approach, their virtues of steadiness and fidelity.

Women, Friendship and Marriage

Lord Herbert's was a marriage of convention, made for him at fifteen; he was not discontented with it, but looked only to the advantages it brought of perpetuating his family on the basis of a great fortune. He paid, in act, what he considered a dutiful attention to the bond; his thoughts travelled elsewhere; and while forming a high ideal of the companionship of minds in marriage, he seems never to have doubted that its realization must be postponed to some other state of being. Dante, almost immediately after the death of Beatrice, married a lady chosen for him by his friends, and Boccaccio, in describing the miseries that attended, in this case,

> "The form of an union where union is none,"

speaks as if these were inevitable to the connection, and as if the scholar and poet, especially, could expect nothing but misery and obstruction in a domestic partnership with Woman.

Centuries have passed since, but civilized Europe is still in a transition state about marriage; not only in practice but in thought. It is idle to speak with contempt of the nations where polygamy is an institution, or seraglios a custom, while practices far more debasing haunt, well-nigh fill, every city and every town, and so far as union of one with one is believed to be the only pure form of marriage, a great majority of societies and individuals are still doubtful whether the earthly bond must be a meeting of souls, or only supposes a contract of convenience and utility. Were Woman established in the rights of an immortal being, this could not be. She would not, in some countries, be given away by her father, with scarcely more respect for her feelings than is shown by the Indian chief, who sells his daughter for a horse, and beats her if she runs away from her new home. Nor, in societies where her choice is left free, would she be perverted, by the current of opinion that seizes her, into the belief that she must marry, if it be only to find a protector, and a home of her own. Neither would Man, if he thought the connection of permanent importance, form it so lightly. He would not deem it a trifle, that he was to enter into the closest relations with another soul, which, if not eternal in themselves, must eternally affect his growth. Neither, did he believe Woman capable of friendship, would he, by rash haste, lose the chance of finding a friend in the person who might, probably, live half a century by his side. Did love, to his mind, stretch forth into infinity, he would not miss his chance of its revelations, that he might the sooner rest from his weariness by a bright fireside, and secure a sweet and graceful attendant "devoted to him alone." Were he a step higher, he would not carelessly enter into a relation where he might not be able to do the duty of a friend, as well as a protector from external ill, to the other party, and have a being in his power pining for sympathy, intelligence and aid, that he could not give.

What deep communion, what real intercourse is implied in sharing the joys and cares of parentage, when any degree of equality is admitted between the parties! It is true that, in a majority of instances, the map looks upon his wife as an adopted child; and places her to the other children in the relation of nurse or governess, rather than that of parent. Her influence with them is sure; but she misses the education which should enlighten that influence, by being thus treated. It is the order of nature that children should complete the education, moral and mental, of parents, by making them think what is needed for the best culture of human beings, and conquer all faults and impulses that interfere with their giving this to these dear objects, who represent the world to them. Father and mother should assist one another to learn what is required for this sublime priesthood of Nature. But, for this, a religious recognition of equality is required.

Where this thought of equality begins to diffuse itself, it is shown in four ways.

First; – The household partnership. In our country, the woman looks for a "smart but kind" husband; the man for a capable, sweet-tempered" wife. The man furnishes the house; the woman regulates it. Their relation is one of mutual esteem, mutual dependence. Their talk is of business; their affection shows itself by practical kindness. They know that life goes more smoothly and cheerfully to each for the other's aid; they are grateful and content. The wife praises her husband as a "good provider", the husband, in return, compliments her as a "capital housekeeper." This relation is good so far as it goes.

Next comes a closer tie, which takes the form either of mutual idolatry or of intellectual companionship. The first, we suppose, is to no one a pleasing subject of contemplation. The parties weaken and narrow one another; they lock the gate against all the glories of the universe, that they may live in a cell together. To themselves they seem the only wise; to all others, steeped in infatuation; the gods smile as they look forward to the crisis of cure; to men, the woman seems an unlovely syren; to women, the man an effeminate boy.

The other form, of intellectual companionship, has become more and more frequent. Men engaged in public life, literary men, and artists; have often found in their wives companions and confidants in thought no less than in feeling. And, as the intellectual development of Woman has spread wider and risen higher, they have, not unfrequently, shared the same employment; as in the case of Roland and his wife, who were friends in the household and in the nation's councils, read, regulated home affairs, or prepared public documents together, indifferently. It is very pleasant, in letters begun by Roland and finished by his wife, to see the harmony of mind, and the difference of nature; one thought, but various ways of treating it.

This is one of the best instances of a marriage of friendship. It was only friendship, whose basis was esteem; probably neither party knew love, except by name. Roland was a good man, worthy to esteem, and be esteemed; his wife as deserving of admiration as able to do without it.

Madame Roland is the fairest specimen we yet have of her class; as clear to discern her aim, as valiant to pursue it, as Spenser's Britomart ; austerely set apart from all that did not belong to her, whether as Woman or as mind. She is an antetype of a class to which the coming time will afford a field — the Spartan matron, brought by the culture of the age of books to intellectual consciousness and expansion. Self-sufficingness, strength, and clear headedness were, in her, combined with a power of deep and calm affection. She, too, would have given a son or husband the device for his shield, "Return with it or upon it;" and this, not because she loved little, but much. The page of her life is one of unsullied dignity. Her appeal to posterity is one against the injustice of those who committed such crimes in the name of Liberty. She makes it in behalf of herself and her husband. I would put beside it, on the shelf, a little volume, containing a similar appeal from the verdict of contemporaries to that of mankind, made by Godwin on behalf of his wife, the celebrated, by most men detested, Mary Wollstonecraft. In his view, it was an appeal from the injustice of those who did such wrong in the name of virtue. Were this little book interesting for no other cause, it would be so for the generous affection evinced under the peculiar circumstances. This man had courage to love and honor this woman in the face of the world's sentence, and of all that was repulsive in her own past history. He believed he saw of what soul she was, and that the impulses she had struggled to act out were noble, though the opinions to which they had led might not be thoroughly weighed. He loved her, and he defended her for the meaning and tendency of her inner life. It was a good fact.

Mary Wollstonecraft, like Madame Dudevant (commonly known as George Sand) in our day, was a woman whose existence better proved the need of some new interpretation of Woman's Rights than anything she wrote. Such beings as these, rich in genius, of most tender sympathies, capable of high virtue and a chastened harmony, ought not to find themselves, by birth, in a place so narrow, that, in breaking bonds, they become outlaws. Were there as much room in the world for such, as in Spenser's poem for Britomart, they would not run their heads so wildly against the walls, but prize their shelter rather. They find their way, at last, to light and air, but the world will not take off the brand it has set upon them. The champion of the Rights of Woman found, in Godwin, one who would plead that cause like a brother. He who delineated with such purity of traits the form of Woman in the Marguerite, of whom the weak St. Leon could never learn to be worthy, – a pearl indeed whose price was above rubies, – was not false in life to the faith by which he had hallowed his romance. He acted, as he wrote, like a brother. This form of appeal rarely fails to touch the basest man: – "Are you acting toward other women in the way you would have men act towards your sister?" George Sand smokes, wears male attire, wishes to be addressed as "Mon Frere;" – perhaps, if she found those who were as brothers indeed, she would not care whether she were brother or sister. We rejoice to see that she, who expresses such a painful contempt for men in most of her works, as shows she must have known great wrong from them, depicts, in "La Roche Mauprat," a man raised by the workings of love from the depths of savage sensualism to a moral and intellectual life. It was love for a pure object, for a steadfast woman, one of those who, the Italian mind, could make the "stair to heaven."

This author, beginning like the many in assault upon bad institutions, and external ills, yet deepening the experience through comparative freedom, sees at last that the only efficient remedy must come from individual character. These bad institutions, indeed, it may always be replied, prevent individuals from forming good character, therefore we must remove them. Agreed; yet keep steadily the higher aim in view. Could you clear away all the bad forms of society, it is vain, unless the individual begin to be ready for better. There must be a parallel movement in these two branches of life. And all the rules left by Moses availed less to further the best life than the living example of one Messiah.

Still the mind of the age struggles confusedly with these problems, better discerning as yet the ill it can no longer bear, than the good by which it may supersede it. But women like Sand will speak now and cannot be silenced; their characters and their eloquence alike foretell an era when such as they shall easier learn to lead true lives. But though such forebode, not such shall be parents of it. Those who would reform the world must show that they do not speak in the heat of wild impulse; their lives must be unstained by passionate error; they must be severe lawgivers to themselves. They must be religious students of the divine purpose with regard to man, if they would not confound the fancies of a day with the requisitions of eternal good. Their liberty must be the liberty of law and knowledge. But as to the transgressions against custom which have caused such outcry against those of noble intention, it may be observed that the resolve of Eloisa to be only the mistress of Abelard, was that of one who saw in practice around her the contract of marriage made the seal of degradation. Shelley feared not to be fettered, unless so to be was to be false. Wherever abuses are seen, the timid will suffer; the bold will protest. But society has a right to outlaw them till she has revised her law; and this she must be taught to do, by one who speaks with authority, not in anger or haste.

Elizabeth Cady Stanton and Committee

July 19, 1848

This declaration was presented and passed in the Woman's Rights Convention held at Seneca Falls in 1848 on 19-20 July. It was drafted by Elizabeth Cady Stanton and is a para by para rewriting of the American Declaration of Independence. More than a hundred women signed the document. The declaration is in itself a step forward in the assertion of political and human rights and marks an important stage in the history of woman's suffrage.

Seneca Falls Declaration of Sentiments and Resolutions

Declaration of Sentiments

When in the course of human events, it becomes necessary for one portion of the family of man to assume among the people of the earth a position different from that which they have hitherto occupied, but one to which the laws of nature and nature's God entitle them, a decent respect to the opinions of mankind requires that they should declare the causes that impel them to such a course.

We hold these truths to be self-evident: that all men and women are created equal; that they are endowed by their Creator with certain inalienable rights; that among these are life, liberty, and the pursuit of happiness; that to secure these rights governments are instituted, deriving their just powers from the consent of the governed. Whenever any form of government becomes destructive of these ends, it is the right of those who suffer from it to refuse allegiance to it, and to insist upon the institution of a new government, laying its foundation on such principles, and organizing its powers in such form, as to them shall seem most likely to effect their safety and happiness. Prudence, indeed, will dictate that governments long established should not be changed for light and transient causes; and accordingly all experience hath shown that mankind are more disposed to suffer while evils are sufferable, than to right themselves by abolishing the forms to which they (are) accustomed. But when a long train of abuses and usurpations, pursuing invariably the same object, evinces a design to reduce them under absolute despotism, it is their duty to throw off such government, and to provide new guards for their future security. Such has been the patient sufferance of women under this government, and such is now the necessity which constrains them to demand the equal station to which they are entitled.

The history of mankind is a history of repeated injuries and usurpations on the part of man toward woman, having in direct object the establishment of an absolute tyranny over her. To prove this, let facts be submitted to a candid world.

He has never permitted her to exercise her inalienable right to the elective franchise.

He has compelled her to submit to laws, in the formation of which she had no voice.

He has withheld from her rights which are given to the most ignorant and degraded men – both native and foreigner.

Having deprived her of this first right of a citizen, the elective franchise, thereby leaving her without representation in the halls of legislation, he has oppressed her on all sides.

He has made her, if married, in the eye of the law, civilly dead.

He has taken from her all right in property, even to wages she earns.

He has made her, morally, an irresponsible being, as she can commit many crimes with impunity, provided they can be done in the presence of her husband. In the covenant of marriage, she is compelled to promise obedience to her husband, he becoming, to all intents and purposes, her master – the law giving him power to deprive her of her liberty, and to administer chastisement.

He has so framed the laws of divorce, as to what shall be the proper causes, and in case of separation, to who, the guardianship of the children shall be given, as to be wholly regardless of the happiness of women – the law, in all cases, going upon a false supposition of the supremacy of man, giving all power into his hands.

After depriving her of all rights as a married woman, if single, and the owner of property, he has taxed her to support a government which recognizes her only when her property can be made profitable to it.

He has monopolized nearly all the profitable employments, and from those she is permitted to follow, she receives but a scanty remuneration. He closes against her all the avenues to wealth and distinction which he considers most honorable to himself. As a teacher of theology, medicine, or law, she is not known.

He has denied her the facilities for obtaining a thorough education, all colleges being closed against her.

He allows her in Church, as well as State, but a subordinate position, claiming Apostolic authority for her exclusion from the ministry, and, with some exceptions, from any public participation in the affairs of the Church.

He has created a false public sentiment by giving to the world a different code of morals for men and women, by which moral delinquencies which exclude women from society, are not only tolerated, but deemed of little account in man.

He has usurped the prerogative of Jehovah himself, claiming it as his right to assign for her a sphere of action, when that belongs to her conscience and to her God.

He has endeavored, in every way that he could, to destroy her confidence in her own powers, to lessen her self-respect and to make her willing to lead a dependent and abject life.

Now, in view of this entire disfranchisement of one-half the people of this country, their social and religious degradation – in view of the unjust laws above mentioned, and because women do feel themselves aggrieved, oppressed and fraudulently deprived of their most sacred rights, we insist that they have immediate admission to all the rights and privileges which belong to them as citizens of the United States.

In entering upon the great work before us, we anticipate no small amount of misconception, misrepresentation, and ridicule; but we shall use every instrumentality within our power to effect our object. We shall employ agents, circulate tracts, petition the State and National legislatures, and endeavor to enlist the pulpit and the press in our behalf. We hope this Convention will be followed by a series of Conventions embracing every part of the county.

Resolutions

Whereas, The great precept of nature is conceded to be, that "man shall pursue his own true and substantial happiness". Blackstone in his Commentaries remarks, that this law of Nature being coeval with mankind, and dictated by God himself, is of course superior in obligation to any other. It is binding over all the globe, in all countries and at all times; no human laws are of any validity if contrary to this, and such of them as are valid, derive their force, and all their validity, and all their authority mediately and immediately from this original; therefore,

Resolved, That all laws which prevent woman from occupying such a station in society as her conscience shall dictate, or which place her in a position inferior to that of man, are contrary to the great precept of nature, and therefore of no force or authority.

Resolved, That woman is man's equal – was intended to be so by the Creator, and the highest good of the race demands that she should be recognized as such.

Resolved, That the women of this country ought to be enlightened in regard to the laws under which they live, that they may no longer publish their degradation by declaring themselves satisfied with their present position, nor their ignorance, by asserting that they have all the rights they want.

Resolved, That inasmuch as man, while claiming for himself intellectual superiority, does accord to woman moral superiority, it is pre-eminently his duty to encourage her to speak and teach, as she has an opportunity, in all religious assemblies.

Resolved, That the same amount of virtue, delicacy, and refinement of behavior that is required of woman in the social state, should also be required of man, and the same transgressions should be visited with equal severity on both man and woman.

Resolved, That the objection of indelicacy and impropriety, which is so often brought against woman when she addresses a public audience, comes with a very ill-grace from those who encourage, by their attendance, her appearance on the stage, in the concert, or in feats of circus.

Resolved, That woman has too long rested satisfied in the circumscribed limits which corrupt customs and a perverted application of the Scriptures have marked out for her, and that it is time she should move in the enlarged sphere which her great Creator has assigned her.

Resolved, That it is the duty of women of this country to secure to themselves their sacred right to the elective franchise.

Resolved, That the equality of human rights results necessarily from the fact of the identity of the race in capabilities and responsibilities.

Resolved, That the speedy success of our cause depends upon the zealous and untiring efforts of both men and women, for the overthrow of the monopoly of the pulpit, and for the securing to women an equal participation with men in the various trades, professions, and commerce.

Resolved, therefore, That, being invested by the creator with the same capabilities, and the same consciousness of responsibility for their exercise, it is demonstrably the right and duty of woman, equally with man, to promote every righteous cause by every righteous means; and especially in regard to the great subjects of morals and religion, it is self – evidently her right to participate with her brother in teaching them, both in private and in public, by writing and by speaking, by any instrumentalities proper to be used, and in any assemblies proper to be held; and this being a self-evident truth growing out of the divinely implanted principles of human nature, any custom or authority adverse to it, whether modern or wearing the hoary sanction of antiquity, is to be regarded as a self-evident falsehood, and at war with mankind.

Pandita Ramabai Saraswati

(1858-1922)

If ever there was an eventful life marked by courage and determination, it was Pandita Ramabai's. It was a life full of challenges, controversies and struggle. Ramabai was the youngest of three children and was virtually brought up by her mother who taught her Sanskrit.

Her father Ananta Shastri had moved to the hills, virtually the forest, as his parents were resistant to the notion of female education. Ramabai found herself all alone fairly early in life as first her parents, then her sister and later her brother all died. But her travels with her family and her education stood her in good stead.

Left alone, after the death of her brother, she married a Bengali lawyer according to civil marriage rites, both of them having outgrown religious orthodoxies. Thus in everything, hers was an unusual family and she an unusual woman who, on being widowed, went on to pursue her former occupation as lecturer. She converted to Christianity, but did not hesitate to ask uncomfortable questions of her mentors and advisors. In later years she set up a home for women near Pune known as Sharda Sadan.

The High Caste Hindu Woman (1888), from which this extract has been taken, was published in Philadelphia and was aimed at a foreign audience/reader. Chapter by chapter it goes through the different stages of a woman's life and examines how it has been curbed by the code propagated by male thinkers like Manu.

This was not the only book she wrote. In fact, she was one of the few women who did make a living out of writing. Earlier in 1882 she had written a book on morals for women *Stree Dharma* which helped her pay for her trip to England. She also wrote several other books, one of them being *My Testimony*.

Woman's Place in Religion and Society

The Hindu religion commands:

> "Women must be honored and adorned by their fathers, brothers, husbands, and brothers-in-law, who desire their own welfare."
>
> "Where women are honored, there the gods are pleased; but where they are not honored, no sacred rite yields rewards."
>
> "Where the female relations live in grief, the family soon wholly perishes; but that family where they are not unhappy ever prospers."
>
> "The houses on which female relations, not being duly honored, pronounce a curse, perish completely, as if destroyed by magic."
>
> "Hence men who seek their own welfare, should always honor women on holidays and festivals with (gifts of) ornaments, clothes and dainty food."
>
> "In that family where the husband is pleased with his wife, and the wife with her husband, happiness will assuredly be lasting."
>
> "For if the wife is not radiant with beauty, she will not attract her husband; but if she has no attractions for him, no children will be born."
>
> "If the wife is radiant with beauty, the whole house is bright; but if she is destitute of beauty, all will appear *dismal."—Manu,* iii., 55-62.

These commandments are very significant. Our Aryan Hindus did, and still do honor woman to a certain extent. The honor bestowed upon the *mother* is without parallel in any other country. Although the woman is looked upon as an inferior being, the mother is nevertheless the chief person and worthy to receive all honor from the son. One of the great commandments of the Hindu Scriptures is, "Let thy mother be to thee like unto a god."[1]

The mother is the queen of the son's household. She wields great power there, and is generally obeyed as the head of the family by her sons and by her daughters-in-law.

But there is a reverse side to the shield that should not be left unobserved. This is best studied in the laws of Manu, as all Hindus, with a few exceptions believe implicitly what that law-giver says about women:

> "It is the nature of women to seduce men in this world; for that reason the wise are never unguarded in the company of females."
>
> "For women are able to lead astray in this world not only a fool, but even a learned man, and to make him a slave of desire and anger."—*Manu*, ii., 213-214.
>
> "Women do not care for beauty, nor is their attention fixed on age; thinking 'it is enough that he is a man,' they give themselves to the handsome and to the ugly."
>
> "Through their passion for men, through their mutable temper, through their natural heartlessness, they become disloyal towards their husbands, however carefully they may be guarded in this world."
>
> "Knowing their disposition, which the Lord of creatures laid in them at the creation, to be such, every man should most strenuously exert himself to guard them."
>
> "When creating them, Manu allotted to women a love of their bed, of their seat and of ornament, impure desires, wrath, dishonesty, malice and bad conduct."
>
> "For women no sacramental rite is performed with sacred texts, thus the law is settled; women who are destitute of strength and destitute of the knowledge of Vedic texts, are as impure as falsehood itself, that is a fixed rule."—*Manu*, ix., 14-18.

Such is the opinion of Manu concerning all women; and all men with more or less faith in the law regard women, even though they be their own mothers, "as impure as falsehood itself."

> "And to this effect many sacred texts are chanted also in the Vedas, in order to make fully known the true disposition of women; hear now those texts which refer to the expiation of their sins."
>
> "If 'my mother, going astray and unfaithful, conceived illicit desires, may my father keep that seed from me,' that is the scriptural text."—*Manu*, ix., 19, 20.

Such distrust and such low estimate of woman's nature and character in general, is at the root of the custom of seclusion of women in India. This mischievous custom has greatly increased and has become intensely tyrannical – since the Mahomedan invasion; but that it existed from about the sixth century, B.C., cannot be denied. All male relatives are commanded by the law to deprive the women of the household of all their freedom:

> "Day and night women must be kept in dependence by the males of their families, and if they attach themselves to sensual enjoyments, they must be kept under one's control."
>
> "Her father protects her in childhood, her husband protects her in youth, and her sons protect her in old age; a woman is never fit for independence."—*Manu*, ix., 2, 3.
>
> "Women must particularly be guarded against evil inclinations, however trifling they may appear; for if they are not guarded, they will bring sorrow on two families."
>
> "Considering that the highest duty of all castes, even weak husbands must strive to guard their wives."—*Manu*, ix., .5, 6.
>
> "No man can completely guard women by force; but they can be guarded by the employment of the following expedients:"
>
> "Let the husband employ his wife in the collection. and expenditure of his wealth, in keeping everything clean, in the fulfilment of religious duties, in the preparation of his food, and in looking after the household utensils."—*Manu*, ix., 10, 11.

Those who diligently and impartially read Sanscrit literature in the original, cannot fail to recognize the law-giver Manu as one of those hundreds who have done their best to make woman a hateful being in the world's eye. To employ her in housekeeping and kindred occupations is thought to be the only means of keeping her out of mischief, the blessed enjoyment of literary culture being denied her. She is forbidden to read the sacred scriptures, she has no right to pronounce a single syllable out of them. To appease her uncultivated, low kind of desire by giving her ornaments to adorn her person, and by giving her dainty food together with an occasional bow which costs nothing, are the highest honors to which a Hindu woman is entitled. She, the loving mother of the nation, the devoted wife, the tender sister and affectionate daughter is never fit for independence, and is "as impure as falsehood itself." She is never to be trusted; matters of importance are never to be committed to her.

I can say honestly and truthfully, that I have never read any sacred book in Sanscrit literature without meeting this kind of hateful sentiment about women. True, they contain here and there a kind word about them, but such words seem to me a. heartless mockery after having charged them, as a class, with crime and evil deeds.

Profane literature is by no means less severe or more respectful towards women. I quote from the ethical teachings, parts of a catechism and also a few proverbs:

Q. What is cruel?
A. The heart of a viper.
Q. What is more cruel than that?
A. The heart of a woman.
Q. What is the cruelest of all?
A. The heart of a sonless, penniless widow.

A catechism on moral subjects written by a Hindu gentleman of high literary reputation says:

Q. What is the chief gate to hell?
A. A woman.
Q. What bewitches like wine?
A. A woman.

Q. Who is the wisest of the wise?
A. He who has not been deceived by women who may be compared to malignant fiends.
Q. What are fetters to men?
A. Women.
Q. What is that which cannot be trusted?
A. Women.
Q. What poison is that which appears like nectar?
A. Women.

Proverbs.

"Never put your trust in women."
"Women's counsel leads to destruction."
"Woman is a great whirlpool of suspicion, a dwelling-place of vices, full of deceit, a hindrance in the way of heaven, the gate of hell."

Having fairly illustrated the popular belief about woman's nature, I now proceed to state woman's religion. Virtues such as truthfulness forbearance, fortitude, purity of heart and uprightness, are common to men and women, but religion, as the word is commonly understood, has two distinct natures in the Hindu law; the masculine and the feminine. The masculine religion has its own peculiar duties, privileges and honors. The feminine religion also has its peculiarities.

The sum and substance of the latter may be given in a few words:—to look upon her husband as a god, to hope for salvation only through him, to be obedient to him in all things, never to covet independence, never to do anything but that which is approved by law and custom.

"Hear now the duties of women," says the law-giver, Manu:

"By a girl, by a young woman, or even by an aged one, nothing must be done independently, even in her own house."

"In childhood, a female must be subject to her father, in youth, to her husband, when her lord is dead, to her sons; a woman must never be independent."

"She must not seek to separate herself from her father, husband, or sons; by leaving them she would make both her own and her husband's families contemptible."

"She must always be cheerful, clever in the management of her household affairs, careful in cleaning her utensils, and economical in expenditure."

"Him to whom her father may give her, or her brother with the father's permission, she shall obey as long as he lives, and when he is dead, she must not insult his memory."

"For the sake of procuring good fortune to brides, the recitation of benedictory texts, and the sacrifice to the Lord of creatures are used at weddings; but the betrothal by the father or guardian is the cause of the husband's dominion over his wife."

"The husband who wedded her with sacred texts, always gives happiness to his wife, both in season and out of season, in this world and in the next."

"Though destitute of virtue, or seeking pleasure elsewhere, or devoid of good qualities, yet a husband must be constantly worshipped as a god by a faithful wife."

"No sacrifice, no vow, no fast must be performed by women apart from their husbands; if a wife obeys her husband, she will for that reason alone, be exalted in heaven."

"A faithful wife, who desires to dwell after death with her husband, must never do anything that might displease him who took her hand whether he be alive or dead."—*Manu*, v., 147-156.

"By violating her duty towards her husband, a wife is disgraced in this world, after death she enters the womb of a jackal, and is tormented by diseases, the punishment of her sin."

"She who, controlling her thoughts, words and deeds, never slights her lord, resides after death with her husband in heaven, and is called a virtuous wife."

"In reward of such conduct, a female who controls her thoughts, speech and actions, gains in this life highest renown, and in the next world a place near her husband."—*Manu*, ix., 45.

Marital Rights

"He only is a perfect man who consists of three persons united, his wife, himself and his offspring; thus says, the Veda, and

> learned Brahmanas propound this maxim likewise, 'The husband is declared to be one with the wife."—*Manu*, ix., 45.
>
> "The wife is declared to be 'the "marital property" of her husband, and is classed with cows, mares, female camels, slave-girls, buffalo-cows, she-goats and ewes."—*Manu*, ix., 48-51.

The wife is punishable for treating her husband with aversion:

> "For one year let a husband bear with a wife who hates him; but after a lapse of a year, let him deprive her of her property and cease to live with her."
>
> "She who shows disrespect to a husband who is addicted to some evil passion, is a drunkard, or diseased, shall be deserted for three months, and be deprived of her ornaments and furniture."—*Manu*, ix., 77, 78.
>
> "She who drinks spirituous liquor, is of bad conduct, rebellious, diseased, mischievous or wasteful, may at any time be superseded by another wife."
>
> "A barren wife may be superseded in the eighth year, she whose children all die in the tenth, she who bears only daughters in the eleventh, but she who is quarrelsome without delay."—*Manu*, ix., 80, 71.
>
> "A wife who, being superseded, in anger departs from her husband's house, must either be instantly confined or cast off in the presence of the family."—*Manu*, ix., 83.
>
> "Though a man may have accepted a damsel in due form, he may abandon her if she be blemished or diseased, and if she have been given with fraud."—*Manu*, ix., 72.

But no such provision is made for the woman; on the contrary, she must remain with and revere her husband as a god, even though he be "destitute of virtue, and seek pleasure elsewhere, or be devoid of good qualities, addicted to evil passion, fond of spirituous liquors or diseased," and what not!

How much impartial justice is shown in the treatment of womankind by Hindu law, can be fairly understood after reading the above quotations. In olden times these laws were enforced by the community; a husband had absolute power over his wife; she could do nothing but submit to his will without uttering a word of protest. Now, under the so-called Christian British rule, the woman is in no better condition than of old. True, the husband cannot as in the golden age, take her wherever she may be found, and drag her to his house, but his absolute power over her person has not suffered in the least. He is now bound to bring suit against her in the courts of justice to claim his "marital property," if she be unwilling to submit to him by any other means.

A near relative of mine had been given in her childhood in marriage to a boy whose parents agreed to let him stay and be educated with her in her own home. No sooner however, had the marriage ceremony been concluded than they forgot their agreement; the boy was taken to the home of his parents where he remained to grow up to be a worthless dunce, while his wife through the kindness and advanced views of her father, developed into a bright young woman and well accomplished.

Thirteen years later, the young man came to claim his wife, but the parents had no heart to send their darling daughter. with a beggar who possessed neither the power nor the sense to make an honest living, and was unable to support and protect his wife. The wife too, had no wish to go with him since he was a stranger to her; under the circumstances she could neither love nor respect him. A number of orthodox people in the community who saw no reason why a wife should not follow her husband even though he be a worthless man, collected funds to enable him to sue her and her parents in the British Court of Justice. The case was examined with due ceremony and the verdict. was given in the man's favor, according to Hindu law.[2] The wife was doomed to go with him. Fortunately she was soon released from this sorrowful world by cholera. Whatever may be said of the epidemics that yearly assail our country, they are not unwelcome among the unfortunate women who are thus persecuted by social, religious and State laws. Many women put an end to their earthly sufferings by committing suicide. Suits at law between husband and wife are remarkable for their rarity in the British Courts in India, owing to the ever submissive conduct of women who suffer silently, knowing that the gods and justice always favor the men.

The case of Rakhmabai, that has lately profoundly agitated Hindu society, is only one of thousands of the same class. The remarkable thing about her is that she is a well-educated lady, who was brought up under the loving care of her father, and had learned from him how to defend herself against the assaults of social and religious bigotries. But as soon as her father died the man who claimed to be her husband, brought suit against her in the court of Bombay. The young woman bravely defended herself, declining to go to live with the man on the ground that the marriage that was concluded without her consent could not be legally considered as such. Mr. Justice Pinhey, who tried the case in the first instance, had a sufficient sense of justice to refuse to force the lady to live with her husband against her will. Upon hearing this decision, the conservative party all over India rose as one man and girded their loins to denounce the helpless woman and her handful of friends. They encouraged the alleged husband to stand his ground firmly, threatening the British government with public displeasure if it failed to keep its agreement to force the woman to go to live with the husband according to Hindu law. Large sums were collected for the benefit of this man, Dadajee, to enable him to appeal against the decision to the full bench, whereupon, to the horror of all right-thinking people, the Chief Justice sent back the case to the lower court for re-trial on its merits, as judged by the Hindu laws. The painful termination of this trial, I have in a letter written by my dear friend Rakhma herself, bearing date Bombay, March 18th, 1887, I quote from her letter:

> "The learned and civilized judges of the full bench are determined to enforce, in this enlightened age, the inhuman laws enacted in barbaric times, four thousand years ago. They have not only commanded me to go to live with the man, but also have obliged me to pay the costs of the dispute. Just think of this extraordinary decision! Are we not living under the impartial British government, which boasts of giving equal justice to all, and are we not ruled by the Queen-Empress Victoria, herself a woman? My dear friend, I shall have been cast into the State prison when this letter reaches you this is because I do not, and cannot obey the order of Mr. Justice Farran.

> There is no hope for women in India, Whether they be under Hindu rule or British rule; some are of the opinion that my case so cruelly decided, may bring about a better condition for woman by turning public opinion in her favor, but I fear it will be otherwise. The hard-hearted mothers-in-law will now be greatly strengthened, and will induce their sons, who have for some reason or other, been slow to enforce the conjugal rights to sue their wives in the British Courts, since they are now fully assured that under no circumstances can the British government act adversely to the Hindu law."

Taught by the experience of the past, we are not at all surprised at this decision of the Bombay court. Our only wonder is that a defenceless woman like Rakhmabai dared to raise her voice in the face of the powerful Hindu law, the mighty British government, the one hundred and twenty-nine million men and the three hundred and thirty million gods of the Hindus, all these having conspired together to crush her into nothingness. We cannot blame the English government for not defending a helpless woman; it is only fulfilling its agreement made with the male population of India. How very true are the words of the Saviour, "Ye cannot serve God and Mammon." Should England serve God by protecting a helpless woman against the powers and principalities of ancient institutions, Mammon would surely be displeased, and British profit and rule in India might be endangered thereby. Let us wish it success, no matter if that success be achieved at the sacrifice of the rights and the comfort of over one hundred million women.

Meanwhile, we shall patiently await the advent of the kingdom of righteousness, wherein the weak, the lowly and the helpless shall be made happy because the great judge Himself "shall wipe away all tears from their eyes."

Notes

1. My readers would perhaps be interested to see these commandments; they are as follows: "After having taught the Veda, the teacher instructs the pupil:

Say what is true.

Do thy duty.

Do not neglect the study of the Veda.

After having brought to thy teacher his proper reward, do not cut off the line of children (i.e. Do not remain unmarried).

Do not swerve from the truth.

Do not swerve from duty.

Do not neglect what is useful.

Do not neglect the learning and teaching of the Veda.

Do not neglect the sacrificial works due to the gods and fathers.

Let thy mother be to thee like unto a god.

Let thy father be to thee like unto a god.

Let thy teacher be to thee, like unto a god.

Let thy guests be to thee like unto a god.

Whatever actions are blameless those should be regarded, not others.

Whatever good works have been performed by us, should be observed by thee, not others."- *Taittiriya Upanishad,* Valli, i. An. xi., 1, 2.

2. In all cases except those directly connected with life and death, the British Government is bound according to the treaties concluded with the inhabitants of India, not to interfere with their social and religious customs and laws; judicial decisions are given accordingly.

Virginia Woolf

(1882-1941)

Largely identified with the 'stream of consciousness' novel, Woolf's contribution to feminist thought has not been properly highlighted or recognised. And when it comes to her feminist thought, *A Room of One's Own* (1929) is treated as the main text. The extract in this anthology has been taken from *Three Guineas* (1938) which is a longer book and examines the larger social dimension as well as the political decisions a nation takes without really consulting its female population. The seriousness is disguised in a mock-heroic argument which, the moment one gets behind the mock-heroism, strikes one as a powerful argument.

Besides her numerous novels like *Jacob's Room* (1922) *Mrs. Dalloway* (1925), *To the Lighthouse* (1927), *The Waves* (1931), she wrote a great deal of literary criticism which focused largely on the gender tradition. Her work *Orlando* (1928) moves through a world of fantasy and imagination and traces the history of the youthful Orlando through four centuries and both male and female manifestations. The essays in *The Common Reader* (2 vols. 1925 and 1932), and *Granite and Rainbow* (1958) also examine the gender dimensions of writing.

Woolf came from a literary family and was the daughter of Leslie Stephen and Julia Duckworth. She married Leonard Woolf in 1912 but always had a turbulent emotional life, which sent her into periods of depression. The last of her attacks led to her drowning herself in the Ouse, near her home at Rodmell, Sussex.

Daughters of Educated Men

One

Three years is a long time to leave a letter unanswered, and your letter has been lying without an answer even longer than that. I had hoped that it would answer itself, or that other people would answer it for me. But there it is with its question – How in your opinion are we to prevent war? – still unanswered.

It is true that many answers have suggested themselves, but none that would not need explanation, and explanations take time. In this case, too, there are reasons why it is particularly difficult to avoid misunderstanding. A whole page could be filled with excuses and apologies; declarations of unfitness, incompetence, lack of knowledge, and experience: and they would be true. But even when they were said there would still remain some difficulties so fundamental that it may well prove impossible for you to understand or for us to explain. But one does not like to leave so remarkable a letter as yours – a letter perhaps unique in the history of human correspondence, since when before has an educated man asked a woman how in her opinion war can be prevented? – unanswered. Therefore let us make the attempt; even if it is doomed to failure.

In the first place let us draw what all letter-writers instinctively draw, a sketch of the person to whom the letter is addressed. Without someone warm and breathing on the other side of the page, letters are worthless. You, then, who ask the question, are a little grey on the temples; the hair is no longer thick on the top of your head. You have reached the middle years of life not without effort, at the Bar; but on the whole your journey has been prosperous. There is nothing parched, mean or dissatisfied in your expression. And without wishing to flatter you, your prosperity – wife, children, house – has been deserved. You have never sunk into the contented apathy of middle life, for, as your letter from an office in the heart of London shows, instead of turning on your pillow and prodding your pigs, pruning your pear trees – you have a few acres in Norfolk – you are writing letters, attending meetings, presiding over this and that, asking questions, with the sound of the guns in your ears. For the rest, you began your education at one of the great public schools and finished it at the university.

It is now that the first difficulty of communication between us appears. Let us rapidly indicate the reason. We both come of what, in this hybrid age when, though birth is mixed, classes still remain fixed, it is convenient to call the educated class. When we meet in the flesh we speak with the same accent; use knives and forks in the same way; expect maids to cook dinner and wash up after dinner; and can talk during dinner without much difficulty about politics and people; war and peace; barbarism and civilization – all the questions indeed suggested by your letter. Moreover, we both earn our livings. But... those three dots mark a precipice, a gulf so deeply cut between us that for three years and more I have been sitting on my side of it wondering whether it is any use to try to speak across it. Let us then ask someone else – it is Mary Kingsley – to speak for us. 'I don't know if I ever revealed to you the fact that being allowed to learn German was *all* the paid-for education I ever had. Two thousand pounds was spent on my brother's, I still hope not in vain.' Mary Kingsley is not speaking for herself alone. She is speaking, still, for many of the daughters of educated men. And she is not merely speaking for them; she is also pointing to a very important fact about them, a fact that must profoundly influence all that follows: the fact of Arthur's Education Fund. You, who have read *Pendennis,* will remember how the mysterious letters A.E.F. figured in household ledgers. Ever since the thirteenth century English families have been paying money into that account. From the Pastons to the

Pendennises, all educated families from the thirteenth century to the present moment have paid money into that account. It is a voracious receptacle. Where there were many sons to educate it required a great effort on the part of the family to keep it full. For your education was not merely in book-learning; games educated your body; friends taught you more than books or games. Talk with them broadened your outlook and enriched your mind. In the holidays you travelled; acquired a taste for art; a knowledge of foreign politics; and then, before you could earn your own living, your father made you an allowance upon which it was possible for you to add the letters K.C. to your name. All this came out of Arthur's Education Fund. And to this your sisters, as Mary Kingsley indicates, made their contribution. Not only did their own education, save for such small sums as paid the German teacher, go into it; but many of those luxuries and trimmings which are, after all, an essential part of education – travel, society, solitude, a lodging apart from the family house – they were paid into it too. It was a voracious receptacle, a solid fact– Arthur's Education Fund – a fact so solid indeed that it cast a shadow over the entire landscape. And the result is that though we look at the same things, we see them differently. What is that congregation of building there, with a semi-monastic look, with chapels and halls and green playing-fields? To you it is your old school; Eton or Harrow; your old university, Oxford or Cambridge; the source of memories and of traditions innumerable. But to us, who see it through the shadow of Arthur's Education Fund, it is a schoolroom table; an omnibus going to a class, a little woman with a red nose, who is not well educated herself but has an invalid mother to support; an allowance of £50 a year with which to buy clothes, give presents and take journeys on coming to maturity. Such is the effect that Arthur's Education Fund has had upon us. So magically does it change the landscape that the noble courts and quadrangles of Oxford and Cambridge often appear to educated men's daughters like petticoats with holes in them, cold legs of mutton, and the boat train starting for abroad while the guard slams the door in their faces.

The fact that Arthur's Education Fund changes the landscape – the halls, the playing grounds, the sacred edifices – is an important one; but that aspect must be left for future discussion. Here we are only concerned with the obvious fact, when it comes to considering this important question – how we are to help you prevent war – that education makes a difference. Some knowledge of politics, of international relations, of economics, is obviously necessary in order to understand the causes which lead to war. Philosophy, theology even, might come in usefully. Now you the uneducated, you with an untrained mind, could not possibly deal with such questions satisfactorily. War, as the result of impersonal forces, is you will agree beyond the grasp of the untrained mind. But war as the result of human nature is another thing. Had you not believed that human nature, the reasons, the emotions of the ordinary man and woman, lead to war, you would not have written asking for our help. You must have argued, men and women, here and now, are able to exert their wills; they are not pawns and puppets dancing on a string held by invisible hands. They can act, and think for themselves. Perhaps even they can influence other people's thoughts and actions. Some such reasoning must have led you to apply to us; and with justification. For happily there is one branch of education which comes under the heading 'unpaid-for education' – that understanding of human beings and their motives which, if the word is rid of its scientific associations, might be called psychology. Marriage, the one great profession open to our class since the dawn of time until the year 1919; marriage, the art of choosing the human being with whom to live life successfully, should have taught us some skill in that. But here again another difficulty confronts us. For though many instincts are held more or less in common by both sexes, to fight has always been the man's habit, not the woman's. Law and practice have developed that difference, whether innate or accidental. Scarcely a human being in the course of history has fallen to a woman's rifle; the vast majority of birds and beasts have been killed by you, not by us; and it is difficult to judge what we do not share.

* * *

Thus all the weapons with which an educated man can enforce his opinion are either beyond our grasp or so nearly beyond it that even if we used them we could scarcely inflict one scratch. If the men in your profession were to unite in any demand and were to say: 'If it is not granted we will stop work', the laws of England would cease to be administered. If the women in your profession said the same thing it would make no difference to the laws of England whatever. Not only are we incomparably weaker than the men of our own class; we are weaker than the women of the working class. If the working women of the country were to say: 'if you go to war, we will refuse to make munitions or to help in the production of goods,' the difficulty of war-making would be seriously increased. But if all the daughters of educated men were to down tools to-morrow, nothing essential either to the life or to the war-making of the community would be embarrassed. Our class is the weakest of all the classes in the state. We have no weapon with which to enforce our will.

The answer to that is so familiar that we can easily anticipate it. The daughters of educated men have no direct influence, it is true; but they possess the greatest power of all; that is, the influence that they can exert upon educated men. If this is true, if, that is, influence is still the strongest of our weapons and the only one that can be effective in helping you to prevent war, let us, before we sign your manifesto or join your society, consider what that influence amounts to. Clearly it is of such immense importance that it deserves profound and prolonged scrutiny. Ours cannot be profound; nor can it be prolonged; it must be rapid and imperfect – still, let us attempt it.

What influence then have we had in the past upon the profession that is most closely connected with war – upon politics? There again are the innumerable, the invaluable biographies, but it would puzzle an alchemist to extract from the massed lives of politicians that particular strain which is the influence upon them of women. Our analysis can only be slight and superficial; still if we narrow our enquiry to manageable limits, and run over the memoirs of a century and a half we can hardly deny that there have been women who have influenced politics. The famous Duchess of Devonshire, Lady Palmerston, Lady Melbourne, Madame de Lieven, Lady Holland, Lady Ashburton – to skip from one famous name to another – were all undoubtedly possessed of great political influence. Their famous houses and the parties that met in them play so large a part in the political memoirs of the time that we can hardly deny that English politics, even perhaps English wars, would have been different had those houses and those parties never existed. But there is one characteristic that all those memoirs possess in common; the names of the great political leaders – Pitt, Fox, Burke, Sheridan, Peel, Canning, Palmerston, Disraeli, Gladstone – are sprinkled on every page; but you will not find either at the head of the stairs receiving the guests, or in the more private apartment of the house, any daughter of an educated man. It may be that they were deficient in charm, in wit, in rank, or in clothing. Whatever the reason, you may turn page after page, volume after volume, and though you will find their brothers and husbands – Sheridan at Devonshire House, Macaulay at Holland House, Matthew Arnold at Lansdowne House, Carlyle even at Bath House, the names of Jane Austen, Charlotte Bronte, and George Eliot do not occur; and though Mrs Carlyle went, Mrs Carlyle seems on her own showing to have found herself ill at ease.

But, as you will point out, the daughters of educated men may have possessed another kind of influence – one that was independent of wealth and rank, of wine, food, dress and all the other amenities that made the great houses of the great ladies so seductive. Here indeed we are on firmer ground, for there was of course one political cause which the daughters of educated men had much at heart during the past 150 years: the franchise. But when we consider how long it took them to win that cause, and what labour, we can only conclude that influence has to be combined with wealth in order to be effective as a political weapon, and that influence of the kind that can be exerted by the daughters of educated men is very low in power, very slow in action, and very painful in use. Certainly the one great political achievement of the educated man's daughter cost her over a century of the most exhausting and menial labour; kept her trudging in processions, working in offices, speaking at street corners; finally, because she used force, sent her to prison, and would very likely still keep her there, had it not been, paradoxically enough, that the help she gave her brothers when they used force at last gave her the right to call herself, if not a full daughter, still a stepdaughter of England.

Mahadevi Varma

(1907-1987)

Well known Hindi poetess and writer, Mahadevi Varma was born in 1907 in Farukkabad. Her primary education was carried on in the Mission School at Indore. Mahadevi's father was fairly modern and liberal while her mother was traditional. At an early age Mahadevi was exposed to Mira's bhajans and other religious songs, which must have made an impact on her young mind and influenced her writing in later years.

Despite this harmonious background and the fact that she was the only girl child in seven generations, she was married off at the young and immature age of nine in 1916. Fortunately the marriage did not disrupt her education, she resumed studies, graduated in 1929, began teaching and worked her way upto the Vice-Chancellorship of the women's university in 1960.

Her major poetry was written during the thirties of which *Deepshikha* (1942) is one of her most highly acclaimed poetry collections. Her work shows the impact of Romantic modernism. Her prose, ordinarily looked upon as being of secondary importance, is equally significant. The present essay is from the collection *Shrankala Ki Kadiyan* (1942) which has been translated as *Links in the Chain* by Neera Kuckreja Sohani (Katha, 2003). The essays in this volume are all related to women's condition their confines, their problems and their relationship to society and point out the interrelatedness of education, gender, politics and culture. Problematising the category of the individual, Mahadevi Varma, explores the clash with conventional role models. This essay is also a follow up of Pandita Ramabai's exposition in *The High Caste Hindu Women.*

The Hindu Woman's Wifehood

Both development and destruction, though rooted in change, are different in their outcomes. This is because one transforms a particular object such that its hidden virtues become more apparent, whereas the other alters and distorts the same virtues such that they begin to seem like flaws. The changes that occur in flowing water after it crashes into a rock are positive, but only deplorable distortion will be found in the change that takes place in stagnant water.

The history of Indian woman's social status is also the story of its deterioration. The past centuries failed to become the founding stones for her social edifice, instead, they acted like thunderbolts to bring it down. Consequently, instead of becoming stronger and better, her condition became progressively weaker and despicable.

The last few years did however turn a new page in the history of her life, compelling society to view the woman's situation with a new perspective. At this point in time, although the Indian woman has not been able to acquire a new form by discarding her old values and beliefs, like the women of Turkey, Russia and other nations, there is little doubt that she is beginning to view her own situation and the pitiful condition born of it with astonishment. It would not be an overstatement to say that the surprise we feel at our feebleness is itself a proof of our belief in our strength, because one who does not trust his or her own strength quite naturally believes in his or her own weakness and therefore, does not find it surprising.

In a woman's life, there has always been a dearth of political rights and economic independence. Her social situation too has not been enviable. Her life's primary goal was considered to be wifehood, and the ultimate one, motherhood. Therefore only one path and only one means of livelihood was open to her. If society can face the bitter truth it will shamefully acknowledge that it assigned to the woman the most degrading means of earning a living. She is forced to live only as an exhibition of man's wealth and as a means of his recreation. No value is attached to her life as an individual and as a citizen. Motherhood is revered because it keeps the society alive and wifehood is lauded because it caters to man's fulfilment. But can it be conceded that the physical and mental state of all women will fit these two roles alone? Can the physical and mental faculties and interests not inspire any woman towards another but equally commendable goal?

The moment a girl is born, her parent's attention is drawn to the difficulties of getting her married. If she inherits some disease from her sick parents, then too, her parents become anxious to hand her over in marriage, cursing her repeatedly as a bitter fruit of their sins and calling her *parai dharohar*, – someone else's property held in trust. The girl may be afflicted with leprosy, tuberculosis or any other illness, but to deprive her of the responsibilities of marriage would be a disgrace to the family! Whether she is physically incapable or mentally unprepared for married life, she has no means of livelihood other than marriage. No one worries about her willingness or unwillingness, acceptance or lack of acceptance, and eligibility or ineligibility, nor do they feel the need to do so. If the daughter is ugly and is not fit to be displayed in the marriage market, another who is beautiful is shown in her place. Likewise, if she is sick, then her illness is hidden and another who is healthy is shown in her place. In essence, bribery, deception, lies and all other means fair or foul are used to arrange a marriage for her, because that is the only means for her subsistence. It is true that society does not worry about men's suitability or unsuitability to marry either, but for men the marital bond is a source of pleasure, not of livelihood. Therefore, in a way, men remain unfettered.

The manner in which daughters are traded off, without much thought or discussion in families that invoke ancient traditions, is indeed a matter of shame. But the practice of checking out the marriageable girl like cattle on sale in the families which worship modernity, is again hardly a matter of pride. The manner in which prospective in-laws scrutinize a girl by making her walk, laugh, read and write is quite shameful. Listening to their remarks about the girl's height, weight, figure, facial features and so on unfailingly evokes the memory of female slaves on sale during the age of slavery. Usually, a girl has to pass the test of not only beauty but also that of education, talent and good qualities even for men who are emaciated, ugly and unemployed but educated. In such a social milieu, where every woman has to become a wife under any circumstance purely for survival's sake, should the dearth of perfect wives or ideal mothers be a matter of surprise?

It is pointless to even talk about the mentality of young men desirous of becoming husbands. Usually before assuming the burden of the wife's subsistence, they want to extract from the prospective father-in-law the highest possible penalty for giving birth to a daughter. One demands that his expenses for going abroad be met, another seeks money to pay for his university education, a third asks for a substantial amount of money for investing in business. In short, each man puts himself up for auction to the highest bidder.

The question then arises: Can this buying and selling, this business of marriage be deemed the most sacred bond in the woman's life? Can she become a Saubhagyavati, the fortunate one, by having a husband who lacks self-pride, the ability to support his wife and is dependent on others? If not, then purely for the sake of her subsistence, how long can she continue to accept this bond, which cannot elevate her to the rank of an ideal wife or an ideal mother? Granted, this is not the age of male valour as in the past, when a suitor's eligibility was tested by such feats as lifting and stringing a heavy bow or piercing the eye of a rotating fish with an arrow looking only at the reflection of the fish in water. Even so, the woman expects at least that much self reliance in the man as will prevent him from weighing her wifehood on a commercial scale.

There are many such people who deem any new viewpoint as ruinous for society and religion, and try their level best to prevent any change from taking place. As a result, drawing strength from opposition, the flow of change becomes so forceful, that it demolishes the sanctity of the past. Such a rebellion would not have been required if the ocean of our society had been deep enough to receive new currents of thought.

The woman's ultimate fulfilment may lie in motherhood but she should accept this duty willingly, after weighing her mental and physical strengths, and not under duress. Something that is accepted under compulsion or in the absence of alternatives cannot be called duty.

Rather than fretting over the marriage of girls right from their birth, it is desirable that the society worries instead about the means for their advancement. If the doors to education, fine arts, business and other professions are thrown open to them and they are free to choose from them according to their leanings, they can become self-reliant. And, if they are free to choose their life partner after becoming aware of their capability and desire, the marriage would become for them a pilgrimage which would remove their narrow mindedness, purge their selfishness and make their future bright. At present, to take pride in their sacrifice is as ridiculous as praising the singing of a caged bird, serenading the sacrifice of her life in captivity.

Time, like an arrow, always moves forward. The conditions of life that we have left behind can never be restored. Therefore, to continue to mould ourselves according to those conditions would mean going round in circles. If we had been able to touch even the shadow of that ancient culture in whose favour we want to obstruct the path to progress, our actions would not have been so meaningless and our outlook so narrow. A past that was capable of absorbing countless cultures, different points of views and mutually opposed streams of thought, may not have helped us to advance, but it certainly would not have caused us to regress. Our mindless conservatism and the excess of bestiality even in the most sacred of our relationships, proves that we have strayed and are headed in a direction that was never our goal.

We worry about women's marriage not because we fear there will be a dearth of capable wives and mothers in our nation or race but because we are unable to think of alternate means for their livelihood. Whether the parents are rich or poor, they are neither glad to take upon themselves any of the girl's responsibilities nor can they find a way other than marriage to get rid of her. Widows pose a similar problem before our society. The moment a woman is widowed, the problem of sustenance and safety looms ahead. If she has no worry regarding her sustenance, even then, the problem of safety persists because she is surrounded by temptations that can lead her to immoral ways. And if she is without means, her needs alone, in the absence of other alternatives, compel her to accept the deviant path.

If we wish to uphold the significance of the institution of home, we will need housewives who will assume their responsibilities willingly and happily after giving the matter due thought and not because they are forced to do so for their livelihood or are incapable of defending themselves.

It should be mandatory for parents to allow their daughters to get education in accordance with their interests and capabilities, so that their talents develop properly and they are able to work in various fields if they so desire and deem necessary. It can well be a woman's duty to give worthy children to the nation but to make all her citizenship rights hinge on that alone can only be called injustice.

It is because of her helplessness that the woman is not considered man's equal partner. Indeed, with feet shackled by fetters, like a prisoner, can woman ever earn the title of a comforting partner? When taking a woman as his wife, every man feels as though he is doing her a favour, But if he is made to wait lifelong for a mate, if he has to make the effort to search for her and has to prove himself eligible to take on the responsibility of marriage, then this feeling of charity which is the cause of grief in a majority of households, would not last a moment.

Today, men are neither required to triumph over rivals in order to be garlanded by the bride as in the swayamvars nor have they to prove themselves as worthy suitors by defeating their adversaries through matchless bravery, nor do they have to prove their intellect. They merely have to accept the lifelong services of a maidservant, in lieu of which they can demand anything. Therefore, how and why should they think of this bond as sacred or significant? Even when they do not want to get married, they are surrounded by fathers of dozens of marriageable girls, who offer a lot of wealth along with flattery and still feel obliged about giving away their beautiful, talented and educated daughters. How else is such a marriage to be regarded, except as an affront to womanhood!

In the ancient society, grahastha ashram, the householder phase in life, was considered the best from the viewpoint of utility. There were some religious and social reasons as well as for deeming it indispensable. In ancient times, the newly arrived Aryan race felt the acute need for maximum possible children to consolidate its social situation. This is clear from those Vedic hymns that constantly beseech the gods to bless the household with brave sons and animals. In this new predominantly agricultural nation, brave sons were as indispensable for their expansion as cattle for their food. Therefore, no woman, whatever her clan, was worth rejecting. Thus, even a brahmin, belonging to the highest caste, could accept a woman of any caste as his wife.

After a period of time, possibly to keep away the low caste relatives of the girl, the principle of isolation was given the form of a religious mandate, whereby having given their daughter in marriage, the parents had to consider their son-in-law's house out of bounds. Even today, we have parents who believe it a sin to accept food, drink or hospitality at their daughter's house or take any kind of help from her. This sentiment was responsible for parents making a distinction between the daughter and the son because once married, the daughter could be of no help to parents while the son would be a support for life. That is why, other than giving her some dowry to help her start her married life, no share in parental property or wealth was secured for her.

However, the instances of the presence of a large number of brahamacharinis, women pledged to spinsterhood, and that of princesses marrying sages, prove that in ancient times, the woman was not as subjugated as she is today. After having observed brahamacharya up to a certain age, she had the right to choose her own companion and become a householder, and after a certain age she could also take leave of the grahastha ashram.

Today, we continue to subscribe to the distorted form of those ancient traditions but do not wish to examine the circumstances under which they prevailed. There is absolutely no link between that historic past and the girl-mothers of today raising skeleton-like, emaciated, sick children. Nor do children, born to destitute beggars, starving, bare-bodied, shivering in the cold, burdened with the diseases inherited from the parents, prove the utility of marriage. These youths with decrepit bodies and lifeless spirit, and old men mocking death but donning the bridegroom's diadem are not the creations of the ashram system of yore.[1] Nor can this scientific society, giving its sanction to birth control after being overwhelmed with population growth, be called a reflection of the circumstances of the past. In fact, the new age has its new curses that can only be rectified in new ways. Due to our foolishness we have built a decrepit hut easily shaken by the wind on the firm and beautiful foundation of the past instead of erecting a magnificent palace reaching the skies. To make a building befitting the foundation, we will have to demolish the existing structure. It would be our short sightedness if we sacrifice the present in order to revive the past because the past can only aid in life's advancement, not be its goal.

When we hear of the changes taking place in countries, where men had earlier held similar beliefs towards women as men in our society, we are filled with trepidation. When we see their women functioning as efficiently as men in all fields and choosing their life partners not out of necessity but out of free choice, our hearts begin to tremble with fear. Giving no thought to the changing conditions, we become all the more actively engaged in keeping the women of our country out of sight. We close our eyes to the fact that just as we cannot confine the rays of light that pierce the darkness at dawn, similarly, we cannot imprison the tide of awakening sweeping through a nation. Moreover, with so many means of communication available for the spread of ideas, change can at best be delayed for some time but cannot be entirely prevented.

Today, who can say of a Turkish woman that she is the descendent of women who were kept locked in great numbers in man's harem, who hid their faces even from the light outside, whose utility was nothing besides being a source of pleasure to the man and ensuring the continuation of his clan? When we see Russian women holding positions of soldiers, judges and the like in the army, navy, bureaus of technology and courts, can we believe they are the same at whom the Russian saying, "Beat your fur and you make it warmer, beat a woman and you make her wiser," was aimed? Earlier, in Russia, the bride's father used to present the bridegroom with a new whip, a symbol of his authority, to be used exclusively to beat the bride. And this whip was commonly hung above the new couple's bed. The plight of the women was the same in other civilized European countries as well. But today, while they may not carry the burden of divinity as Indian women do, they are definitely beginning to be considered human. The question now is how long can the women of our country be content with being merely a beloved and a wife? It does not, of course, follow that if Indian women were to renounce the duties of wifehood and motherhood, and start working like men in all the fields, their situation would become worthy of being called progressive.

Marriage is the oldest custom of the uncivilized as well as the civilized human race. But for it to become a moral and religious bond along with a social one, it will have to be further refined. At present, the Indian man picks a woman to domesticate and rear, just as he picks exotic colourful birds as pets for his pleasure or a cow or horse for his use. He thinks he has the same right over her body and mind as the right he has over his pet birds and animals. To see the living proof of man's thoughtless conduct in our society, we only need observe a young girl, healthy and blooming like a rose, five years after her marriage. We will find a prematurely aged, sickly mother of many emaciated children, whose helplessness and tragic story is sure to brings tears to our eyes.

Many people believe that if we make girls self-reliant they will refuse to marry, which will lead to immoral conduct in the society and also cause chaos in the institution of marriage. But they forget that the desire for companionship should be primary in a marriage and not the compulsion of economic necessity. Also, if the desire for lifelong companionship with someone was not inherent in human beings, then no trace of the custom of marriage would have remained in countries where women are self-reliant in all respects. As for immoral conduct, it is undeniably true that the ease with which a person discontented with the social situation can adopt the immoral path, a contented person cannot. We live beneath the open sky enclosed by the walls of our homes and so does a prisoner. But when we get home in the evening, tired and weary, we lock ourselves behind our doors to feel safe whereas the prisoner, fully secure, spends the whole night wondering how to escape. The sole reason for this contrasting mental state is that while one is kept secure against his wishes, the other is free to come and go as he/she pleases. If the woman's social situation does not remain so pitiable and her heart is not so hurt, being enchained, she will never willingly acquiesce to follow a path that leads to suicide.

The belief that equipped with the means of being self-reliant, the woman will view the housewife's duties as lowly, thereby causing anarchy at home, is bound to prove erroneous. All the gentle grace of the woman is centred in motherhood. It will be a rare woman who will show no concern for the concurrence of the life partner she has accepted of her own will, who will leave her precious children uncared for, who will be driven solely by her desire for economic self-reliance and will busy herself in acquiring material assets in an extremely demanding work sphere. If she is compelled to do this due to economic circumstances and in order to run her household satisfactorily, it must then be considered praiseworthy.

In our society even today, women married to labourers or farmers manage the household and also help their husbands in earning a livelihood. Prompted by the worry that they may defy the man's authority because of economic independence, if they are taught nothing but the art of pleasing their husbands, the outcome would be suicidal. It would be suicidal not only for them but for society as well because they can never become true social beings and citizens.

As far as education is concerned, not even two per cent of Indian women are educated. This is so because the parents do not wish to spend anything on educating their daughters and even if they do educate them, it is merely to increase the daughters' value in the marriage market, and not for their advancement. Rebelling against this very inevitability of wifehood, many well-educated women refuse to marry because of the fear that their partners will not be able to tolerate their independent personality.

Unfortunately, there is no dearth of instances which support this belief. No matter how well-educated, no Indian man has been able to move so far away from his ingrained attitude that he does not consider his wife an extension of his glory. Her knowledge, wisdom, talent and beauty are all merely the means of his self-praise. Whenever this living image of display desires to express her separate individuality and reveals her own distinct inclinations, ideas and opinions, the man unfailingly becomes agitated at first and then discontented.

At one time, the Indian woman may have been a source of the country's dignity, but today she is just a source of its mockery. If society fails to understand her plight, her discontentment at her condition will force her to do that which will destroy its remaining dignity.

Note

1. In the Vedic age, man's life was divided into four stages. The first, brahmacharya ashram was the phase of studenthood and celibacy. Grahastha ashram, the most productive phase, imposed on the

individual the duties and responsibilities of a householder. Vanaprastha ashram meant the handing over of the affairs of a householder to the next generation and becoming detached from worldly affairs. The last, the sanyasa ashram was a phase of renunciation and meditation, a stage to prepare the individual's soul for attaining moksha.

Simone de Beauvoir
(1908-1986)

Simone de Beauvoir's best known work is *The Second Sex* (1949) and has overshadowed her work as a novelist, essayist and playwright. Born in a middle class family of comfortable means, she studied at the Sorbonne from where she took a degree in Philosophy, and went on to have a teaching career from 1931-1943.

Early in her life she adopted atheism and decided to become a writer, a promise she fulfilled in every way. Amongst her books are *The Blood of Others* (1945), *She Came to Stay* (1949), the *Mandarins* (1957) and *Memoirs of a Dutiful Daughter* (1958). Her most important philosophical work is *The Ethics of Ambiguity* (1948). While the *Mandarins* is a four part autobiography, another novel *The Coming of Age* is a critique of society's treatment of the elderly. Her mother's death lead her to write *A Very Easy Death*.

Simone de Beauvoir met Sartre after her studies in the Sorbonne. This was the beginning of a friendship which lasted until his death in 1980. After his death she published another book *Adieux A Farewell to Sartre* which is a dairy she had maintained during his slow, lingering death.

The Second Sex problematises gender and all that constructs it – the epistemological framework, the social institutions and the processes of socialization. She asserts that 'woman is not born but made' and goes on to detail the history of women's oppression. Her stand is an assertion of independence. The present extract provides us with a political history of the feminist struggle for public space.

Since the French Revolution: The Job and the Vote

It might well have been expected that the Revolution would change the lot of woman. It did nothing of the sort. The middle-class Revolution was respectful of middle-class institutions and values and it was accomplished almost exclusively by men. It is important to emphasize the fact that throughout the Old Régime it was the women of the working classes who as a sex enjoyed most independence. Woman had the right to manage a business and she had all the legal powers necessary for the independent pursuit of her calling. She shared in production as seamstress, laundress, burnisher, shopkeeper, and so on; she worked either at home or in small places of business; her material independence permitted her a great freedom of behaviour: a woman of the people could go out, frequent taverns, and dispose of her body as she saw fit almost like a man; she was her husband's associate and equal. It was on the economic, not on the sexual plane that she suffered oppression. In the country the peasant woman took a considerable part in farm labour; she was treated as a servant; frequently she did not eat at the table with her husband and sons, she slaved harder than they did and, and the burdens of maternity added to her fatigue. But as in ancient agricultural societies, being necessary to man she was respected by him; their goods, their interests, their cares were all in common; she exercised great authority in the home. These are the women who, out of the midst of their hard life, might have been able to assert themselves and demand their rights; but a tradition of timidity and of submissiveness weighed on them. The *cahiers* of the States-General contained but few feminine claims, and these were restricted to keeping men out of women's occupations. And certainly women were to be seen beside their men in demonstrations and riots; these women went to seek at Versailles ' the baker, his wife, and his little journeyman'. But it was not the common people who led the Revolution and enjoyed its fruits.

As for the middle-class women, some ardently took up the cause of liberty, such as Mme Roland and Lucile Desmoulins. One of them who had a profound influence on the course of events was Charlotte Corday when she assassinated Marat. There was some feminist agitation. Olympe de Gouges proposed in 1789 a 'Declaration of the Rights of Woman', equivalent to the 'Declaration of the Rights of Man', in which she asked that all masculine privilege be abolished; but she perished before long on the scaffold. Short-lived journals appeared, and fruitless efforts were made by a few women to undertake political activities.

In 1790 the right of the eldest and the masculine prerogative in inheritance were abolished; girls and boys became equals in this respect. In 1792 a law was passed establishing divorce and thus relaxing matrimonial bonds. But these were only insignificant victories. Middle-class women were too well integrated in the family to feel any definite solidarity as a sex; they did not constitute a separate caste capable of imposing claims: economically they led a parasitic existence. Thus it was that while women who, in spite of their sex, could have taken part in events were prevented from doing so on account of their class, those belonging to the active class were condemned to stand aside as being women. When economic power falls into the hands of the workers, then it will become possible for the working-woman to win rights and privileges that the parasitic woman, noble or middle-class, has never obtained.

During the Revolution woman enjoyed a liberty that was anarchic. But when society underwent reorganization, she was firmly enslaved anew. From the feminist point of view, France was ahead of other countries; but unfortunately for the modern Frenchwoman, her status was decided during a military dictatorship; the Code Napoléon, fixing her lot for a century, greatly retarded her emancipation. Like all military men, Napoléon preferred to see in woman only a mother; but as heir to a bourgeois revolution, he was not one to disrupt the structure of society and give the mother pre-eminence over the wife. He forbade the investigation of paternity; he set stern conditions for the unwed mother and the natural child. The married woman herself, however, did not find refuge in her dignity as mother; the feudal paradox was perpetuated. Girl and wife were deprived of the attribute of citizenship, which prevented them from practising law and acting as guardian. But the celibate woman, the spinster, enjoyed full civil powers, while marriage preserved the old dependency. The wife owed *obedience* to her husband; he could have her condemned to solitary confinement for adultery and get a divorce from her; if he killed her, caught in the act, he was excusable in the eyes of the law; whereas the husband was liable to penalty only if he brought a concubine into the home, and it was in this case only that the wife could obtain a divorce from him. The man decided where to live and had much more authority over the children than did the wife; and, except where the wife managed a commercial enterprise, his authorization was necessary for her to incur obligations. Her person and property were both under rigorous marital control.

During the nineteenth century jurisprudence only reinforced the rigours of the Code. Divorce was abolished in 1826, and was not restored until 1884, when it was still very difficult to obtain. The middle class was never more powerful, but it was uneasy in its authority, mindful of the menaces implied in the industrial revolution. Woman was declared made for the family, not for politics; for domestic cares and not for public functions. Auguste Comte declared that there were radical differences, physical and moral, between male and female which separated them profoundly, especially in the human race. Femininity was a kind of 'prolonged infancy' that set woman aside from 'the ideal of the race' and enfeebled her mind. He foresaw the total abolition of female labour outside the home. In morality and love woman might be set up as superior; but man acted, while she remained in the home without economic or political rights.

Balzac expressed the same ideal in more cynical terms. In the *Physiologie du marriage* he wrote: 'The destiny of woman and her sole glory are to make beat the hearts of men... she is a chattel and properly speaking only a subsidiary to man.' Here he speaks for the antifeminist middle class, in reaction against both eighteenth-century licence and the threatening progressive ideas of the time. Balzac showed that bourgeois marriage where love is excluded naturally leads to adultery, and he exhorted husbands to keep a firm rein, deny their wives all education and culture, and keep them as unattractive as possible. The middle class followed this programme, confining women to the kitchen and the home, closely watching their behaviour, keeping them wholly dependent. In compensation they were held in honour and treated with the most exquisite politeness. 'The married woman is a slave whom one must be able to set on a throne', said Balzac. She must be yielded to in trifles, given first place; instead of making her carry burdens as among primitives one must rush forward to relieve her of any painful task and of all care – and at the same time of all responsibility. Most bourgeois women accepted this gilded confinement, and the few who complained were unheard. Bernard Shaw remarks that it is easier to put chains on men than to remove them, if the chains confer benefits. The middle-class woman clung to her chains because she clung to the privileges of her class. Freed from the male, she would have to work for a living; she felt no solidarity with working-women, and she believed that the emancipation of bourgeois women would mean the ruin of her class.

The march of history, however, was not stopped by such obstinate resistance; the coming of the machine destroyed landed property and furthered the emancipation of the working class along with that of women. All forms of socialism, wresting woman away from the family, favour her liberation: Plato envisioned a communal regime and promised women an autonomy in it such as they enjoyed in Sparta. With the utopian socialisms of Saint-Simon, Fourier, and Cabet was born the utopia of the 'free woman'; the slavery of worker and of woman was to be abolished, for women like men were human beings. Unfortunately this reasonable idea did not prevail in the school of Saint-Simonism. Fourier, for example, confused the emancipation of women with the rehabilitation of the flesh, demanding for every individual the right to yield to the call of passion and wishing to replace marriage with love; he considered woman not as a person but only in her amorous function. Cabet promised the complete equality of the sexes, but he restricted woman's share in politics. Others demanded better education for women rather than emancipation. The lofty notion of woman the regenerating influence persisted through the nineteenth century and appears in Victor Hugo. But woman's cause was rather discredited by the ineptitude of woman's partisans. Clubs, magazines, delegations, movements like 'Bloomerism' – all went down in ridicule. The most intelligent women of the time, like Mme do Staël and George Sand, remained apart from these movements while fighting their own battles for freedom. But feminism was favoured in general by the reform movement of the nineteenth century because it sought justice in equality. Proudhon was a remarkable exception. He broke the alliance between feminism and socialism, relegating the honest woman to the home and to dependence on the male, and attempting to demonstrate her inferiority. 'Housewife or harlot' was the choice he offered. But like all anti-feminists he addressed ardent litanies to 'the true woman', slave and mirror of the male. In spite of this devotion, he was unable to make his own wife happy: the letters of Mme Proudhon are one long lament.

These theoretical debates did not affect the course of events: rather they were a hesitant reflection of things taking place. Woman regained an economic importance that had been lost since prehistoric times, because she escaped from the hearth and assumed in the factory a new part in production. It was the machine that made possible this upheaval, for the difference in physical strength between male and female workers was to a large extent annulled. As the swift growth of industry demanded a larger working force than the males alone could furnish, the collaboration of women became necessary. That was the grand revolution of the nineteenth century, which transformed the lot of woman and opened for her a new era. Marx and Engels gauged its whole range, and they promised women liberation implied in that of the proletariat. In fact, 'woman and the worker have this in common: that they are both oppressed,' said Bebel. And both would escape together from oppression, thanks to the importance their work would take on through technological evolution. Engels showed that the lot of woman has been closely tied to the history of private property; a calamity put the patriarchate in place of the matrilineal régime and enslaved woman to the patrimony. But the industrial revolution was the counterpart of that loss of rights and would lead to feminine emancipation.

* * * * *

One of the basic problems of woman, as we have seen, is the reconciliation of her reproductive role and her part in productive labour. The fundamental fact that from the beginning of history doomed woman to domestic work and prevented her taking part in the shaping of the world was her enslavement to the generative function. In female animals there is a physiological and seasonal rhythm that assures the economizing of their strength; in women, on the contrary, between puberty and the menopause nature sets no limits to the number of her pregnancies. Certain civilizations forbid early marriage, and it is said that in certain Indian tribes a rest of at least two years between childbirths is assured to women; but in general, woman's fecundity has been unregulated for many centuries. Contraceptives have been in existence since antiquity, usually to be used by the woman: potions, suppositories, vaginal tampons; but they remained the secret of prostitutes and doctors. Perhaps this secret was known to those Roman women of the decline whose sterility was attacked by the satirists. But contraceptives were practically unknown to the Middle Ages in Europe; scarcely a trace of them is to be found up to the eighteenth century. For many women life in those times was an uninterrupted succession of pregnancies; even women of easy virtue paid for their licentious lovemaking by frequent childbearing.

At certain epochs man has strongly felt the need to reduce the size of the population; but at the same time nations have feared becoming weak. In times of crisis and misery the birth rate may have been reduced by late marriage, but it remained the general rule to marry young and have as many children as the woman could produce; infant mortality alone reduced the number of living children.

As for abortion, it is nowhere officially sanctioned by the laws. Roman law accorded no especial protection to embryonic life; it regarded the *nasciturus* (to be born) as a part of the maternal body, not as a human being. In the period of the decline abortion seemed to be a normal practice, and even the legislator who wished to encourage childbearing did not venture to forbid it. If a wife rejected her infant against her husband's will, he could have her punished, but it was her disobedience that constituted the offence. Throughout the whole of Oriental and Greco-Roman civilization abortion was permissible.

Christianity revolutionized moral ideas in this matter by endowing the embryo with a soul; for then abortion became a crime against the foetus itself. According to St. Augustine, 'Any woman who acts in such a way that she cannot give birth to as many children as she is capable of makes herself guilty of that many murders, just as with the woman who tries to injure herself after conception.' Ecclesiastical law developed gradually, with interminable discussions on such questions as when the soul actually enters the body of the foetus. St Thomas and others set the time of animation at about the fortieth day for males and the eightieth day for females. Different degree of guilt were attached to abortion in the Middle Ages according to when it was performed and why: 'There is a great difference between the poor woman who destroys her infant on account of the difficulty of supporting it, and her who has no aim other than hiding the crime of fornication,' said the book of penitence. An edict of Henri II in 1556 was the basis for regarding abortion as murder and punishable with death. The Code of 1791 excused the woman but punished her accomplices. In the nineteenth century the idea that abortion is murder disappeared; it was regarded rather as a crime against the State. The French law of 1810 forbade it absolutely, with heavy penalties; but physicians always practised it whenever it was a question of saving the mother's life. The law was too strict and at the end of the century few arrests were made and still fewer convictions reached. New laws were passed in 1923 and 1939, with some variations in the penalties; and in 1941 abortion was decreed a crime against the safety of the State. In other countries the crime and its punishment have been variously regarded, but in general laws and courts have been much more lenient with the woman having the abortion than with her accomplices. The Catholic Church, however, has in no way softened its rigour, and in 1917 the code of canon law called for the excommunication of all concerned in an abortion. The Pope has again quite recently declared that as between the life of the mother and that of the infant, the former must be sacrificed: of course the mother, being baptized, can gain entrance to heaven – oddly enough, hell never enters these calculations – whereas the foetus is doomed to limbo for eternity. Abortion has been officially recognized during a brief period only: in Germany before Nazism and in Russia before 1936. But in spite of religion and the law, it holds a place of considerable importance in all countries. In France abortions number each year from 800,000 to 1000,000 – about as many as there are births – two-thirds of those aborted being married women, many already having one or two children.

Thus it is, then, that in spite of prejudices, opposition, and the survival of an outdated morality, we have witnessed the passage from free fecundity to a fecundity controlled by the State or by individuals. Progress in obstetrical science has considerably reduced the dangers of confinement; and the pain of childbirth is reduced. At this time – March 1949 – legislation has been passed in England requiring the use of certain anaesthetic methods; they are in general application in the United States and are beginning to spread in France. Artificial insemination completes the evolutionary advance that will enable humanity to master the reproductive function. These changes are of tremendous importance for woman in particular; she can reduce the number of her pregnancies and make them a rationally integral part of her life, instead of being their slave. During the nineteenth century woman in her turn emancipated herself from nature; she gained mastery of her own body. Now protected in large part from the slavery of reproduction, she is in a position to assume the economic role that is offered her and will assure her of complete independence.

The evolution of woman's condition is to be explained by the concurrent action of these two factors: sharing in productive labour and being freed from slavery to reproduction. As Engels had foreseen, woman's social and political status was necessarily to be transformed. The feminist movement, sketched out in France by Condorcet, in England by Mary Wollstonecraft in her *Vindication of the Rights of Woman,* and taken up again at the beginning of the nineteenth century by the Saint-Simonists, had been unable to accomplish definite results, as it lacked concrete bases. But now, with woman in industry and out of the home, her demands began to take on full weight. They were to make themselves heard at the very centre of the bourgeoisie. In consequence of the rapid development of industrial civilization, landed property lost importance in relation to personal property, and the principle of the unity of the family group lost force. The liquidity of capital allowed its holder, instead of being possessed by it, to possess it without reciprocal cares of ownership, and to dispose of it at will. It was through the patrimony that woman had been most strongly attached to her spouse; with the patrimony a thing of the past, they were simply in juxtaposition, and not even their children united them with a firmness comparable to that of property interest. Thus the individual was to gain independence against the group.

This process was especially striking in America, where modern capitalism triumphed: divorce was to flourish and husband and wife to seem no more than provisional associates. In France, where the rural population was a factor of importance and the Code Napoleon placed the married woman under guardianship, the process of evolution was bound to be slow. In 1884 divorce was restored, and the wife could obtain it if the husband committed adultery. In the matter of penology, however, the sex difference was retained: adultery was a legal offence only when committed by the wife. The power of trusteeship, granted with reservations in 1907, was fully obtained only in 1917. In 1912 the determination of natural paternity was authorized. The status of the married woman was modified in 1938 and 1942: the duty of obedience was then abrogated, though the father remained the head of the family. He determined the place of residence, though the wife could oppose his choice if she had good arguments. Her legal powers were increased; but in the confused statement: 'the married woman has full legal powers. These powers are limited only by the marriage contract and the law', the last part of the article contradicts the first. The equality of husband and wife was not yet an accomplished fact.

As for political rights, we can say that they were not easily achieved in France, England and the United States..... New Zealand gave woman full rights in 1893, and Australia followed in 1908. But in England and America the victory was difficult. Victorian England isolated woman in the home; Jane Austen hid herself in order to write; scientists proclaimed that woman was 'a sub-species destined only for reproduction'. Feminism was very timid until about 1903, when the Pankhurst family founded in London the Women's Social and Political Union and feminist agitation took on a singular and militant character. For the first time in history women were to be seen taking action as women, which gives a special interest to the 'suffragette' adventure. For fifteen years they exerted pressure, at first without violence, marching with banners, invading meetings, at first without violence, marching with banners, invading meetings, provoking arrest, putting on hunger strikes, marching on Parliament with shawled workers and great ladies in line together, holding meetings, inciting further arrests, parading in columns miles long when votes on suffrage were being taken in Parliament. In 1912 more violent tactics were adopted: they burned houses, slashed pictures, trampled flowerbeds, threw stones at the police, overwhelmed Asquith and Sir Edward Grey with repeated deputations, interrupted public speeches. The war intervened. English women got the vote with restrictions in 1918, and the unrestricted vote in 1928. Their success was in large part due to the services they rendered during the war.

Nayantara Sahgal

(b 1927)

Nayantara Sahgal has been active on the Indian literary scene for nearly half a century and her work continues to be meaningful and relevant to present day concerns. Better known as a novelist, she has also written political journalism, essays, two volumes of autobiography and a book on Indira Gandhi.

Born in 1927 in Allahabad, she is the daughter of an inter-lingual marriage, her father being a Maharashtrian and her mother a Kashmiri brahmin. Both her parents were actively involved in the freedom struggle, in fact her first volume of autobiography is titled *Prison and Chocolate Cake.* Though she belongs to a political family, she has never refrained from critiquing oppressive stances. During the Emergency, she travelled abroad and lectured in the States. These lectures have been put together in a volume titled *A Voice for Freedom*. A volume of correspondence has also been published.

From her early semi-autobiographical novels she moved on to writing historical novels concentrating on the peak years of the freedom struggle 1929-1947, and going back and forth to analyse causes and consequences. Sahgal has a wry sense of humour and uses language with a great deal of control. Very subtly it shocks one into a new awareness.

Her political and historical concerns have in no way detracted from her aesthetic concerns and another book of writings *Point of View,* from which the present essay has been taken, carries several of these essays. Her latest work is *Lesser Breeds* which uses the epigraph from Kipling's poem to bring the western presumption and the eastern response face to face. The present essay is political and questions the west-centred normative patterns. Power is a myth which rests on imaginative fictions. Both imperialism and globalisation are mono-cultural ideologies which do not respect alternative cultural constructs, instead they go on to construct frameworks to control differences.

Illusion and Reality

I can only share with you some thoughts I have on the collection of islands and continents we call the world, which are the subject of this conference, and to talk about some ideas that have governed this world and their effects on us, for it is my belief that writing comes as much out of this heritage as the heritage known as a literary tradition.

I have to speak personally, and as an Indian. How else can one speak, except from one's own time, experience and position, with all the limitations that these impose'? And when I say 'we' or 'us,' I am referring to the people who lie more or less within the same general ambit of experience, and share a somewhat similar outlook in common. And in these very broad general terms it seems to me that the 'we' I speak of are the people who live out scenarios that have been conceived elsewhere, and been directed from that elsewhere by other people. The real world we have been repeatedly told we live in has not been one whose reality we could believe in. For us, it has been a stage set by others on which we have played the roles assigned to us.

The imperial era I was born into was a stage setting of this kind. Empire itself was no illusion. It was a fact of life, a businesslike arrangement that had divided up the globe into rulers and the ruled, masters and slaves. Under this dispensation huge land masses with names and ancient civilizations of their own became quaintly known as Europe's possessions,' and hung with European ownership titles: British India, Dutch East Indies, French Indo China, German East Africa and so on. Trade routes opened up by these owners carried everything from silk and spices to human flesh westward. All this went on for several hundred years and it was real enough. But the proposition that this scenario was based on was probably the most ingenious and imaginative fiction we have ever heard, mythologizing Europe as the centre of the world, inhabiting it with a superior race, and bestowing upon it a monopoly of civilization, all of which then gave it the right to conquer and make use of non-Europe for its profit and pleasure. Non-Europe in this scenario was a mixed bag of 'lesser breeds' – a wonderfully expressive phrase immortalized by the imperial poet, Kipling, and these 'lesser breeds' were long overdue for European enlightenment.

These flights of fantasy would have faded like the fantasies they were, if they had not yielded so much profit, and had not therefore been glued and hammered into place with blood and iron, and legitimized by a massive scaffolding of words and images and pseudo-scientific theories in their support. Generations grew up and died doomed to inferiority, believing there was no way out of this scenario which posed as a true and natural state of affairs. And outdated and hackneyed though this situation now sounds, it is so very recent that South Africa struggled out of its stranglehold only a few years ago.

What difference can this or any other outer casing make to our lives? Does the lie that others impose on us as history affect ordinary people's on-going lives? Does it affect the aromas of your grandmother's cooking, or the sound of rain on your roof, or your love for your beloved? And aren't these basically what the human process is all about? Yet it is this outer casing that becomes the framework we are compelled to act within, and travel through, burdened with itineraries that may or may not be of our own choosing, but that nevertheless dominate our journey, and colour our mentality. And history does dog our footsteps, even and especially those of us who have left our soil of origin and acquired new nationalities. When has the kind of world we lived in not moved into us, even though we might not even be aware of its major events and upheavals? The mentality that flourished in a flat world was quite different from the grander one that dawned on a globe whose seas men could navigate, and still grander is it now that we live in a boundless cosmos holding worlds upon worlds still waiting to be discovered. Our outer casing affects us powerfully, and we are squaring our account with it in big and intimate ways every day of our lives. In fact, in our own era the line between public and private has been a continually disappearing one, as vast numbers of people have had to face the traumatic consequences of public events in their private lives. The gap between public and private is in any case infinitesimal in all societies that are in transition. When politics enters daily life, those who write, among others, are forced to take sides, and it becomes impossible to separate politics from literature or any other department of life. In such an environment literature would be floating in a void if it did not enter the arena.

When great areas of the world were released from the cast-iron outer casing of empire, the horizon was revealed, the skies expanded, and we came out of our silences. The first thing this set us free to do was to speak, from points of view based on assumptions and findings that had had no hearing till then. We had something of value to contribute: a point of view – another way of looking at the world, an alternative art of politics, of love and marriage, of medicine, philosophy and nutrition. We believed these alternative approaches might even lead to some useful shifts in perspective, and would find their due place in the mainstream of affairs which until then had been undilutedly western. But at this moment another scenario invented elsewhere was launched on us. The bombs dropped on Hiroshima and Nagasaki had let loose a reign of terror in the shape of an escalating arms race that kept the world on the brink of a third world war as the two Super Powers matched weapon for weapon, and fought out their rivalries in proxy wars all over the map. One of them made a hell on earth for ten years in Vietnam, and one of their proxy wars has reduced Afghanistan to ruin and destitution. The illusion on which all this devastation and destruction was founded was that two ideologies could not co-exist. It had to be either-or.

For those of us who did not see life in these black and white categories, or see peace in terms of an armed race and armed camps, it was all rather bewildering. The armed camp called the Free World which the non-aligned were being persuaded to join looked like a cocktail of dictatorships and theocracies besides democracies. But apart from this, taking sides made no sense to those who did not want *to* restrict themselves to the *either* or the *or* on offer. We felt kindly toward both, and though each camp warned us of the evils of the other, we hobnobbed with both the capitalists and the communists and felt both were necessary for a world in need of more than one solution. In India we had a hoary tradition of communal living and common ownership of land and individual enterprise. We had no intention of becoming a trophy of either camp by joining its military alliances. But like it or not, and even if one rejected the straitjacket of either-or, everyone had to revolve around the remarkable fiction that the human race is too tiny to accommodate two ideas.

Khruschev once told a joke against himself at a dinner party at the Indian embassy in Moscow. He said he had been touring the country and had come across an ancient ragged peasant. He thumped him on the back and asked him, "Well, grandfather, and how, has life been treating you since the Great October Revolution?" The ancient one said miserably, *"Look* at me", comrade. Before the Great October Revolution I had two coats to wear. Since the revolution I've had only this one, and it is so tattered it is falling off my back." Khruschev said heartily, "Count your blessings, grandfather. Do you know there are countries in the world where people are running around naked because they have absolutely nothing to wear?" The peasant gave a gloomy nod and said, "In that case, comrade, they must have had *their* Great October Revolution long before ours."

I wasn't there on the occasion but I have wondered why on earth Khruschev didn't come to the adult conclusion that it was time to compromise, and give the Great October Revolution a hefty dose of rugged individualism. He might have saved his country from collapse, as America would have saved itself decades of paranoia if it had admitted there was another view of world affairs besides its own.

A scene from Satyajit Ray's film *Pratidwandi* illustrates the point of view many of us were in sympathy with at the time. In the film the hero appears for a job interview. The interviewer asks him what, in his opinion, is man's greatest modern achievement. He replies that it is the heroism of the Vietnamese. As this is the time when Neil Armstrong has just landed on the moon, one of the interviewers asks him why he has placed Vietnamese valour above the moon landing, and he says the moon landing is a triumph of technology, while Vietnam is a triumph of the human spirit.

The either-or hysteria came to an end when the Soviets opened up their system. With glasnost and perestroika it collapsed of its own weaknesses, and the Soviet Union disintegrated under its new pressures. But no sooner had this happened when we were ushered into yet another version of reality that many of us are having a hard time subscribing to, which is that unrestrained competition holds the key to the kingdom of heaven, and the Lord has proven this by vanquishing communism. This latest figment of imagination from elsewhere is being fitted into place by a process known as the globalization of markets, and the market mantra is now the law. It is now the outer casing, the current interpretation of history that we are having to live within.

There is nothing wrong with globalization. Who doesn't want to be part of a changing world, and reap the benefits thereof? But which world? Is it going to be one we can still recognize ourselves in, and have had some little share in designing? As things stand, we are not even sure of a welcome in some parts of it. In spite of all we hear about boundaries dissolving, never did boundaries look solider than they do now, with immigration barriers rising higher and racism taking to the streets. The perils of passage through those barriers and once through them, the perils of arrival, are not so far items that the globalizers have included on their agenda. Maybe that is yet to come, but so far the agenda is not startlingly new. In a manner of speaking colonization was a form of globalization. It built roads and railways, opened sea routes and extended communications to connect up the empire and speed up commerce. Today it is not a one-way process. The globalizers of markets have to consult national sovereignties and seek permissions. Some of their former possessions have become economies to reckon with. There is discussion and bargaining, in international forums. But it revolves around the ground rules laid down by the financial institutions of the west, and it is they who carry the day. And industrial interests are so heavily backed by their governments that aid can be withdrawn and sanctions imposed when markets cannot be had for the asking and when access to a vital commodity such as oil looks threatened, governments think nothing of going to war, as they did in the Gulf.

Within this compulsory marketization of the world, which a friend of mine calls market terrorism, our colonized minds are still hung over with older inflections. Concepts like modernization and development have automatically been taken to mean what the west understands by them. Levels of industry and technology are judged by western standards. Non-Europe, without its own criteria, has no option but to struggle on in imitation of the models and standards set up in the west. This has its own fallout in poor societies. But apparently this is a race that now has to be run, and in circumstances where essential power, from finance to information and armaments, is largely controlled by the west. The nuclear club, with its one non-western member, is a particularly, terrifying monopoly. How it can demand a ban on the proliferation of nuclear weapons when it refuses to disarm itself, is hard to understand, since the only way to prevent the spread of weapons is by universal disarmament. And why nuclear arsenals should be considered safe in the hands of these club members – one of whom is the only country to have put these bombs to actual use – is another bit of reasoning that is hard to fathom. Old sins have long shadows, and the shadows of the bombs dropped on Hiroshima and Nagasaki still lie over us, with the race for nuclear arms continuing, and armaments a thriving industry without whose sales the prosperous economies would be much less prosperous. The world is not a cosy place at this point in time. Who can rest easy in such a world?

And who can rest assured that the redrawing of maps has made it a world where all human beings have equal status? A few months ago, on the 50th anniversary of the end of World War II, I watched programmes about the holocaust. There was also an official apology from Germany for this crime. I was curious about what slant and coverage would be given to the anniversary of Hiroshima. It was mentioned in the news, of course, but the horrific aspect of the atomic bombs was ignored. Though Japan had expressed remorse for its aggression and its wartime oppression of Asian nations, no international leader was present at the ceremony at the memorial, and only a junior United Nations official. And far from there being an apology from the United States for the worst genocide of all time there were justifications of the event, and a celebration of a golden anniversary, the 50th birthday of the atom bomb. Apparently no one need apologize for exterminating the 'lesser breeds'. You will forgive me if I can't think of this world as globalized. And if you ask me what all this has to do with an ACLALS conference, and the field of literature, I would have to say, what else is consciousness composed of but the age it lives in, and if writers do not in some way reflect that age, what are they writing about?

The aim of globalization seems to be the creation of a mono-culture, so that every place on earth will end up looking like Kansas City. The metaphor of Kansas City occurred to me because of the song in the musical, *Oklahoma,* which goes: "Everything's up-to-date in Kansas City, they've gone about as far as they can go." But this is that brand of packaged programmed change that makes short work of history and continuity, and if you have a lot of those, you have a lot to lose. Once the varieties of human culture have been transformed into varieties of tourism, what need is there for memory? That is the process we, in my part of the world, seem to be caught in, and never did an outer casing make such zombies of us, take hold of body, brain and entrails as fast as this one shows every sign of doing. Globalization of this sort looks like one more form of fundamentalism because it sees itself as the one and only way ahead, the only path to progress, when we know very well that nothing of the sort can be true. The oldest wisdom is that there is no single wisdom. Take the matter of diet. The experts keep coming to us with different rules but no one has yet said the last word on what's good for us. Every other day the last word changes. There's a story about a diet researcher who went to interview a 90-year-old man and asked him how he accounted for his longevity. The 90-year-old raised a trembling finger and said, "No drop of liquor ever touched my lips." The researcher wrote this down and then asked how the old gentleman could put up with all the noise coming from upstairs the singing and dancing and yelling, and the 90-year-old shrugged, "Oh, that's just Dad, drunk as usual."

It seems to me that I've always lived in a world according to elsewhere. The concepts it was based on, the point of view it held, were taught to me in textbooks, not as the west's contribution to knowledge, but as indisputable knowledge, and canonized as truths. These were not only the political scenarios written elsewhere. There have been all kinds of scenarios, resting on all kinds of assumptions, that had no particular validity for us, but which all too often we did not challenge or question, not just because they came from that fashionable, powerful and influential elsewhere, but because there seemed no exit from it, no other intellectual space to move in. Let's take the example of psychology, since Freud and Jung and psychoanalysis have dominated life and literature in this century. Why should we be blown before them like leaves in a wind? Are Greek myths, and Oedipus and other complexes, really pivotal to our understanding of our sexual natures? Are there perhaps other ways of exploring states of consciousness? Why not let those in elsewhere sort out their problems with their sons and lovers on psychiatrists' couches, or spill their guts out on television talk shows? What reason is there to be trapped in an alien point of view? And if this is an age known as post-modern, then wouldn't post-modern, like modern, perhaps have a different meaning and implications for us than these concepts have in elsewhere, where they originated? Concepts travel, and travel changes them. Feminism is a case in point. Though autonomy is the goal of women's struggles for equality everywhere, issues of sheer survival and basic human needs give ours a more tormenting dimensions.

Again, what is so final or inevitable or attractive, for us about the economic system that western post-modernism has laid down, complete with its structure, its goals and its values? Do we really go along with an ideology of no-holds-barred competition, and aggressive individualism, in which family, community, the contacts and responsibilities between generations, the welfare of the weak and vulnerable, play no part? Is it really possible that man is an endless consumer whose happiness lies in endless consumption; that more and more toys must be produced for him to play with; that in effect he's no better than a grunting pig with gargantuan appetites, and stuffing those appetites is the right and proper way for him to live? These theories are not alien only to non-Europe. The idea that life is nourished on greed and grab and there is no moral law beyond material satisfactions, must be repugnant to every society on earth. How and why such notions have found gurus and disciples I cannot say – though these are times when all manner of bizarre cults find huge followings – but obviously this particular cult has to be knocked out of existence, laughed out of court, so that if history has indeed come to a stop, as an American academic would have us believe, we can get it going again without delay and human beings can resume their march to a more civilized level of living, and out of the pigs' trough they have been shoved into by the new economic philosophers.

Quite apart from history being allowed to go on, it would be nice if literature went on too. Will it? I wonder if, those who write will be able to disassociate themselves from any outer wrappings they find uncomfortable, so that they can feel free to transmit their own individual perceptions. Empires, after all, were unmade not merely by new arrangements of words on a page, but the new visions and intensities felt through them. Black immigrant literatures have hacked life and laughter and lyricism out of the unrelenting societies around them by, exercising their own independent imaginations and not the ghosts of others. But these achievements took for granted the presentation of an inner freedom in the absence of external freedom. Great works have come out of unfree conditions, as in 19th century Russia, the Soviet Union, East Europe or Latin America. Whether it can happen in India, in the future that is now upon us, I don't know. I don't live in a metropolitan centre and I try not to keep up with trends, but the impression I have is that the Indian elite are entranced with the excitement of eating a potato chip made with French collaboration, and buying a Maiden form bra. I should explain that until recently India had severely restricted imports in order to build up her own industrial infrastructure, so the flood of foreign goods is a novelty. To judge by the glittering goods advertised, and their skyrocketing prices, or by the magazine articles and TV programmes about the rich and famous, whose celebrity rests on how many times a year they pop over to Paris or New York, one could easily come to the conclusion that we are a jet-propelled society, living in a limbo of limitless luxury, and that there's no such place as India anymore.

Instead of the crackle of ideas there once was, inanity rules the day. Newspapers are remaking themselves to become more marketable, and since markets don't need editors, this disappearing breed has gone into other media jobs and been replaced by marketing managers. Publishers, like some of their counterparts elsewhere, have become purveyors of merchandise. And the electronic media, which now has a unique opportunity to use the latest technology to project the themes and images that concern us, is giving impeccable imitations of tasteless fare from the west. The pornography hitting the market follows suit, and this is truly disappointing as one had expected something more original than the regulation nude centerfolds, and what the textile tycoon's ex-mistress told her rival after their fourth double scotch on the rocks. From the inheritors of Kama Sutra, Khajuraho, and other sophisticated splendours in word and stone, one had hoped for a touch of class. But just as Macdonald's rubbery hamburger may soon drive the sublime shami kebab out of the market, our pornographers have settled for dreary derivative porn instead of blazing a new trail. As we were once interpreted by others through the lenses of the Raj, we are now interpreting ourselves in the jargon, and by the norms and market values, of globalization. As a child I was once shown the newspaper picture of Mahatma Gandhi striding up the stairs of Buckingham Palace in his loincloth, for a meeting with His Majesty the King. Looking back, there is a magnificence about that picture. It seems to symbolize how two cultures *should* meet, each with its dignity and integrity intact.

The Indian scene is much more Indian than the zombie-like rush for buying, selling and mimicking, hallowed by the media and the advertisers. would have us believe. Our virtues and our vices are all our own. Politics, once an altar for self-sacrifice and idealism, now offers dazzling criminal opportunities. The classic villains of fiction and cinema in the 1930s and 40s – the landlords, the moneylenders, the priests – begin to look like babes in arms compared with the dashing new breed. Then we've got militant Hinduism, two words which since time began could never be linked because they were mutually contradictory. Now efforts are being made to join them by politicians who are busy rewriting Indian history, and to listen to the chitchat on the lawns and in the bars of exclusive clubs, about eight hundred years of Hindu-Muslim culture might never have existed. There have been changes at every level, the major one being convulsions in the caste structure that have stood the caste system on its head. The once backward castes govern states, and control positions of wealth and power. The western-educated high caste elite to whom the British transferred power in 1947 have long since had their day. The several hundred million Indians blotted out by the advertisers are demonstrating their clout in ways we like and don't like. Will the writers among us have a sense of the history that has brought all this about? Will they say anything of all this? Will we carry the awareness that will translate into what we alone have to offer, and not just into cleverness and special effects?

The best writers in the west have their national and group experiences branded into them – their French and Russian and American revolutions, their golden ages and disasters. We were branded by training in their histories and literatures and methodologies, more with their experiences than our own. But this was a condition that was passing, when the current known as globalization swept us on the road to Kansas City, and swept everything from sausages to writing into the same market value production line. Gobbled into this new framework from elsewhere, what can a pen put on paper but words that have no past, and probably very little future? There may well be words that will attract investment in the industry that writing has become; words that may take us backward, concocting versions of the orient as it is still expected to be, complete with ethnic flourishes and misty mysticisms and bags of tricks. The Indian writer, Mulk Raj Anand, points out the contrast in angle of vision between his own story of an orphan in his novel *Coolie,* who is a real Indian orphan, and Kipling's colourful fantasy character, Kim, who helps the British to protect their Indian empire from the Russians. Will we be back to variations of *Kim?* Or, will we be seduced by the mechanized, globalized words and images spawned by the new technologies, and divorced from our own context and conditions? For people whose main resource is their imagination, technology may reserve its most death-dealing devices. I know technology is sacrosanct, and has been written into the scripture of what is known as progress, but there must be a point beyond which we do not let it usurp our human functions, and that point may well have been reached. But mesmerized by it, will we in India well and truly return to being creatures of elsewhere?

I am reminded of a friend of mine years ago in Bombay, a cultivated, elegant, much admired woman. There was something about her that used to puzzle me, that I couldn't quite place, until I realized that if I closed my eves and shut out her dark skin and her sari, and thought of her as an upper class Englishwoman, everything about her fell into place. In India the old order died no violent death. It was bowed out. In the drawing rooms of Bombay high society in the late 1950s, it was still very much around. My friend charmingly reflected its accent, its conversation, its culture. These were the masks Indians had once worn in order to be invited to the ball as it were, to be acceptable in ruling circles, and a good many of them had never taken them off. Maybe they had become a second skin and they felt more comfortable with them than with the Indian reality around them or maybe their indoctrination had made them incapable of a relationship with India, except as outsiders and unfit for any role except one in a masquerade. I told her once that I had been to the airport to receive Ho Chi Minh and found him one of the gentlest and most affectionate of men, and this filled her with genuine amazement, for she genuinely believed he was a monster. She also believed India was not going to last out the next decade. The country was going to fall apart. A foreign think-tank had told her so. Thus, when we wear masks, do the demons of others become our demons, and their gods, our gods. And I have an overwhelming sense of deja vu today as I look around me when I go to Delhi, which is more advanced in matters of globalization than Dehra Dun, where I live. It seems to me we are yet again acting and reacting within the confines of a provided framework. Perhaps it is still a case of having to wear a mask or not being invited to the ball. It is certainly still the case that the journeys we make continue to take us westward, to what is still the centre of the world.

It is these journeys to what is still the centre of the world, a Mecca even in our own consciousness, that create the illusion that because varieties of people flock to that Mecca, we are now living in a cosmopolitan era; that literature, too, is becoming cosmopolitan, unfettered by frontiers or a frontier consciousness, and that it no longer needs to start from a place of its own. This bit of logic is like the Miss Universe contest, which chooses the most beautiful woman in the universe from twenty-one glamorous contestants, after which she goes on to advertise Coca Cola. The word cosmopolitan similarly covers a handful compared with the mass of people who feel at home only in a particular soil, many of them untouched by outer trends. 'Cosmopolitan' has about it the exclusive luxurious tinkle of privileged culture. When I hear that the world is fast becoming cosmopolitan, or that it is now a global village, I feel I must be living in another world, not the one all the experts are talking about. And I think this is entirely possible since it is far from being One World.

Speaking at an ACLALS conference a few years ago I asked when post-colonial would stop being post-colonial. Now I wonder when exile stops being exile. I'm not sure I understand the word the way it is now used, to cover so many variations on the theme. I have come across book reviews referring to the book's author as exiled. Recently I came across a book which was partly about the effects of exile on writers and their writing. The dictionary definition, which is banishment, or long absence from one's country, would not fit them all. Can exile, when it is the result of choosing to live somewhere else be exile? Can such a person's state of mind and being, however nostalgic, in any way resemble the sense of displacement and loss that plagues those who have been forced to leave home, as political or economic refugees? Can the label of exile be pinned on all expatriate writing? I read very little and I know nothing about the vocabulary of criticism, so I may be quite wrong in thinking that the word exile has acquired a cult flavour, and come to have extravagant all purpose meanings almost as if Rupert Murdoch, on acquiring American nationality, had become an exile.

In 1992, the *Guardian*, published a series of articles under the heading "Writing Home", in which around the world reflected on their nationality, and described their feelings for the country they called home. I thought I would find in these articles a rejection of the sentiment people once attached to their native soil, even a thankfulness at having shed all that, either metaphorically, or by literally moving to new territory. I thought my own contribution to the series would show up an unfashionable attachment to my roots in an age when cross-cultural connections are supposed to matter more than roots. I thought I would be in a minority of one. To my surprise there were several like me, for whom a national identity was not only *not* out of date, but a source of selfhood. Two of these writers, with opportunities to settle in the west, decided to remain in their authoritarian homelands. The Chinese writer, Zhang Xianliang, had spent 22 years in a labour camp and was still not being published in China, yet these are his words:

> Perhaps there are some who belong to the world and not to one country. I cannot be such a person. In my body and spirit I can belong only to China. I do not believe that there can be a truly universal literature which is not attached to any particular society. Even Shakespeare's works belong in the end to England.

The Czech writer, Ivan Klima, was visiting London when Soviet troops invaded Czechoslovakia, but he went home. In his words:

> home, where at any moment the police could ring the doorbell and search my flat, take me off for interrogation or even arrest me. Home where my wife was continually getting the sack, where I didn't know whether my children would be allowed to study, and where I was banned from publishing.... But I was born here and have accepted it as destiny that my home is here. The worst thing for me would be to discover that my home is nowhere, or that it is everywhere, which is no more than a substitute for ... 'nowhere,' and is intended to fill more easily that empty space in the soul which the loss of home tends to leave behind.

Likewise, Shusako Endo of Japan, who writes about the suffering of the Japanese during the war, the horror of the atomic strikes, the humiliation of defeat, and what Japan has lost in the race to become an industrialized power, concludes: "However, as a Japanese, I cannot desert Japan." And Chinua Achebe of Nigeria, who had no choice but to leave Nigeria if he wanted to stay alive writes: "The hard words Nigeria and I have said to each other look like words of anxious love, not hate." Shusako Endo also writes: "Many Japanese especially the young are gripped by a sense of emptiness. One manifestation of this is the ... large number of people travelling overseas." It would seem that the plant of universalism, at least according to these writers, is itself a product of having stayed rooted. And incidentally, I've often wondered what sort of books Henry James would have written if *he'd* stayed home during the wonderful turbulent years of America's tremendous growth as a nation.

True cosmopolitanism, which would mean partaking of a world culture, cannot exist, there being no world culture, only the Europe centeredness that substitutes for one. On the other hand, wars of identity rage all about us, including here on this once serene island, and few are as fortunate as Naipaul in being able to sort out their enigmas of identity in peaceful, affluent surroundings. Those countries of Europe that are the most advanced and stable areas of the world are just as fiercely obsessed with their identity, and with keeping their racial identity unsullied, when they pass laws to restrain or prohibit non-white immigration. Whether identity bares its teeth and claws in actual battle, or dresses soberly and speaks in suave accents, or is simply the need within us to stay home, it is very much with us.

But if all I have said sounds like a plea for nationalism, my plea is for the very opposite. Separateness is probably the most absurd and dangerous of all illusions. There never was a time when it was a sound idea. My own belief is in a reconciliation of cultures, of the sort that Nelson Mandela and Aung San Su Kyi have come to represent in politics. It is not time for me to become more like you, and to pattern myself on your ways, or to write what pleases you. What it is time for is for us to harmonize our ways of living and thinking, so that we will never be strangers to one another again; so that from a relationship their partakes of all our identities, a truly cosmopolitan world, and a genuinely universal literature can arise.

bell hooks

(b 1952)

Born in 1952, bell hooks nee Gloria Watkins, studied at the universities of Stanford, Wisconsin and California. She began with writing plays and poems, but soon felt compelled to challenge the notion of 'white feminism' and its claim to represent all women. It failed to take note of the differences and multiplicities present in social reality. In 1981 came out hooks's statement on black feminism in *Ain't I a Woman* to be followed by *Feminist Theory: From Margin to Center* (1984), *Talking back, thinking feminist, thinking black* (1989), and several other books. hook's fascination with the lower case tells its own story of her need to obliterate hegemonic structures and power symbols. This also finds a reflection in her pedagogical concerns which move outside the classroom in *Teaching to Transgress*.

When *Ain't I a Woman: Black Women and Feminism* came out, it was initially met with tremendous resistance and hostility because it brought in race as a category and interrogated the assumption that women 'share a common plight', an assumption which would automatically rest everything on the biological sex than on social constructs and environment.

bell hooks traces the history of black feminism through the resistance of the slaves, and points out that histories go a long way to create the basis both of protest and of antagonisms. There is an underlying statement that women of any one category need to look at the experience of women of other categories in order to address feminist positions in any meaningful way.

Critical of the blurring of differences which lead to intensification of power on one side and erasure on the other. hooks stresses the socio-cultural specificities which mark the existence of third world women.

Black Women and Feminism

More than a hundred years have passed since the day Sojourner Truth stood before an assembled body of white women and men at an anti-slavery rally in Indiana and bared her breasts to prove that she was indeed a woman. To Sojourner, who had traveled the long road from slavery to freedom, the baring of her breasts was a small matter. She faced her audience without fear, without shame, proud of having been born black and female. Yet the white man who yelled at Sojourner, "I don't believe you really are a woman," unwittingly voiced America's contempt and disrespect for black womanhood. In the eyes of the 19th century white public, the black female was a creature unworthy of the title woman; she was mere chattel, a thing, an animal. When Sojourner Truth stood before the second annual convention of the women's rights movement in Akron, Ohio, in 1852, white women who deemed it unfitting that a black woman should speak on a public platform in their presence screamed: "Don't let her speak!" Sojourner endured their protests and became one of the first feminists to call their attention to the lot of the black slave woman who, compelled by circumstance to labor alongside black men, was a living embodiment of the truth that women could be the work-equals of men.

It was no mere coincidence that Sojourner Truth was allowed on stage after a white male spoke against the idea of equal rights for women, basing his argument on the notion that woman was too weak to perform her share of manual labor that she was innately the physical inferior to man. Sojourner quickly responded to his argument, telling her audience:

> ...Well, children, whar dar is so much racket dar must be something out o' kilter. I tink dat twixt de niggers of de Souf and de women at de Norf all a talking' bout rights, de white men will be in a fix pretty soon. But what's all dis here talkin' bout? Dat man over dar say dat women needs to be helped into carriages, and lifted ober ditches, and to have de best places...and ain't I a woman? Look at me! Look at my arm!.... I have plowed, and planted, and gathered into barns, and no man could head me – and aint I a woman? I could work as much as any man (when I could get it), and bear de lash as well – and aint I a woman? I have borne five children and I seen 'em mos all sold off into slavery, and when I cried out with a mother's grief, none but Jesus hear – and ain't I a woman?

Unlike most white women's rights advocates, Sojourner Truth could refer to her own personal life experience as evidence of woman's ability to function as a parent; to be the work-equal of man; to undergo persecution, physical abuse, rape, torture; and to not only survive but emerge triumphant.

Sojourner Truth was not the only black woman to advocate social equality for women. Her eagerness to speak publicly in favor of women's rights despite public disapproval and resistance paved the way for other politically minded black women to express their views. Sexism and racism have so informed the perspective of American historiographers that they have tended to overlook and exclude the effort of black women in discussions of the American women's rights movement. White female scholars who support feminist ideology have also ignored the contribution of black women. In contemporary works, like *The Remembered Gate: Origins of American Feminism* by Barbara Berg, *Herstory* by June Sochen, *Hidden from History* by Sheila Rowbothan, *The Women's Movement* by Barbara Deckard, to name a few, the role black women played as advocates for women's rights in the 19th century is never mentioned. Eleanor Flexner's *Century of Struggle,* which was first published in 1959, remains one of the very few book-length historical works on the women's rights movement that documents the participation of black women.

Most women involved in the recent move toward a feminist revolution assume that white women have initiated all feminist resistance to male chauvinism in American society, and further assume that black women are not interested in women's liberation. While it is true that white women have led every movement toward feminist revolution in American society, their dominance is less a sign of black female disinterest in feminist struggle than an indication that the politics of colonization and racial imperialism have made it historically impossible for black women in the United States to lead a women's movement.

Nineteenth century black women were more aware of sexist oppression than any other female group in American society has ever been. Not only were they the female group most victimized by sexist discrimination and sexist oppression, their powerlessness was such that resistance on their part could rarely take the form of organized collective action. The 19th century women's rights movement could have provided a forum for black women to address their grievances, but white female racism barred them from full participation in the movement. Furthermore, it served as a grave reminder that racism had to be eliminated before black women would be recognized as having an equal voice with white women on the issue of women's rights. Women's organizations and clubs in the 19th century were almost always racially segregated, but that did not mean that black female participants in such groups were any less committed to women's rights than white participants.

Contemporary historiographers tend to over-emphasize the 19th century black female's commitment to eliminating racism so as to make it seem that their involvement with anti-racist work precluded involvement in women's rights activities. An example of this trend can be found in June Sochen's work *Herstory,* where she discusses white women's organizations in a chapter titled "The Women's Movement" but discusses black women's organization in a chapter titled "Old Problems: Black American," a categorization which implies that black women's organizations emerged as part of the general effort of black people to end racism, not as part of their participation in the women's movement. Sochen writes:

> Black women's clubs were organized locally to perform charitable and educational services. Similar in purpose and nature to white women's clubs, the National Association of Colored Women was formed in 1896 and, led by Mary Church Terrell (1863-1954), it had more than 100,000 members in 26 states within four years. While one local chapter would be organizing a hospital for blacks, another would be developing a kindergarten program for the black children of its community.
>
> One of the first black women to graduate from Oberlin College, Mary Church Terrell was an articulate and prominent spokeswoman for black Americans' rights. An extraordinary person, she spent her long life working for the freedom of black people. She was a good speaker and writer for a variety of causes. In addition to heading the NACW, Mrs. Terrell campaigned against lynching, became a charter member of the NAACP, and worked for the suffrage movement as well. She represented black women at many national and international meetings.

From the information provided in these paragraphs, readers might easily conclude that Mary Church Terrell was a passionate spokesperson for black American rights who was not overly concerned with rights for women. This was not so. As president of the National Association of Colored Women, Mary Church Terrell worked arduously to involve black women in the women's rights struggle. She was particularly concerned that they struggle to obtain social equality for their sex in the educational sphere. That Mary Church Terrell, like most black women's rights advocates, was also committed to uplifting her race as a whole in no way diminished the fact that the focus of her attention was on changing the role of women in society. Had Terrell considered herself to be spokesperson for the black race as a whole she would not have published "A Colored Woman in a White World," a narrative that discussed the social status of black women and the impact of racism and sexism on their lives.

No white feminist historian would write about the efforts of Lucy Stone, Elizabeth Stanton, Lucretia Mott and others to initiate social reforms that would affect primarily white women as if their efforts were completely divorced from the issue of women's rights.

Yet historians who label themselves feminists continually minimize the contribution of black women's rights advocates by implying that their focus was solely on racial reforms measures. Because of white racial imperialism, white women could organize groups like the Women's Christian Temperance Union, Young Women's Christian Association, General Federation of Women's Clubs, without explicitly stating in their heading that these organizations were exclusively white. Black women identified themselves racially calling their groups Colored Women's League, National Federation of Afro-American Women, National Association for Colored Women, and because they identified themselves by race scholars assume that their interest in the elevation of blacks as a group overshadowed their involvement with woman's effort to effect social reform. In fact, black female reform organizations were solidly rooted in the women's movement. It was in reaction to the racism of white women and to the fact that the U.S. remained a society with an apartheid social structure that compelled black women to focus on themselves rather than all women.

Black activist Josephine St. Pierre Ruffin tried to work with white women's organizations and found that black women could not depend on racist white women to encourage them to fully participate in the women's reform movement; consequently, she demanded that black women organize to address issues for themselves. At the First National Conference of Colored Women held in Boston in 1895, she told her audience:

> The reasons why we should confer are so apparent that it would seem hardly necessary to enumerate them, and yet there is none of them but demand our serious consideration. In the first place we need to feel the cheer and inspiration of meeting with each other, we need to gain the courage and fresh life that comes from the mingling of congenial souls, of those working for the same ends. Next, we need to talk over not only those things which are of vital importance to us as women, but also the things that are of especial interest to us as colored women, the training of our children, opening for our boys and girls how they can be prepared for occupations and occupations may be found or opened for them, what we especially can do in the moral education of the

> race with which we are identified, our mental elevation and physical development, the home training it is necessary to give our children in order to prepare them to meet the peculiar conditions in which they shall find themselves, how to make the most of our own, to some extent limited opportunities, these are some of our own peculiar questions to be discussed. Besides these are the general questions of the day, which we cannot afford to be indifferent to....

Ruffin did not encourage black women's rights advocates to work solely to improve their own lot, she maintained that black women needed to organize so that they could lead a women's movement that would address the concerns of all women:

> Our woman's movements is a woman's movement that is led and directed by women for the good of women and men, for the benefit of all humanity, which is more than any one branch or section of it. We want, we ask the active interest of our men, and, too, we are not drawing the color line; we are women, American women, as intensely interested in all that pertains to us as such as all other American women; we are not alienating or withdrawing, we are only coming to the front, willing to join any others in the same work and cordially inviting and welcoming any others to join us.

Other black women's rights advocates echoed Ruffin's sentiments. Despite the fact that white racial imperialism excluded black women from participating in groups with white women, they remained committed to he belief that women's rights could be attained only if women joined together to present a united front. Addressing the World Congress of Representative Women, black suffragist Fannie Barrier Williams made it known that black women were as committed to the struggle for women's rights as any other group of women. In her address she voiced the belief that women joined in political solidarity would have a tremendous impact on American culture:

> The power of organized womanhood is one of the most interesting studies of modern sociology. Formerly women knew so little of each other mentally, their common interests were so sentimental and gossipy, and their knowledge of all the larger

> affairs of human society was so meager that organization among them, in the modern sense, was impossible. Now their liberal intelligence, their contact in all the great reformatory movements of the age has created in them a grater respect for each other, and furnished the elements of organization for large and splendid purposes. The highest ascendancy of woman's development has been reached when they have become mentally strong enough to find bonds of association interwoven with sympathy, loyalty, and mutual trustfulness. Today union is the watchword of woman's onward march.

Although racial segregation was the norm in women's organization, reform measures initiated by white and black women's groups were not radically different. They differed only in that black women included in their reform efforts measures that were aimed at solving specific problems they faced. One such problem was the general tendency among white Americans and even some brainwashed blacks to regard all black women as sexually immoral, licentious, and wanton – a negative stereotype that had its origin in American Sexist mythology. Consequently, while white women's organizations could concentrate their attentions on general reform measures, black women had to launch a campaign to defend their 'virtue'. As part of their campaign they wrote articles and speeches upholding black female sexual morality.

White women's organizations could confine their attention to issues such as education, charity, or to the formation of literary societies, while black women were concerned with issues such as poverty, care for the elderly and disabled, or prostitution. Black female clubs and organizations were potentially more feminist and radical in nature than white women's clubs because of the difference in their circumstance created by racist oppression. White women as a group did not have to launch an attack on prostitution as did black women. Many young black women leaving the South and migrating north were compelled to work as prostitutes. In some cases, they would come North on what was called a justice ticket, supplied them by employment agencies or labor agents. In exchange for transportation and the guarantee of a job on arrival, black women signed contracts to work where the agent placed them and agreed to pay a fee equivalent to one or two month's wages. On arriving north they would find their jobs were mainly as maids in houses of prostitution. Unable to survive on the low salary paid them, they would be encouraged to become prostitutes by white "pimps." The National League for the Protection of Colored Women was formed to inform and aid southern black women migrating north. In 1897, black activist Victoria Earle Matthews formed the White Rose Working Girl's Home and a Black Protection and Women's Rights Society in the Women's Loyal Union of New York and Brooklyn. To further acquaint the public with the plight of white women, Victoria Matthews delivered a lecture on "The Awakening of the Afro-American Woman." Her work was not done in isolation. Numerous black women's organizations were formed to help black women in their struggle for self-improvement.

Of those black women who advocated social equality for women, Anna Julia Cooper was one of the most outstanding. She was one of the first black activists to urge black women to articulate their own experiences and to make the public aware of the way in which racism and sexism together affected their social status. Ann Cooper wrote:

> The colored woman of today occupies, one might say, a unique position in this country. In a period of itself transitional and unsettled, her status seems one of the ascertainable and definitive of all the forces which makes for our civilization. She is confronted by a woman question and a race problem, and is as yet an unknown or unacknowledged factor in both.

Anna Cooper wanted the U.S. public to recognize the role black women played not just as spokespersons for their race but as advocates of rights for women. To spread her views on women's rights, she published *A Voice from the South in 1892,* one of the first feminist discussions of the social status of black women and a lengthy discussions of woman's right to higher education. In *A Voice from the South,* Cooper reiterated her belief that black women should not assume a passive subordinate position in relationship to black men. She also criticized black males for their refusal to support woman's effort to obtain equal rights. Since it was common for black leaders to question whether or not black female involvement in the struggle for women's rights would undermine their involvement in the struggle to eliminate racism, Cooper maintained that social equality of the sexes would mean that black women would be able to serve as leaders in the struggle against racism. She further argued that they had in fact shown themselves to be as committed to the black liberation struggle as black men, if note more so.

Included in *A Voice from the South* was an essay by Cooper on "The Higher Education of Women" in which she argued that women as a collective group should have the right to acquire higher education. Like many modern-day feminists, Cooper believed in the existence of a distinct "feminine principle" and argued that "a great want of the world in the past has been a feminine force," a force which could have "its full effect only through the untrammeled development of women."

> All I claim is that there is a feminine as well as a masculine side to truth; that these are related not as inferior and superior, not as better and worse, not as weaker and stronger, but as complements – complements in one necessary and symmetric whole. That as the man is more noble in reason, so the woman is more quick in sympathy. That as he is indefatigable in pursuit of abstract truth, so is she in caring for the interests by the way striving tenderly and lovingly that not one of the least of these "little ones" should perish. That while we not unfrequently see women who reason, we say, with the coolness and precision of a man, and men as considerate of helplessness as a woman, still there is a general consensus of mankind that one trait is essentially masculine and the other is peculiarly feminine. That both are needed to be worked into the training of children, in order that boys may supplement their virility by tenderness and sensibility, and our girls may round out their gentleness by strength and self-reliance. That, as both are alike necessary in giving symmetry to the individual, so a nation or a race will degenerate into mere emotionalism on the one hand, or bullying on the other, if dominated by either exclusively; lastly, and most emphatically, that the feminine factor can have its proper effect only through woman's development and education so that she may fitly and intelligently stamp her force on the forces of her

> day, and add her modicum to the riches of the world's thought....

Even though Anna Cooper, like other 19th century women's rights advocates, continued to believe that woman could best serve her country by using education to enhance the sex role assigned her by patriarchy, she was aware that higher education would also enable women to explore worlds outside the traditional realm of home and family. To answer those who argued the higher education interfered with marriage, Cooper replied:

> I grant you that intellectual development, with the self-reliance and capacity for earning a livelihood which it gives, renders woman less dependent on the marriage relation for physical support (which, by the way, does not always accompany it). Neither is she compelled to look to sexual love as the one sensation capable of giving tone and relish, movement and vim to the life she lives. Her horizon is extended. Her sympathies are broadened and deepened and multiplied. She is in closer touch with nature....

Nineteenth century black women believed that were they given the right to vote, they could change the educational system so that women would have the right to pursue fully their educational goals. To achieve this end they wholeheartedly supported woman suffrage. Black woman activist Frances Ellen Watkins Harper was more outspoken on the subject of woman suffrage than any other black woman of her day. In 1888 she addressed the International Council of Women in Washington and spoke on the importance of suffrage to black and white women. At the Columbian Exposition in Chicago in 1893 she delivered an address titled "Woman's Political Future" expressing her views on suffrage:

> I do not believe in unrestricted and universal suffrage for either men or women. I believe in moral and educational tests. I do not believe that the most ignorant and brutal man is better prepared to add value to the strength and durability of the government than the most cultured, upright, and intelligent woman.... The ballot in the hands of woman means power added to influence. How well she will use that power I cannot foretell. Great evils stare us in the face that need to be throttled by the combined

> power of an upright manhood and an enlightened womanhood; and I know that no nation can gain its full measure of enlightenment and happiness if one-half of it is free and the other half is fettered. China compressed the feet of her women and thereby retarded the steps of her men.

As in the 19th century struggle over the issue of woman suffrage, in the 20th century struggle, race and sex became interlocking issues. Like their predecessors, white women consciously and deliberately supported white racial imperialism, openly disavowing feelings of empathy and political solidarity with black people. In their efforts to secure the ballot, white women's rights advocates willingly betrayed the feminist belief that voting was the natural right of every woman. Their willingness to compromise feminist principles allowed the patriarchal power structure to co-opt the energy of women suffragists and sue the votes of women to strengthen the existing anti-woman political structure. The great majority of white women did not use their voting privileges to support women's issues; they voted as their husbands, fathers, or brothers voted. The more militant white suffragists had hoped that women would use the vote to form their own party rather than supporting major parties that denied women social equality with men. Voting privileges for women changed in no fundamental way the lot of women in society, but they did enable women to help support and maintain the existing white raciest imperialist patriarchal social order. To a very grave extent women obtaining the right to vote was more victory for racist principle than a triumph of feminist principles.

Black female suffragists found that the vote had little impact on their social status. The most militant wing of the 1920s women's movement, the National Woman's Party, was both racist and classist. Even though the party pledged to work for full equality for women, it actively worked to promote solely the interests of white middle and upper class women. In *Herstory*, June Sochen makes this comment on the attitude of white suffragists toward black women:

> After the woman's suffrage amendment was passed in 1920, some reformers wondered whether it would benefit black

women as well a white women – the South where black men had been virtually disenfranchised by the white power-holders. Over two million newly enfranchised black women lived in the South. When suffragists suggested to Alice Paul that the voting rights of black women would be a continuing vital issue, she replied that the year 1920 was not the time to discuss that question. Rather, she said, the suffragists should enjoy their new political power and make plans for other battles in the future. Yet as the reformers had foreseen, when black women went to the polls in Alabama or Georgia, they found that white election officials had a bag of tricks ready to prevent them from voting. If a black woman could read a complicated text put before her, the white official would find some other obscure reason why she was ineligible to vote. And any woman who persisted was threatened with violence if she did not obediently slink away.

When women suffrage failed to alter in any way the social status of black women, many black female suffragist became disillusioned with women's rights. They had supported woman suffrage only to find their interests betrayed, only to find that "woman suffrage" would be used as a weapon to strengthen white oppression of black people. They found that obtaining rights for women would have little impact on their social status as long as white racial imperialism automatically denied them full citizenship. While white women were rejoicing over obtaining the right to vote, a system of racial apartheid was being institutionalized throughout the U.S. that would threaten the freedom of black women far more crucially than sexual imperialism. That system of racial apartheid was called Jim Crow. In *The Strange Career of Jim Crow,* C. Vann Woodward describes this resurgence of racism:

> In the postwar era there were new indications that the Southern Way was spreading as the American Way in race relations. The great migration of the Negro into the residential slum areas and the industrial plants of the big northern cities increased tension between races. Northern labor was jealous of its status and resentful of the competition of Negroes, who were excluded from unions. Negroes were pushed out of the more desirable jobs in industries that they had succeeded in invading during the

> manpower shortage of the war years. They were squeezed out of federal employment more and more. Negro postmen began to disappear from their old routes as they did from the police beats. They began to lose their grip upon crafts such as that of the barbers, which had once been a virtual monopoly in the South.
>
> Racism in regimented form was spread over the whole country in the twenties by the new Ku Klux Klan....
>
> There was no apparent tendency toward abatement or relaxation of the Jim Crow code of discrimination and segregation in the 1920's, and none in the thirties until well along in the depression years. In fact the Jim Crow laws were elaborated and further expanded in those years. Much social and economic history is reflected in the new laws. When women began to bob their hair and became patrons of the barbershops, Atlanta passes an ordinance in 1926 forbidding Negro barbers to serve women or children under fourteen years of age. Jim Crow kept step with the march of progress in transportation and industry, as well as with the changed in fashion.

As Jim Crow apartheid threatened to strip black people of the rights and achievements they had acquired during Reconstruction, it was only natural that black female activists ceased to struggle over women's rights issues and concentrated their energies on resisting racism.

Black women activists were not the only group of women to shift their attention away from women's rights issues. Because much of the energy of female activists had focused on the vote, once it was obtained many women saw no further need for a women's movement. Although white women in the Woman's Party continued feminist struggle, black women were rarely active participants. Their energies were focused on resisting mounting racial oppression.

In the forty years from the mid-1920s to mid-1960s black female leaders no longer advocated women's rights. The struggle for black liberation and the struggle for women's liberation were seen as inimical largely because black civil rights leaders did not want the white American public to see their demands for full citizenship as synonymous with a radical demand for equality of the sexes. They made black liberation synonymous with gaining full participation in the existing patriarchal nation-state and their demands were for the elimination of racism, not capitalism or patriarchy. Just as white women had publicly disavowed any political connection with black people when they believed that such an alliance was inimical to their interests, black women disassociated themselves from feminist struggle when they were convinced that to appear feminist, i.e. radical, would hurt the cause of black liberation. Black men and women wanted entrance they felt it was necessary for them to be conservative.

Black women's organizations, which at one time had concentrated on social services like child care, homes for working women and help for prostitutes, became de-politicized and focused more on social affairs like debutante balls and fundraisers. Black women club members imitated the behavior of middle class white women. Those black women who believed in social equality of the sexes learned to suppress their opinions for fear attention might be shifted from racial issues. They believed they should first support freedom for black people, then later, when that freedom was obtained, work for women's rights. Unfortunately, they did not foresee the strength of black male resistance to the idea that women should have equal status with men.

Lorraine Hansberry's play was a foretelling of future conflicts between black women and men over the issue of sex-role patterns. This conflict was exaggerated and brought to public attention by the 1965 publication of Danial Moynihan's report *The Negro Family: The Case for National Action.* In his report Moynihan argued that the black American family was being undermined by female dominance. He claimed that racist discrimination against black men in the work force caused black families to have a matriarchal structure which he asserted was out of line with the white American norm, the patriarchal family structure, and that this prevented black race from being accepted into the mainstream of American life. Moynihan's message was similar to that of black women who admonished black men for not assuming the patriarchal role. The difference in the two perspectives was that Moynihan placed a measure of the responsibility for the black male's inability to assume a patriarchal role on black women, whereas black women felt that racism and black male indifference were the forces that caused black men to reject the role of sole economic provider.

By labeling black women matriarchs, Moynihan implied that those black women who worked and headed households were the enemies of black manhood. Even though Moynihan's supposition that the black family was matriarchal was based on data that showed that only one-fourth of all black families in America were female-headed households, he used this figure to make generalizations about black families as a whole. His generalizations about black family structure, though erroneous, had a tremendous impact upon the black male psyche. Like the American white male in the 50s and 60s, black men were concerned that all women were becoming too assertive and domineering.

The notion that modern women were emasculating men had its origin not in the conflict between black women and black men over sex-role patterns but in the overall conflict in American society over the issue of sex roles. Women as castrator was an image first evoked not in reference to black women and certainly not by Daniel Moynihan; it was popularized by certain psychoanalysts who had their heyday in the 50s. They imposed upon the consciousness of the American public the notion that any career woman, any woman who competed with men, was envious of male power and was likely to be a castrating bitch.

Black women came to be depicted as female castrators par excellence, though not because they were inherently more assertive and independent than white women. History shows that white women were actively competing in the male-dominated power structure long before black women because there was no racial barrier to make entrance into that sphere completely impossible. Black women became the target for many misogynist attacks on female independence largely because of racist scapegoating. Just as the 19th century white public had portrayed black women as embodying all negative traits that were usually attributed to the female sex as a whole while portraying white public continued this practice. They idealized and elevated the status of the white female group by debasing and degrading the black female group. Daniel Moynihan did not attempt to document the fact that the so-called "matriarchal" role black women assumed in the female-headed household was the same as the one white women assumed in the female-headed household. Instead, he continued to perpetuate one of the United States most popular sexist-racist myths about black womanhood – the myth that black women are inherently more assertive, independent, and domineering than white women.

Sexist ideology was the core of the matriarchy myth. Implicit in the assertion that black women were matriarchs was the assumption that patriarchy should be maintained at all costs and that the subordination of the female was necessary for the healthy achievement of manhood. In effect, Moynihan suggested that the negative effects of racist oppression of black people could be eliminated if black females were more passive, subservient and supportive of patriarchy. Once again, woman's liberation was presented as inimical to black liberation.

The extent to which black men absorbed this ideology was made evident in the 60s black liberation movement. Black male leaders of the movement made the liberation of black people from racist oppression synonymous with their gaining the right to assume the role of patriarch, of sexist oppressor. By allowing white men to dictate the terms by which they would define black liberation, black men chose to endorse sexist exploitation and oppression of black women. And in so doing they were compromised. They were not liberated from the system but liberated to serve the system. The movement ended and the system had not changed; it was no less racist or sexist.

Chandra Talpade Mohanty
(b 1955)

Chandra Talpade Mohanty, India born, educated in Mumbai, and now working in United States is a third world feminist. She takes bell hooks's argument even further but shifts it into a different direction. Neither colour nor sex in itself governs the feminist struggle instead it is the notion of power which needs to be addressed.

In her introductory chapter to *Feminism Without Borders* she writes: "In my own life, borders have come in many guises, and I live with them inside as well as across racialized women's communities. I grew up in Mumbai, where the visible demarcations between India and Pakistan, Hindu and Muslim, rich and poor, British and Indian, women and men, Dalit and Brahmin were a fact of everyday life". But this very Mumbai was also the home of multiple languages and cultures and learning and knowledge permeated these borders. Similarly moving from one city to another in the States, she has experienced the need to cross borders. Borders are both exclusionary and enabling according to her.

The new threat to women is from globalization. Mohanty addresses the question of being a woman in this society where the reference points are constantly shifting and challenges to feminism have "grown exponentially".

There is, in her work, a constant interrogation of capitalist positions and a recognition that differences cannot be ignored. At the same time there is strong need to work together in spite of the differences. She has emerged as one of those voices which have not allowed the dialogue with western concepts to overtake or shadow issues of her origins – location and history are not at war. How does one *write* and experience 'minorityism' is an ongoing concern in her work.

This extract is from *Feminism Without Borders* and forms the concluding section of Chapter II, "Cartographies of Struggle".

Anthropology and the Third World Woman as "Native"

One of the most crucial forms of knowledge produced by, indeed born of, colonial rule is the discipline of anthropology. While I do not intend to offer a comprehensive analysis of the origins of this discipline in the racialized and sexualized relations of colonial rule, a brief example of these links clarifies my point. I want to suggest that anthropology is an important discursive context in this cartography and that it is an example of disciplinary knowledge that signifies the power of naming and the contests over meaning of definitions of the self and other. Trinh T. Minh-ha (1989) formulates the racial and sexual basis of the "object of anthropological study" thus:[1]

> It seems clear that the favorite object of anthropological study is not just any man but a specific kind of man: the Primitive, now elevated to the rank of the full yet needy man, the Native. Today, anthropology is said to be "conducted in two ways: in the pure state and in the diluted state."...The "conversation of man with man" is, therefore, mainly a conversation of "us" with "us" about "them," of the white man with the white man about the primitive-native man. The specificity of these three "man" grammatically leads to "men"; a logic reinforced by the modern anthropologist who, while aiming at the generic "man" like all his colleagues, implies elsewhere that in this context, man's mentality should be read as men's mentalities. (Trinh 1989, 64-65)

The quotation illustrates both the fundamentally gendered and racial nature of the anthropological project during colonial rule and the centrality of the white, Western masculinity of the anthropologist. A number of anthropologists have engaged the discursive and representational problems of classical anthropology in recent years. In fact, one of the major questions feminist anthropology has had to address is precisely the question of both representing Third World women in anthropological texts (as a corrective to masculinist disciplinary practices) and simultaneously speaking for Third World women.[2] As Trinh states, we must be concerned with the question of Third World women:

> Why do we have to be concerned with the question of Third World women? After all it is only one issue among others. Delete "Third World" and the sentence immediately unveils its value-loaded clichés. Generally speaking, a similar result is obtained through the substitution of words like *racist* for *sexist*, or vice versa, and the established image of the Third World Woman in the context of (pseudo-) feminism readily merges with that of the Native in the context of (neo-colonialist) anthropology. The problems are interconnected. (Trinh 1989, 85)

Here Trinh suggests that there is a continuity between definitions of the "Native" (male) and the "Third World Woman." Both draw on sexist and racist stereotypes to consolidate particular relations of rule in both cases, gender and race (white men and white women) are central to the definition of superior/inferior. This, then, is an example of the interconnectedness of the processes of racialization and sexualization in the production of knowledge conducive to colonial rule. Anthropology and its "nativization" of Third World women thus forms a significant context for understanding the production of knowledge "about" Third World women. Knowledge production in literary and social-scientific disciplines is clearly an important discursive site for struggle. The practice of scholarship is also a form of rule and of resistance, and constitutes an increasingly important arena of Third World feminisms. After all, the material effects of this knowledge production have ramifications for institutions (e.g., laws, policies, educational systems) as well as the constitution of selves and of subjectivities. For instance, Rey (1991) addresses such paradigms when she suggests that Chinese women "disappear" in popular and academic discourses on China, only to reappear in "case studies" or in the "culture garden." Similarly, in chapter 1, I discuss the discursive production of the "Third World woman" in the discourse of international development studies. Questions of definition and self-definition inform the very core of political consciousness in all contexts, and the examination of a discourse (anthropology) that has historically authorized the objectification of Third World women remains a crucial context to map Third World women as subjects of struggle.

Consciousness, Identity, Writing

Numerous texts on Third World women's political struggles have focused on their participation in organized movements, whether in nationalist or antiracist liberation struggles, organized peasant working-class movements, middle-class movements pertaining to the legal, political, and economic rights of women, or struggles around domestic violence. In fact, the focus of the three previous sections detailing historical and contextual issues (colonialism, class, gender; citizenship, the state, and racial formation; and multinational production and social agency) has also been on such macrostructural phenomena and organized movements. However, not all feminist struggles can be understood within the framework of "organized" movements. Questions of political consciousness and self-identity are a crucial aspect of defining Third World women's engagement with feminism. And while these questions have to be addressed at the level of organized movement, they also have to be addressed at the level of everyday life in times of revolutionary upheaval as well as in times of "peace."

This section foregrounds the interconnections of consciousness, identity, and writing and suggests that questions of subjectivity are always multiply mediated through the axes of race, class/caste, sexuality, and gender. I do not provide a critique of identity politics here, but I do challenge the notion "I am, therefore I resist!" That is, I challenge the idea that simply being a woman, or being poor or black or Latino, is sufficient ground to assume a politicized oppositional identity. In other words, while questions of identity are crucially important, they can never be reduced to automatic self-referential, individualist ideas of the political (or feminist) subject.

This section focuses on life story-oriented written narratives, but this is clearly only one, albeit important, context in which to examine the development of political consciousness. Writing is itself an activity marked by class and ethnic position. However, testimonials, life stories, and oral histories are a significant mode of remembering and recording experience and struggles. Written texts are not produced in a vacuum. in fact, texts that document Third World women's life histories owe their existence as much to the exigencies of the political and commercial marketplace as to the knowledge, skills, motivation, and location of individual writers.

For example, critics have pointed to the proliferation of experientially oriented texts by Third World women as evidence of "diversity" in U.S. feminist circles. Such texts now accompany "novels" by black and Third World women in women's studies curricula. However, in spite of the fact that the growing demand among publishers for culturally diverse life (hi)stories indicates a recognition of plural realities and experiences as well as a diversification of inherited Eurocentric canons, often this demand takes the form of the search for more "exotic" and "different" stories in which individual women write as truth-tellers and authenticate "their own oppression," in the tradition of Euro-American women's autobiography. In other words, the mere proliferation of Third World women's texts, in the West at least, owes as much to the relations of the marketplace as to the conviction to "testify" or "bear witness." Thus, the existence of Third World women's narratives in itself is not evidence of decentring hegemonic histories and subjectivities. It is the way in which they are read, understood, and located institutionally that is of para-mount importance. After all, the point is not just to record one's history of struggle, or consciousness, but how they are recorded; the way we read, receive, and disseminate such imaginative records is immensely significant. It is this very question of reading, theorizing, and locating these writings that I touch on in the examples below.

The consolidation and legitimation of testimonials as a form of Latin American oral history (history from below) owes as much to the political imperatives of such events as the Cuban revolution as to the motivations and desires of the intellectuals and revolutionaries who were/are the agents of these testimonials. The significance of representing "the people" as subjects of struggle is thus encapsulated in the genre of testimonials, a genre that is, unlike traditional autobiography, constitutively public, and collective (for and of the people).[3]

Similarly, in the last two decades, numerous publishing houses in different countries have published autobiographical or life story-oriented texts by Third World feminists. This is a testament to the role of publishing houses and university and trade presses in the production, reception, and dissemination of feminist work, as well as to the creation of a discursive space where (self-)knowledge is produced by and for Third World women. Feminist analysis has always recognized the centrality of rewriting and remembering history, a process that is significant not merely as a corrective to the gaps, erasures, and misunderstandings of hegemonic masculinist history but because the very practice of remembering and rewriting leads to the formation of politicized consciousness and self-identity. Writing often becomes the context through which new political identities are forged. It becomes a space for struggle and contestation about reality itself. If the everyday world is not transparent and its relations of rule – its organizations and institutional frameworks – work to obscure and make invisible inherent hierarchies of power (Smith 1987), it becomes imperative that we rethink, remember, and utilize our lived relations as a basis of knowledge. Writing (discursive production) is one site for the production of this knowledge and this consciousness.

Written texts are also the basis of the exercise of power and domination. This is clear in Barbara Harlow's (1989) delineation of the importance of literary production (narratives of resistance) during the Palestinian intifada. Harlow argues that the Israeli state has confiscated both the land and the childhood of Palestinians, since the word "child" has not been used for twenty years in the official discourse of the Israeli state. This language of the state disallows the notion of Palestinian "childhood," thus exercising immense military and legal power over Palestinian children. In this context, Palestinian narratives of childhood can be seen as narratives of resistance, which write childhood, and thus selfhood, consciousness, and identity, back into daily life. Harlow's analysis also indicates the significance of written or recorded history as the basis of the constitution of memory. In the case of Palestinians, the destruction of all archival history, the confiscation of land, and the rewriting of historical memory by the Israeli state mean not only that narratives of resistance must undo hegemonic recorded history, but that they must also invent new forms of encoding resistance, of remembering. Honor Ford-Smith,[4] in her introduction to a book on "life stories of Jamaican women," encapsulates the significance of this writing:

> The tale-telling tradition contains what is most poetically true about our struggles. The tales are one of the places where the most subversive elements of our history can be safely lodged, for over the years the tale tellers convert fact into images which are funny, vulgar, amazing or magically real. These tales encode what is overtly threatening to the powerful into covert images of resistance so that they can live on in times when overt struggles are impossible or build courage in moments when it is. To create such tales is a collective process accomplished within a community bound by a particular historical purpose.... They suggest an altering or re-defining of the parameters of political process and action. They bring to the surface factors which would otherwise disappear or at least go very far underground. (Sistren with Ford-Smith 1987, 3-4)

I quote Ford-Smith's remarks because they suggest a number of crucial elements of the relation of writing, memory, consciousness, and political resistance: the codification of covert images of resistance during nonrevolutionary times; the creation of a communal (feminist) political consciousness through the practice of storytelling; and the redefinition of the very possibilities of political consciousness and action through the act of writing. One of the most significant aspects of writing against the grain in both the Palestinian and the Jamaican contexts is thus the invention of spaces, texts, and images for encoding the history of resistance. Therefore, one of the most significant challenges here is the question of decoding these subversive narratives. Thus, history and memory are woven through numerous genres: fictional texts, oral history, and poetry, as well as testimonial narratives – not just what counts as scholarly or academic ("real"?) historiography. An excellent example of the recuperation and rewriting of this history of struggle is the 1970s genre of U.S. black women's fiction that collectively rewrites and encodes the history of American slavery and the oppositional agency of African American slave women. Toni Morrison's *Beloved* and Gayl Jones's *Corregidora* are two examples that come to mind.

Ford-Smith's discussion also suggests an implicit challenge to the feminist individualist subject of much of liberal feminist theory, what Norma Alarcon, in a different context, calls "the most popular subject of Anglo-American feminism ... an autonomous, self-making, self-determining subject who first proceeds according to the logic of identification with regard to the subject of consciousness, a notion usually viewed as the purview of man, but now claimed for women" (Alarcon 1989, 3). Alarcon goes on to define what she calls the "plurality of self" of women of color as subjects in the book *This Bridge Called My Back* (1981) in relation to the feminist subject of Anglo-American feminism. Both Ford-Smith and Alarcon suggest the possibility, indeed the necessity, of conceptualizing notions of collective selves and consciousness as the political practice of historical memory and writing by women of color and Third World women. This writing/speaking of a multiple consciousness, one located at the juncture of contests over the meanings of racism, colonialism, sexualities and class, is thus a crucial context for delineating Third World women's engagement with feminisms This is precisely what Gloria Anzaldúa refers to as a "mestiza consciousness" (Anzaldúa 1987).[5] A mestiza consciousness is a consciousness of the borderlands, a consciousness born of the historical collusion of Anglo and Mexican cultures and frames of reference. It is a plural consciousness in that it requires understanding multiple, often opposing ideas and knowledges, and negotiating these knowledges, not just taking a simple counterstance:

> At some point, on our way to a new consciousness, we will have to leave the opposite bank, the split between the two mortal combatants somewhat healed so that we are on both shores at

> once, and at once see through the serpent and the eagle eyes.... The work of mestiza consciousness is to break down the subject-object duality that keeps her a prisoner and to show in the flesh and through the images in her work how duality is transcended. The answer to the problem between the white race and the colored, between males and females, lies in healing the split that originates in the very foundation of our lives, our culture, our languages, our thoughts. A massive uprooting of dualistic thinking in the individual and collective consciousness is the beginning of a long struggle, but one that could, in our best hopes, bring us to the end of rape, of violence, of war. (Anzaldúa 1987, 78-80)

This notion of the uprooting of dualistic thinking suggests a conceptualization of consciousness, power, and authority that is fundamentally based on knowledges that are often contradictory. For Anzaldúa, a consciousness of the borderlands comes from a recentering of these knowledges – from the ability to see ambiguities and contradictions clearly, and to act collectively, with moral conviction. Consciousness is thus simultaneously singular and plural, located in a theorization of being "on the border". Not any border, but a historically specific one: the United States-Mexican border. Thus, unlike a Western, postmodernist notion of agency and consciousness that often announces the splintering of the subject, and privileges multiplicity in the abstract, this is a notion of agency born of history and geography. It is a theorization of the materiality and politics of the everyday struggles of Chicanas.

Some of these questions are also taken up by Lourdes Torres in her 1991 essay on the construction of the self in U.S. Latina autobiographies. Torres speaks of the multiple identities of Latinas and of the way particular autobiographical narratives create a space to theorize the intersection of language and sexuality, and to examine and define the historical and cultural roots of survival in Anglo society.

Finally, the idea of plural or collective consciousness is evident in some of the revolutionary testimonials of Latin American women, speaking from within rather than for their communities. Unlike the autobiographical subject of Anglo-American feminism characterized by Alarcon, testimonials are strikingly nonheroic and impersonal. Their primary purpose is to document and record the history of popular struggles, foreground experiential and historical "truth" which has been erased or rewritten in hegemonic, elite, or imperialist history, and bear witness in order to change oppressive state rule. Thus testimonials do not focus on the unfolding of a singular woman's consciousness (in the hegemonic tradition of European modernist autobiography); rather, their strategy is to speak from within a collective, as participants in revolutionary struggles, and to speak with the express purpose of bringing about social and political change. As Doris Sommer argues, testimonials are written so as to produce complicity in the reader. Thus they are fundamentally about constructing relationships between the self and the reader, in order to invite and precipitate change (revolution). Sommer identifies the "plural" or "collective" self of Latin American women's testimonials as "the possibility to get beyond the gap between public and private spheres and beyond the often helpless solitude that has plagued Western women even more than men since the rise of capitalism" (Sommer 1988, 110).

Alarcon, Ford-Smith, Anzaldúa, and Sommer thus together pose a serious challenge to liberal humanist notions of subjectivity and agency. In different ways, their analyses foreground questions of memory, experience, knowledge, history, consciousness, and agency in the creation of narratives of the (collective) self. They suggest a conceptualization of agency that is multiple and often contradictory but always anchored in the history of specific struggles. it is a notion of agency that works not through the logic of identification but through the logic of opposition. This is a complex argument that I want to introduce rather than work through here.

At the furthest limit of the question of oppositional agency is a problem addressed by Rosalind O'Hanlon (1988) in her analysis of the work of the South Asian subaltern studies group which focuses on the histories of peasants, agricultural laborers, factory workers, and tribals. In her examination of the "history from below" project of *Subaltern Studies,* O'Hanlon suggests the crux of the difficulty in defining and understanding the subjectivity of the subaltern as outside the purview of liberal humanism:

> In speaking of the presence of the subaltern, we are, of course, referring primarily to a presence which is in some sense resistant: which eludes and refuses assimilation into the hegemonic, and so provides our grounds for rejecting elite historiography's insistence that the hegemonic itself is all that exists with the social order. Our question, therefore, must in part be what kind of presence, what kind of practice, we would be justified in calling a resistant one: what is the best figure for us to cast it in, which will both reflect its fundamental alienness, and yet present it in a form which shows some part of that presence at least to stand outside and momentarily to escape the constructions of dominant discourse. (O'Hanlon 1988, 219)

O'Hanlon suggests one aspect of the dilemma with which I began this discussion: how do we theorize and locate the links between history, consciousness, identity, and experience in the writings of Third World women, writings and narratives that are constitutively about remembering and creating alternative spaces for survival, which figure self- and political consciousness? If, as I suggested earlier, certain narratives by Third World women operate not through a logic of identification but through one of opposition, how is domination and resistance theorized? Firstly, resistance clearly accompanies all forms of domination. However, it is not always identifiable through organized movements; resistance inheres in the very gaps, fissures, and silences of hegemonic narratives. Resistance is encoded in the practices of remembering, and of writing. Agency is thus figured in the small, day-to-day practices and struggles of Third World women. Coherence of politics and of action comes from a sociality that itself perhaps needs to be rethought. The very practice of remembering against the grain of "public" or hegemonic history, of locating the silences and the struggle to assert knowledge that is outside the parameters of the dominant, suggests a rethinking of sociality itself.

Perhaps Dorothy Smith's concept of relations of rule can provide a way of linking institutions and structures with the politics of everyday life that is the basis of this formulation of struggle and agency. For instance, the notion "the personal is political" must be rethought if we take seriously the challenge of collective agency posed by these narratives. Similarly, the definition of personal/public life as it has been formulated in feminist theoretical work has to undergo a radical reexamination. I introduce these questions here in an attempt to suggest that we need to renegotiate how we conceive of the relation of self- and collective consciousness and agency; and specifically the connections between this and historical and institutional questions. These narratives are thus an essential context in which to analyze Third World women's engagement with feminism, especially since they help us understand the epistemological issues which arise through the politicization of consciousness, our daily practices of survival and resistance.

To summarize, the first part of this chapter delineates the urgency and necessity to rethink feminist praxis and theory within a cross-cultural, international framework, and discusses the assumption of Third World women as a social category in feminist work and definitions and contests over feminism among Third World women. The second part suggests five provisional contexts for understanding Third World women's engagement with feminism. The first three chart political and historical junctures: decolonization and national liberation movements in the Third World, the consolidation of white, liberal capitalist patriarchies in Euro-America, and the operation of multinational capital within a global economy.* The last two contexts for understanding Third World women's engagement with feminism focus on discursive contexts: first, on anthropology as an example of a discourse of dominance and self-reflexivity, and second, on storytelling or autobiography (the practice of writing) as a discourse of oppositional consciousness and agency. Again, these are necessarily partial contexts meant to be suggestive rather than comprehensive - this is, after all, one possible cartography of contemporary struggles. And it is admittedly a cartography which begs numerous questions and suggests its own gaps and fissures. However, I write it in an attempt to "pivot" the center of feminist analyses, to suggest new beginnings and middles, and to argue for more finely honed historical and context-specific feminist

* This part of the chapter is not included in the present extract which deals with only two of the five contexts discussed.

methods. I also write out of the conviction that we must be able and willing to theorize and engage the feminist politics of women, for these are the very understandings we need to respond seriously to the challenges of race, class, and our postcolonial condition.

Notes

1. Spivak's work also addresses similar questions. See especially Spivak 1987.
2. For a comprehensive analysis of these questions, see Moore 1988. Two particularly influential (self-critical) texts that develop the notion of the politics of interpretation and representation in the constitution of anthropology as a discipline are Marcus and Fischer 1986 and Clifford and Marcus 1986. For a feminist critique of these texts and their premises, see Mascia-Less et al. 1989.
3. Doris Sommer makes this point in her excellent essay in Brodzki and Schenck 1988. My discussion of testimonies draws on Sommer's analysis. For a theoretical extension of these issues, see Stone-Mediatore.
4. Sistren with Ford-Smith 1987. Another text that raises similar questions of identity, consciousness, and history is Menchu 1984.
5. For texts that document the trajectory of Third World women's consciousness and politics, see also the recent publications of the following feminist publishers: Firebrand Press, Crossing Press, Spinsters/Aunt Lute, Zed Press, South End Press, Women's Press, and Sheba Feminist Publishers.

References

Alarcon, Narma. 1989. "The Theoretical Subject(s) of *This Bridge Called My Back* and Anglo-American Feminism", *Chicana Criticism in a Social Context*. Eds. H. Calderon and J.D. Saldivar. Durham, N.C.: Duke University Press.

Anzaldúa, Gloria. 1987. *Borderlands/La Frontera: The New Mestiza*. San Francisco: Spinsters/Aunt Lule.

Brodzki, Bella and Celeste Schenk, eds. 1988. *Life/Lines: Theorizing Women's Autobiographies*. Ithaca: Cornell University Press.

Clifford, James, and George Marcus, eds. 1986. *Writing Culture: The Poetics and Politics of Ethnography*. Berkeley: University of California Press.

Harlow, Barbara. 1989. "Narrative in Prison: Stories from the Palestinian Intifada". *Modern Fiction Studies* 35, no. 1: 29-46.

Marcus, G. and M. Fischer. 1986. *Anthropology as Cultural Critique*. Chicago: Chicago University Press.

Mascia-Lees, F.E. et al. 1989. "The Postmodernist Turn in Anthropology: Cautions from a Feminist Perspective", *Signs* 15, no. 1 (autumn): 7-33.

Menchu, Rigoberta. 1984. *I. Rigoberta Menchu: An Indian Woman in Guatemala*. London: Verso Books.

Minh-ha Trinh T. 1989. *Women, Native, Other*. Bloomington: Indiana University Press.

O'Hanlon, Rosalind. 1988. "Recovering the Subject: Subaltern Studies and Histories of Resistance in Colonial South Asia", *Modern Asian Studies*, 22, no. I: 189-224.

Sistern with Ford Smith. 1987. *Lionhart Gal: Life Stories of Jamaican Women*. Toronto: Sister Vision Press.

Smith, Dorothy. 1987. *The Everyday World as Problematic: A Feminist Sociology*. Boston: Northeastern University Press.

Sommer, Doris. 1988. "Not Just a Personal Story: Women's Testimonies and the Plural Self." In *Life/Lines: Theorizing Women's Autobiography*. Edited by Bella Brodzki and Celeste Schenk, 107-130. Ithaca: Cornell University Press.

Spivak, Gayatri Chakravorty. 1987. In *Other Worlds: Essays in Cultural Politics*. New York: Methuen.

Urmila Pawar

(b 1945)

Urmila Pawar is a well-known writer of Marathi. Her work *Aamahihi Itihas Gadwala (We Also Have Made History)*, written in collaboration with Meenatai, is a record of dalit women's struggle for freedom and dignity. She has also written short stories and the one included here, is an autobiographical narrative based upon her own childhood memories.

Born in a dalit family, Urmila states that she can lay no claims to a literary heritage. But the very fact that her father was a teacher, though having qualified only upto the seventh class, does go to show that he had an advantage over many who were totally illit erate. Urmila herself completed her school in 1964 before taking up a job. She has gone on to take her Masters' degree even though her education has run an interrupted course.

She recalls how her mother used to weave baskets and the manner in which the upper caste people humiliated and abused them. Her father's shifting his residence from a village to a city further dislocated them and alienated them even from their village kin.

Yet she has been more fortunate than many and even her marriage, which took place in 1966, was not to a complete stranger. He was known to their tenants and had learned to value Urmila for her qualities. Mother of two daughters, she has had to take many a public position in defence of their rights.

Urmila's writing is based upon her experience and is invested with the candour necessary to its aesthetic value. She does not allow it to dissolve into self-pity or confession. It is almost brittle in its objective analysis. Her work reflects the new realism, which is increasingly being reflected in dalit writing, in its use of strong, even abusive language and its stark, down-to-earth images.

My Four Enemies

'Write something for the children', a well-known editor of a children's magazine told me, Goodness! It was not so easy to become a child again and to write for the children. I put the letter aside and got busy with my work. But I do not know when, one day, my childhood caught hold of me by the neck. Not only did it catch me by the neck, but it also swiftly turned the time back. It took me back by thirty five years... and pushed me into the enemy camp... in the midst of those who had been my enemies thirty-five years ago.

When I was young I took all older people to be my opponents. Perhaps all children feel that way. But my enemies were of a different kind. I had four main opponents. Enemy number one – my father! Enemy number two – my mother! Number three – my brother, and the fourth was my teacher – Harlekar Guruji. These four antagonists of mine shaped my life, and whatever I am today I am because of these four.

Beside these four, I took a few other unimportant people to be my foes, for they were always picking up quarrels with me, making up stories about me, and insisting that my mother should not let me step out of the house, and carrying tales to my mother about me – 'this girl of yours has stolen fruit from our garden', or 'if you throw stones at the berry tree or the guava tree we will break your legs and hand the broken pieces to you', or 'run away from here. Go away or you will touch us!' They had many ways to show how much they disliked me.

I did not bother about these petty enemies. But I had to confront my important foes every day. These four were always seeking new ways to tighten their hold on me. My enemy number one was my father who died at a young age, and I lost one of the four terrifying opponents. The other three were, however, still living.

I was in class three when my father passed away. I have a very clear recollection of him – if anyone were to ask me to draw his picture, I would need only two colours – white and black. Father was very thin, short and dark. He was always dressed in a white shirt and dhoti, a black coat and wore a white Gandhi cap on his head. His eyes were always wide open. White staring eyes in his dark face. He had white shining teeth. Now tell me why did I need any other colour?

Have you even seen a small crab hopping about in the sand? My father walked in the same manner – always on the run. In summer, during the monsoons, when there was no sun or rain, even then. He was always running. Father always carried a black umbrella. This umbrella was like his third hand, which often fell on our back with full force.

Father was a school teacher and like all teachers of his generation, he was very good at beating. He did not only hit, but as soon as he started on the job, he would lose all control. He was the only educated man in our wadi – the area in which our community lived. What do you think how many classes had he studied? He had read upto the seventh class. Some of the elders of our community had given him a swollen head because he had been able to study this much although he belonged to a backward caste. Father would be immensely pleased with himself whenever he heard this praise. He was always exhorting people to study, the way a doctor would prescribe and dispense medicines. When father came home, he would make us sit down to study in the dim light of the lantern. We would sit with our heads bent over our books till our necks would start aching. If we did not study, we would be badly beaten up and our stupid mother would watch us being thrashed.

Once father had gone to a nearby village where we had an aunt. When he learnt that her son had bunked school, father started hitting him. Aunt told him 'let him not study. How does it matter to you?' But Father did not heed her and beat him black and blue. My aunt split a kokum nut and applied the red juice on her son's buttocks and began wailing – 'Look! What has this butcher done to my son! He has thrashed him so badly that the boy is passing blood!' She slapped her face with her hands and wept loudly. The whole village, the elders of the community abused my father and he had to flee the village.

I remember another interesting anecdote about him. My father was the priest of our community. He read the almanac, performed Satyanarayan's puja and officiated at weddings of the community. His father and before him, his grandfather and great grandfather were all priests. Father did all this along with his job at the school, and was seldom at home. When he would come back after performing a wedding, he would bring rice and coconut tied up in a new piece of cloth. Mother would open the various knots and we would sit watching her keenly like crows. Dried dates, shredded pieces of coconut, almonds, walnuts would all be mixed up in the rice. And when the bundle was untied, we would all fall on the rice. One of us would try to snatch the material, 'this is for my shirt!' When enough material for a shirt had been collected, then they will all be stitched together and a new dress would be ready. Did it make any difference if one sleeve of the shirt was of one colour and the other of another? Often, there would also be some coins in the rice and we would all try to snatch them. Father would slap us on our heads – 'Is this your father's money?' How did we know whose father's money was it?

Just don't ask how miserly he was! He never spent a single paisa on himself. Never bought a single cup of tea for himself. When his dhoti wore out, he would mend it and go on wearing it. A torn and darned shirt could be hidden under the coat. If we ever asked him for any money, even to buy a pencil, it would annoy him. He looked like the demon hiding in the moon when he was angry with his black and white glaring eyes.

He enjoyed irritating us! When he came home at night, he would take some chinapod powder and roll up some tablets the size of small berries and make us swallow them. If one were to take these tablets after dinner and to drink some castor oil in the morning, it would have the effect of destroying not only the worms existing in one's belly but all the future generations of worms. We had no need to drink castor oil for the worms in our bellies were killed by his glaring red eyes as he sat rolling the chinapod tablets in the light of the lantern.

Once I was unable to swallow the tablets and started shouting. Father got up and putting the tablet in my mouth, hit me hard on the chest. I fell back and the tablet went down my throat. He gave a burst of laughter. I was furious. I wished that he should never come home from the school, he was teaching in.

There was a Hanuman temple near our school. This temple gave me a great sense of security. Whenever I wanted to avoid going to school, I would sit in this temple with my school bag. I would often say in my heart – "O God, don't send my father home!"

Perhaps God heard my prayer. When I was in class three, my father fell ill. Mother told us that his blood had turned to water. I visited him once in the hospital with my mother. He lay on the bed, his body covered by a white sheet. I could not look at his face. His stomach was swollen like a pregnant woman's. As we stood near the head of his bed, he started weeping like a child and kept on telling mother 'educate the children.'

That day I didn't want father to die. He should have lived. How much had he wanted my elder sister to study! It was beyond him to teach her and therefore, he had sent her away to some other people so that she could study. But she was rather dumb, and she was married off. I wanted to tell father – 'I will not be like her. I will study, and go to school. I will also take the chinapod tablets, but please don't die!' But he did not live. He died on Friday. We sat around his body the whole night.

The next day was a Saturday, and we had early morning school. I don't know what happened to me, but I picked up my bag and asked mother, 'Aai, may I go to school?' Mother turned away her face. I had never been so enthusiastic about school earlier and was never after that day.

Father was gone. Aai had started looking forlorn and broken down. I thought this was good for now she will not shout at me and not get after me to go to school. I would be free to run about. But this did not happen. Father had given her one purpose in life before his death – 'educate the children'. This was enough for her to take on his mantle and act like him. It seemed to me that mother was very fond of emulating father's role as a teacher.

Aai was also thin like father, but she was tall and fair. She had a fixed look of sadness on her face. She was always dressed in a nine yard sari coming up to her knees.

Our house was on the road. Children could be seen going to and coming from school. Aai would sit under the tree weaving baskets. Small, big, deep and shallow. She knew only two things – crying and weaving baskets. You could see her weaving a fan or a basket early in the morning. And she would sit there in the same manner till it was time to sleep. In between, she would get up to cook. Father was always on his feet and Aai's hands were always working.

Once in a while, the children passing by on the road would stop to watch her weaving her baskets. They would stare at her and I would be embarrassed. Their mothers were beautiful – wore fine clothes and jewellery, with enchanting smiles on their faces and there was my Aai – always irritated and annoyed with me – 'Go to school. Study!' She herself could not read a single word. She spoke wrong and ungrammatical Marathi. But she was always hectoring us like a teacher.

She had surpassed father in miserliness. She cooked a watery thin dal with rice. Only once in a while she would cook vegetables, but we got very small helpings – enough to cover a peanut. Once in a while, she cooked dried fish or shrimp. She did not make anything sweet, even on festivals. When father had been alive, she had sometimes cooked kheer with broken rice and jaggery, but she had stopped doing that now. She would sit there and shed tears. My friends brought such tasty food to school that it made my mouth water, but it had no effect on my mother when I told her this.

Let alone food, we did not even know what it was to dress up. Once every week, my mother would boil water with washing soda and scrub my hair and ears. After my hair dried, she would oil and comb it with a fine toothed comb so as to rid it of all the lice. Then she would tie my hair in a tight plait. It seemed as if she was not bathing us but condemning us to death by hanging. I would see butterflies flitting and fireflies twinkling before my shut eyes. Finally, she would tie up my plaited hair with a thin piece torn from her worn out sari. This stiff plait hung down my back like a scorpion's sting for the whole week. My friends wore bright ribbons of satin or plastic and would often admire themselves in the mirror, but if I ever peeped into the mirror, mother would immediately declare – 'What is the need to look into the mirror again and again? The face of the man confronting you will tell you how you look!'

Aai appeared to be very simple and truthful. But she was full of lies and pretence. If a customer would shout at her – 'you had said that the basket would be ready today! Why isn't it ready? Give my money back!' My mother would very conveniently declare me to be ill and start crying -'what can I do? This younger one of mine was so sheek (this was how she pronounced sick). It seemed as if she would not live... I will definitely finish the work today. Give me just this one day.' And I would be standing behind her, fit and healthy!

If some baskets were to be delivered, she would call out to me very sweetly – 'Dhaktya'. As I was the youngest, she called me by the name 'Dhaktya', and whenever I heard her sweet tone I knew what I would be asked to do. And if I did not heed her then I would be beaten. One who was so sweet a moment ago, would now be shouting and gnashing her teeth – 'you know only how to eat! You cannot do anything! Go deliver this basket at this address!'

Aai looked meek and as docile as a cow when she was talking to others – 'yes sir, yes sir,' and would shake her head in agreement. But god knows from where she got the energy and sharpness when she shouted at me. If I was ill, then she would caress me and the touch of her hand on my forehead was so gentle and soft. She was however, very restless and would always be muttering to herself – 'I have so much work to do! So many baskets to weave. I have to feed the cow'. She would go on like this, clucking like a hen.

Oh yes, I was telling you about Aai asking me to deliver baskets to her customers. The people I delivered the baskets to were the type who would make me stand at their doorstep. They would sprinkle water on the baskets and the winnowing baskets that I was delivering before they touched them, and would drop money in my hand from above so that they should not touch me. Such behaviour would astonish me. If their hands were to touch mine, would they turn black or would they be scorched? All this

Sane Guruji's life – 'chassi laage chammm chamm' very tunefully to me.

The school had an open compound, and animals would walk in and dirty it with their droppings. Every class took turns to clean it, but when it was the turn of my class, then I alone was made to do this work. We had a beautiful cow Kapila. My mother had brought her from her village to worship the thirty-three crore devis and devtas residing in her belly. Guruji insisted that it was always Kapila who dirtied that compound and it was my duty to clean it up. But it was not the turn of my class today. Even then he was asking me to clean up the compound.

I looked at my friends. They were not friends, they were my foes. They were all laughing at me. I do not know what came over me but I did not stir from my place. Guruji shouted, "Can't you hear me?" Even then I kept standing Guruji was now mad with rage and rushed to beat me, but even then I did not move. Aai had often said that your feet forget to move when you are facing a python. My condition was somewhat like that.

By now Guruji had come up to me. He stood very close to me. Giving me a hard slap he shouted – 'Go away from here!' I gave a scream and ran home weeping bitterly. Aai sat in the verandah weaving her baskets. When she saw me screaming and crying, she asked – 'What happened? Why are you crying?" I could not say anything and kept on sobbing, Aai saw the imprint of Guruji's five fingers on my swollen cheek and said – 'Has Guruji beaten you? All right I'll see him'. She started abusing Guruji and muttered to herself – 'Should I go to school?'

I really wanted Aai to shout at Guruji and to berate him, but I didn't want her to go to my school. I was ashamed of her torn sari which she wore high up to her knees and her tangled hair. My eyes were swollen from weeping, and I watched her sullenly.

She showed her restlessness by fidgeting with her things and suddenly she sat down. She picked up her work and then again putting it to one side she stood up. She dusted the scraps of cane from her sari and then, as if she had recollected something, sat down. This was repeated two or three times. I sat there sobbing.

She applied a paste of alum and turmeric on my cheek and asked – 'Why did Guruji hit you?"

"I .... because I did not clean the cowdung. Guruji says it is Kapila who dirties the compound."

"He is right, you sit here and when Guruji returns from the school in the evening, tell me, I'll fix him."

Saying this Aai got up. My weeping stopped suddenly. What will Aai tell Guruji? I felt that Aai will be struck dumb when she will come face to face with Guruji. Her hands and her tongue were used on me alone.

I dozed during the afternoon, but I forced my eyes open. Aai applied the turmeric and alum paste again on my cheek. The afternoon passed. The evening bell rang in the school. My heart beat fast. When I saw Harlekar Guruji coming down the road with the children I was frightened. My tongue stuck to the roof of my month. But somehow I uttered the two words – "Aai, Guruji!"

As soon as Aai heard this she threw the half-woven basket from her hand and stood up straightening her sari ... like a mother reptile with her hood spread out, ready to strike! As he was about to move ahead Aai pulled her sari onto her head and said – "Just a minute, Guruji!"

Guruji stopped short and looking at Aai said in an arrogant tone "What is it?"

"My daughter studies in your school, right? What did she do today? I mean the way you thrashed her, look at her cheek!" Her voice was sharp. She called out to me and turned my cheek toward him. I did not have the courage to look at him.

"That ... that... your white cow ... it dirties the school..." he stammered. "My cow dirties the school, hain? Have you seen her doing that? Guruji, you are an educated man, and yet you talk like a child. I am an illiterate rustic woman, and live on the road with my children. Do you know why? So that my children can study and become good human beings. And you harass my child like this?"

Aai was using wrong grammar. Then she began threatening Guruji – "see from now on even if you lay a finger on this girl, then I will see how you pass on this road!"